United States Catholic Historical Society
Monograph Series VIII

The Catholic Church in Virginia
(1815-1822)

BY

THE REV. PETER GUILDAY

Docteur ès sciences morales et historiques (Louvain),
Professor of Church History, Catholic University of America
President, American Catholic Historical Society, Philadelphia

Author of "The English Catholic Refugees on the Continent (1558-1795),"
"The Life and Times of John Carroll, First Archbishop
of Baltimore (1735-1815)," "The National Pastorals
of the American Hierarchy (1791-1919)," etc.

NEW YORK
THE UNITED STATES CATHOLIC
HISTORICAL SOCIETY
1924

OFFICE OF THE EXECUTIVE SECRETARY,
NO. 346 CONVENT AVENUE, NEW YORK

Copyright, 1924,
THE UNITED STATES CATHOLIC
HISTORICAL SOCIETY

DEDICATED
TO
THE RIGHT REVEREND DENNIS J. O'CONNELL, D.D.
Third Rector of the Catholic University of America, Bishop of Richmond

Contents

	Page
Foreword	ix-x
Introduction	xi-xxxv

CHAPTER I
The Catholic Church in Virginia Under Archbishop Neale.................................. 1-27

CHAPTER II
The "Letter to Archbishop Neale"................ 28-44

CHAPTER III
The Appeal to the Holy See...................... 45-62

CHAPTER IV
Archbishop Maréchal and the Norfolk Schism.... 63-101

CHAPTER V
Archbishop Maréchal and the Norfolk Schism (Continued) 102-123

CHAPTER VI
The Erection of the See of Richmond.............124-133

CHAPTER VII
Bishop Patrick Kelly............................134-153
Conclusion 154-156
Index 157

The Catholic Church in Virginia
(1815-1822)

Foreword

During the past three years, the writer has been occupied in collecting material, here and abroad, for a *Life and Times of John England, first Bishop of Charleston, 1786-1842.*

The history of the Church in the South before the beginning of Carroll's episcopate in 1790, and from that date to the creation of the Sees of Richmond and Charleston (1820), forms part of one and the same narrative. There are the pre-Colonial attempts at Spanish and French settlement along the eastern coast of the United States; the founding of missions from what is probably the present site of Jamestown down the coast to St. Augustine; the tragic fate of the Virginia mission with its martyrs and of the missions in Orista (South Carolina) and Guale (Georgia) with their martyrology; and then the long stretch of years through the sixteenth and seventeenth centuries when the Spanish outposts north of St. Augustine were gradually but ultimately abandoned. Over the Catholic history of these Southern States, down through the English Colonial period to the American Revolution, there is the same veil of darkness, with only a shadowy fact here and there visible to the eye of the searcher. There are the same hints and the same surprising proofs of a sturdy crypto-Catholicism which perdured in spite of Colonial penal laws. There is the same quick leap forward into an organized religious life after the ban of intolerance had been lifted by the Federal Constitution, and the same vigorous growth of the young American Church in all the chief cities from Richmond to Augusta during the first twenty years of the nineteenth century. There are the same sentiments, the same difficulties, the same antipathies in the Catholic groups of all these busy centres.

It is with one phase of Catholic progress in one of these cities that the present volume chiefly deals. A sub-title for the book might well be: *The Norfolk Schism (1815-1822).*

In sketching the main outlines of the Church's history in the Carolinas, especially in Charleston, during these years, almost at every turn the spirit and influence of the Norfolk schismatics can be seen and felt. Yet, the story of the Norfolk schism has certain individual aspects which prevent a blending of its narrative with that of the more dangerous schism of Charleston. For this reason, as well as for others that are apparent in the narrative itself, the history of the Norfolk Church is here given separately.

Following the method used in the *Life and Times of John Carroll,* the writer has remained in this volume loyal to the new school of ecclesiastical history, founded and brought to perfection by such masters as Jungmann and Cauchie of the Catholic University of Louvain. To them and to their disciples it is the document that dominates. The original source alone is allowed to speak, and to speak abundantly. Interpretation is offered only where collateral documents or secondary sources prompt it. There is no attempt at fine writing; no moralizing. The latter is left to the reader. The fundamental rule of the school is this: *Chaque source sur tous les points du sujet: toutes les sources sur chaque point du sujet.* The Archives of the Sacred Congregation de Propaganda Fide (Rome); the Archiepiscopal Archives of Dublin, Quebec and Baltimore, New York, Bordeaux and Besançon; the Episcopal Archives of St. Louis, Charleston and Savannah, and the manuscript collections in the possession of the American Catholic Historical Society (Philadelphia), were all found to contain valuable documents and papers hitherto unused for this critical episode in the history of Church discipline in the United States. A search in the Diocesan Archives at Waterford resulted in the discovery of only one document belonging to Bishop Kelly's episcopate.

The writer wishes to express his gratitude to a small group of scholars who are interested in the Catholic history of the United States and whose generosity made possible the photographing of all the documents used in this volume; among these are the Most Reverend Michael J. Curley, D.D., Archbishop of Baltimore, and the Right Reverend Dennis J. O'Connell, D.D., Bishop of Richmond. In particular he begs the Most Reverend Sebastian G. Messmer, Archbishop of Milwaukee, to accept his sincere thanks for having read the manuscript of the book.

PETER GUILDAY.

July 2, 1924.
Feast of the Visitation of Our Lady,
Catholic University of America,
Washington, D. C.

Introduction

On Sunday, December 3, 1815, the government of the Catholic Church in the United States passed from the hands of John Carroll, its founder and its first hierarchical head, into those of Leonard Neale, his coadjutor and successor.

I

The first metropolitan of the American Church had ruled the faithful here for thirty years when he was called to his reward. In 1785, when he accepted the burden of spiritual leadership in the new Republic there were under his jurisdiction twenty-four priests—nineteen in Maryland and five in Pennsylvania—and probably twenty-five thousand Catholics; at his death in 1815, the number of priests had increased to about fifty and the faithful numbered about one hundred thousand. In 1808, the vast Diocese of Baltimore had been divided and four other episcopal Sees created: at Boston, New York, Philadelphia and Bardstown. Leonard Neale was appointed coadjutor to Bishop Carroll *cum jure successionis in* 1795, and was consecrated second Bishop of the Church in the United States in 1800. Together for fifteen years, the two prelates successfully governed and moulded the nascent American Church.[1]

Many and serious were the problems with which they coped during these critical years (1800-1815): problems arising from the administration of Church property; problems of racial and national antipathies; problems of clerical discipline and problems of lay coöperation. There was a grave situation in New York, especially during the last five years of Carroll's life when that future metropolis was without a bishop; a graver situation prevailed at Philadelphia, where, a year before his own death, John Carroll witnessed the sad passing of the saintly Egan; at Bardstown, there was a serious conflict on Church property between Bishop Flaget and Father Badin, as yet undecided by the Sacred Congregation de Propaganda Fide. Boston, happily, was enjoying peace and was making spiritual progress, though slowly, under the future Cardinal-Archbishop of Bordeaux, John Cheverus. In his own diocese, which stretched from the northern boundary of

---

1. Cf. Guilday, *Life and Times of John Carroll etc.*, pp. 749-789. New York, 1922.

Maryland to the northern boundary of Florida, and then westward to the Mississippi, Archbishop Carroll bequeathed to his successor two congregations that were to be ecclesiastical storm-centres from the day of his death down to the year 1821. These congregations were those of Norfolk and of Charleston.

During these six years (1815-1821) the eyes of the entire Church in the United States were watching the factionist groups which had barricaded themselves within these two Southern cities; and, indeed, long before the Sees of Richmond and Charleston (July, 1820) were created by the Holy See as a means of appeasing the dissatisfaction existing there, the story of their attempted schism was known and discussed in many of the capitals of Europe and especially in Rome. The cause of the schism at Norfolk and at Charleston was the same as that which was then dividing the churches of New York and of Philadelphia: lay encroachment upon the spiritual power of the American episcopate. Each schismatic group was formidable in itself and boded grave disorder to the Church of God within its own State. But the real danger arose when a coalition was sought by all the elements, cleric and lay, opposed to acknowledging complete spiritual obedience to the American hierarchy of the time. Fortunately, New York and Philadelphia, New York and Norfolk, Philadelphia and Charleston were so much farther apart in those days, that before such a coalition could actually be formed, the successor in name and in spirit of the great Ambrose of Milan succeeded in gaining control of the schismatic elements within his metropolitan jurisdiction. But the actual cause of the discontent which appeared during Carroll's last five years, almost simultaneously, in New York, Philadelphia, Norfolk and Charleston, cannot be said to have been definitely removed until the Fathers of the American Church met in the First Provincial Council of Baltimore in 1829. The history of lay trusteeism from its obnoxious aspect is well summed up in the following words, written by Bishop England, first Bishop of Charleston, and addressed to the laity in a Pastoral, by the Council, on October 17, 1829:

> Yet there have been found amongst you, men, who not fully acquainted with the principles of our Church government, either presumed to reform it upon the model of those who have separated from us, or claimed imaginary rights from the misapprehension of facts and laws with which they were badly, if at all, acquainted; they have sometimes been abetted by ignorant or unprincipled priests; and disastrous schisms have thereby occasionally arisen. We have shed bitter tears

when we beheld those usurping and frequently immoral delinquents, standing in the holy places, and profaning the services of the living God; we have deplored the delusion of their adherents. But we trust those evil days have passed away, and forever. Still, we feel it to be our duty to declare to you, that in no part of the Catholic Church does the right of instituting or dismissing a clergyman to or from any benefice or mission, with or without the care of souls, exist in any one, save the ordinary prelate of the diocese or district in which such benefice or mission is found. We, of course, consider our holy father the Pope, as the ordinary prelate of the whole Church, yet it is not usual for him to interfere, save on very extraordinary occasions; this right never has been conceded by the Church to any other body, nor could it be conceded, consistently with our faith and discipline. We further declare to you, that no right of presentation or patronage to any one of our churches or missions, has ever existed or does now exist canonically, in these United States, and, moreover, even if it were desirable to create such right, which we are far from believing, it would be altogether impossible canonically to do so, from the manner in which the Church-property in these States is vested; and that even did we desire to create such right, it would not be in our power, after what we have learned from eminent lawyers in various States, to point out any mode in which it could be canonically created; the nature of our State constitutions and the dispositions of our State Legislatures regarding Church-property, being so perfectly at variance with the principles upon which such property must be secured before such right could be created. It is our duty, as it is our disposition, so to exercise that power which resides in us, of making or changing the appointments of your pastors, as to meet not only your wants but your wishes, so far as our conscientious convictions and the just desires and expectations of meritorious priests will permit, and we trust that in the discharge of this most important and most delicate duty, we shall always meet with your support; as our only object can be your spiritual welfare, for the attainment of which we are, at the risk of our eternal salvation, to lay aside all prejudice and partiality respecting those whom we appoint.[2]

The trustee disorder with its allied claim of the canonical

---

2. Cf. Guilday, *National Pastorals of the American Hierarchy* (1792-1919), pp. 33-34. Washington, D. C., 1923. For the current viewpoint on the conflict between canon law and civil law on this question, cf. Edwards, *Religious Forces in the United States, 1815-1830*, in the *Mississippi Valley Historical Review,* Vol. V, No. 4, March, 1919.

right of patronage, so clearly denied in the Pastoral Letter of 1829, was synchronous with the years of Neale's and Maréchal's regime as metropolitans of the American Church (1815-1828). To judge trusteeism adequately, it should be viewed as a movement embracing the whole Church of that period; but historic accuracy is not lessened when its most serious development be recognized as a large part of the chronicle of the Norfolk Congregation. As a center of rebellion, the trustees at Norfolk radiated an evil influence over the archdiocese, and each group of malcontents in other parts of the country gained strength as it abetted the formation of the Norfolk Schism. Had this succeeded, and had the Southern schismatics gained their objective, namely: the creation of an "Independent Catholick Church of the United States," subject directly to the Jansenist Archbishop of Utrecht, the seamless garment of the American Church would undoubtedly have been rent for all time by these first rebels, and their followers, against episcopal authority.

II

The following pages are an attempt to chronicle the story of the Church in Virginia during these seven stirring years. The narrative proper runs from the beginning of Archbishop Neale's episcopate to the end of the short episcopate of Virginia's first bishop, Dr. Patrick Kelly, in 1822. To understand, however, the trend of ecclesiastical events in Virginia during the administrations of Neale and Maréchal, a brief survey of the colonial history in that State is necessary.

Eighty-one years before the founding of Jamestown, and probably on the very spot of the English settlement, Ayllon's Virginia colony of 1526 had with it two Dominican priests as its spiritual guides.[3] Forty-four years later (1570) a Jesuit mission

---

3. John Gilmary Shea gives the best account of this settlement in his *Catholic Church in Colonial Days* (1521-1763), pp. 106ss. In a note on p. 107, will be found a list of all the original sources for Ayllon's settlement at San Miguel de Guandape (Jamestown). It does not enter into the design of this present volume to describe the attempts made in the sixteenth century by the Spaniards to plant a colony in what is now the State of Virginia. That story has not yet been written with all the wealth of detail now available through the manuscript collections of early Americana at the University of California and in the possession of the newly-created Florida State Historical Society. Shea made use of all the documents known up to his day, and in his chapter on *Ancient Florida* in the second volume of Winsor's *Narrative and Critical History of America,* the best description of these Spanish settlements will be found. Lowery's *Spanish Settlements etc.,* is based upon new source-material discovered since

INTRODUCTION xv

was begun at Axacan, but was destroyed by unfriendly Indians.[4] In the Jamestown expedition, the presence of Edwin Maria Wingfield, as first President of the colony, is a salient note in Virginia's Catholic history, since Wingfield, whose father was a godson of Queen Mary Tudor and Cardinal Pole, was a Catholic, and tradition has it that he was deprived of his office by the Jamestown settlers on account of his non-conformity to the established Church.[5] From 1634, when the Catholic settlement of Maryland was founded, to 1791, it is generally assumed that the Jesuits of Maryland, at the risk of arrest and imprisonment, frequently visited the Catholic families of Virginia.[6] Magri, the historian

---

Winsor's volumes appeared (Boston, 1889). The *Guides* published by the Department of Historical Research of the Carnegie Institution of Washington, particularly the *Guide to the Materials for the History of the United States in Spanish Archives,* by Wm. R. Shepherd, have opened the way farther to a more thorough scholarship in this field. Brown's *Genesis of the United States* (New York, 1890) contains other documents from English archives for the history of Spain's attitude towards the English settlement of this her ancient colony. Fiske has dealt with the Spanish colony of Virginia in his *Discovery of America* (Boston, 1892), and a sympathetic and at the same time a most thorough narrative of Spanish discovery and colonization is Bourne's *Spain in America* (New York, 1909). Tyler's *Narratives of Early Virginia* (New York, 1907) does not know of the Ayllon settlement. Cf. *The Planting of the Faith in America,* article by Rev. E. I. Devitt, S.J., in the *Records* of the American Catholic Historical Society, Vol. VI (1895), pp. 137-179. The Dominicans were Fathers Anthony de Montesinos and Anthony de Cervantes and Brother Peter de Estrada.

4. Cf. *Axacan: The Martyrs of the Rappahannock,* article by Rev. E. I. Devitt, S.J., in the *Records* ACHS, Vol. XIX (1908), pp. 1-18, where a translation of Rogel's account of Axacan is given from Astrain's *Historia de la Compañia de Jesus en la Asistencia de España* (Vol. II, pp. 295-298, 640-644. Madrid, 1905). Cf. *Catholic World,* vol. XX, p. 847; *Records* ACHS, vol. VI (1895), pp. 141-142, 148; *Researches* (Griffin), XX, vol. XXV, p. 394; vol. XXIII, pp. 332-335; *Catholic Historical Review,* vol. I, pp. 223, 260, 480. Griffin (*Catholics in Colonial Virginia,* in the *Records* ACHS, vol. XXII, p. 85) calls Father Segura, the Superior of the Mission, a Franciscan.
5. Cf. *Edward Maria Wingfield,* article by E. J. McGuire, in the *Historical Records and Studies* (United States Catholic Historical Society), vol. X (1907), pp. 164-171.
6. "The Norfolk County, Virginia, records of September 15, 1687 show Father Edmonds, a Roman Catholic Priest, arrested for marrying a couple; and on November 16, 1687, Father Raymond, at Norfolk, Virginia arrested for saying Mass. . . . No doubt both these priests visited Williamsburg and ministered throughout that section of Virginia. These records show the Catholic mission priests present in Virginia at that early period, and they must have had successors up to the time of the arrival of the Abbe Dubois," cited by Magri, *The Catholic Church in the City and Diocese of Richmond,* p. 37. (Richmond, 1906). Cf. Hughes, *History of the Society of Jesus etc.,*

of the Diocese of Richmond, chronicles an attempt made by Captain George Brent during the reign of James II (1685-88) to establish a Catholic settlement in Virginia.[7]

With some other capitalists, he purchased a tract of land covering thirty thousand acres between the Potomac and Rappahannock Rivers, and proclaimed religious freedom to the settlers, but the change in the political fortunes of James II brought an end to the project. There was one Catholic settlement in Virginia, that of Aquia Creek which was visited by the priests of Maryland. It was considered a mission attached to the Rock Creek Church, where Father John Carroll was pastor from 1774 to 1784.[8]

The penal legislation against the Catholic Church in Virginia from the settlement at Jamestown in 1607, to the adoption of the Federal Constitution of 1787, is to be found in a series of enactments against the presence of "Popery" in the colony. The shadow of the Gunpowder Plot lay heavily upon the reign of James I, and the penal laws enacted during that time exceeded in some respects the barbarity and ferociousness of his predecessor.

The penal laws of Elizabeth's reign had pursued the Catholics from the cradle to the grave. No walk of life was sacred, and the re-enactment of the "Act for the better discovering and repressing of popish recusants" subjected Catholics in England to penalties that baffle description.[9] The Winslade expedition of 1605, projected for the purpose of inducing the harassed Catholics to emigrate "to the Northern parts of America," would have been a means in all likelihood of affording them a refuge beyond the seas; but when that old warrior of the Faith, Father Robert Persons, the Jesuit, opposed the Winslade expedition on the score that it was dishonorable for the Catholics to fly persecution, the movement was checked.[10]

We shall probably never know to what extent faithful Catholics at that time took the oath of supremacy. When the revised oath was first imposed upon the Catholics (1606), there were some who

---

Documents, vol. I, part 1, pp. 31-35, 41-42, 96-99, 103-112, 129-130, 145-147; Text, vol. II, pp. 22-24, speaks of the Jesuit missionary work in Virginia during the seventeenth century.
7. *Op. cit.*, p. 37.
8. "I have care of a very large congregation; I have often to ride 25 to 30 miles to the sick; besides which, I go once a month between fifty and sixty miles to another congregation in Virginia."—Carroll to Plowden, February 28, 1779 (Hughes, *op. cit. Doc.*, vol. I, pt. II, p. 650 note).
9. Dodd-Tierney, *Church History of England*, vol. IV, pp. 67-68 note.
10. Hughes, *op. cit.*, Doc. vol. I, part 1, pp. 2-5, 153 ss.

INTRODUCTION xvii

believed that it could be taken without doing violence to any Catholic doctrine. The clergy were divided upon the lawfulness of taking it, and the controversy, then begun, voiced its weary way down the years until Catholic Emancipation in 1829. Though the oath of 1605 contains, offensively expressed, the doctrine now generally accepted on the question of papal supremacy, it could not have been taken in those days without grave consequences to one's orthodoxy.[11]

The Charter of James I (November 20, 1606) to the London Company expressly decreed the establishment of the Anglican faith: "That the true word, and service of God and Christian faith be preached, planted and used . . . . according to the doctrine, rites and religion now professed and established within our realme of England."[12] The second Charter (May 23, 1609) says: "We should be loath that any person should be permitted to pass, that we suspected to affect the superstitions of the Church of Rome; we do hereby declare that it is our will and pleasure that none be permitted to pass in any voyage . . . . . but such as first shall have taken the oath of supremacy."[13] It was this oath of supremacy which was tendered to Lord Baltimore at Jamestown on October 1, 1629; and his refusal to take it, except in a modified form, furnished the Governor and his Council with the pretext they needed for his expulsion. After the failure of the Avalon expedition, Lord Baltimore came to Virginia (1629), intending to remain there temporarily until patents for the Maryland colony were issued by the crown. He was not allowed to remain. "The Governor and Council insisted that, even for so short a time as his purposes required, he must take the oath of supremacy. As a Roman Catholic, it was impossible for him to acknowledge the ecclesiastical headship of the King of England, but he offered to take a modified oath covering all the necessary questions of allegiance. This the Virginians were not willing to accept, and Baltimore, though a personal friend of Charles, was not allowed to remain in the colony."[14] Cobb, who generally sees a political

---

11. Dodd-Tierney, *op. cit.*, vol. IV, pp. 81-83.
12. Hening, *The Statutes-at-Large, Being a Collection of All the Laws of Virginia* (1619-1792), vol. I, pp. 268-269. New York, 1823.
13. *Ibid.*
14. Cobb, *The Rise of Religious Liberty*, p. 82; Cf. Meerness, *Maryland as a Proprietary Province*, p. 11. New York, 1901. The whole proceeding according to Meerness was a most presumptuous one, since the Governor and the Council had no authority to tender him the oath of allegiance. Cf. Russell, *Maryland the Land of Sanctuary*, pp. 44-45. Baltimore, 1907.

motive in all such intolerant acts, strongly suspects "that this action was due, less to ardor for the royal prerogative and the maintenance of the Established Church, than to jealousy of a new proprietor who designed to found another and rival colony on the borders of Virginia." Five years later, when the Maryland colonists arrived at Point Comfort, Virginia, on February 27, 1634, they were treated courteously by Sir John Harvey, the Governor, but there is evidence of hostility on the part of some of the Virginia settlers. An enactment, dated September, 1632, required the commander of the Fort at Point Comfort to administer the oath of allegiance to all those coming into the colony. Refusal meant seizure and imprisonment.

In England, the bigotry that prevailed in James's day had been somewhat subdued for political reasons during the reign of Charles I (1625-49). There was an attempt at that time to find a new oath, less likely to offend the Catholics, but it never materialized. During the Cromwellian usurpation (1649-60), other matters disturbed the nation, and after the restoration of Charles II, Catholics were allowed a certain amount of religious freedom. The Titus Oates Plot reawakened the old-time demand for the securing of Catholic allegiance by a rigid oath, and again the former controversies among the Catholics arose. Dodd has defined the oath as follows: "It plainly appeared that the oath was never designed to be a test of allegiance, but a State trick, to squeeze money from the party, and nourish an opinion in the common people, that they [*the Catholics*] were enemies to the civil government. It was contrary to the desire, or intention of the ministry, that any of them should take the oath. The vulgar were made to believe that Catholics were persons without either honour or conscience; in which case an oath is a useless expedient."[15]

The history of No Popery in the English Colonies marches in equal pace with the growth of the same political disease in the home country. From one viewpoint, however, it would seem that the colonies which were founded with No Popery clauses in their charters kept reiterating these anti-Catholic legal disabilities, often couched in bloodthirsty terms, even when no Catholic was known to the legislators, as a political trick to show loyalty to the party in power in England.[16] For example, in 1642, a statute was passed by the Virginia House of Delegates, to the

---

15. Dodd-Tierney, *op. cit.*, vol. IV, p. 89.
16. Cobb, *op. cit.*, p. 451.

effect "that no popish recusants should at any time hereafter exercise the place or places of secret counsellors . . . . . that it should be unlawful under the penalties aforesaid for any popish priest that shall hereafter arrive to remain five days after warning given for departure."[17] Apparently, "popish recusant convicts" reached the colony, and laws were passed (1699, 1705, 1753) to declare them incapable of the franchise and of the right to give testimony in court. But these laws are to be interpreted more in the light of a last attempt to postpone disintegration of the Established Church than as rigid penal laws against the Catholic Faith.[18] The extraordinary fears aroused by the French and Indian War brought forth an Act "for disarming Papists."[19] Cobb says of it: "All Papists were required to surrender their arms and ammunition, on penalty of three months' imprisonment, the loss of their arms, and fine. It is clear, however, that the measure, like a similar proposition in Pennsylvania, was more political than religious. The act observed that the Papists were dangerous at this time of war with their fellow-religionists."[20]

On this series of penal enactments, the last before the Revolution, Bruce makes the following interesting comment: "The religion of the Papist . . . . . carried with it necessarily the absolute spiritual supremacy of the Roman See in the hearts of all who professed it. In denying that the King of England was the head of their Church, the dissenters did not attempt to set up another, and that, too, a foreign potentate in his stead; this the Papist openly did; and in that age, it was not unnaturally regarded as a step towards treason in temporal affairs. The Pope, who was denounced by the great body of the English people as Anti-Christ, was the head of the Roman Catholic Church, and his principal design was supposed to be to overthrow both the spiritual and civil order in England; a member of that Church was, therefore, regarded as scheming, so far as lay in his power, to promote the success of this design, presumably so dear to that head, who claimed his entire allegiance."[21]

The principle of an established religion is somewhat uniquely bound up with the Colonial history of Virginia, and the religious liberty gained at considerable cost by the different non-conformist

---

17. Hening, *op. cit.*, vol. I, pp. 268-269.
18. *Ibid.*, vol. VII, p. 35.
19. *Ibid.*
20. *Op. cit.*, p. 108.
21. Bruce, *Institutional History of Virginia in the Seventeenth Century*, vol. I, p. 264. New York, 1910.

bodies, just prior to the American Revolution, brought about the collapse of the official Church.[22] "The Virginia establishment—to use Cobb's phrase—"debased the things of God into a mere setting for the sordidness of earth. In its fall there were few to mourn."[23] The Revolution obliterated a religious corporation, two-thirds of which adhered to the King and to the principles of Loyalism.[24] The State convention of 1776, not only severed all political relations with the home government, but also adopted George Mason's Bill of Rights, the sixteenth section of which (proposed by Patrick Henry) granted, as the original draft had it, "the fullest toleration in the exercise of religion according to the dictates of conscience, unpunished and unrestrained by the magistrate; unless under color of religion any man disturb the peace, happiness, or safety of society."[25] From that day the religious slavery of Virginia was past and Madison expressed the obvious corollary that religion did not come within the cognizance of government.[26] After the passage of the *Act Establishing Religious Freedom*,[27] in October, 1785, there was no further obstacle to the presence of Catholics in the State, and they were free to organize parishes or congregations as they desired.

One curious development of the disestablishment of the Episcopal Church in Virginia and one which was to bring the struggling Catholic congregations almost to disaster, was a provision in the Virginia State Constitution absolutely prohibiting the grant of any "charter of incorporation . . . . to any church or religious denomination," thus forcing church associations to hold their property by the trustee system.[28] It is this clause that the malcontents of Norfolk used as a threat over Archbishop Maréchal during the years (1817-21) that he endeavored to exercise spiritual jurisdiction over their church; and it was the protest of Dr. Patrick Kelly, Virginia's first Catholic bishop, against this constitutional enactment which helped to hasten his departure in 1822 for the more congenial atmosphere of Waterford and Lismore.

---

22. Cobb, *op. cit.*, p. 483.
23. *Op. cit.*, p. 115.
24. Hawks, *Ecclesiastical Contributions*, vol. I, p. 139; AHA Report, 1886-87, p. 23.
25. Cobb, *op. cit.*, p. 491; Jefferson, *Works*, vol. I, p. 39.
26. Hening, *op. cit.*, vol. IX, pp. 312, 469, 579.
27. *Ibid*, vol. XII, p. 84; Cobb, *op. cit.*, p. 494.
28. Zollmann, *American Civil Church Law*, p. 25. New York, 1917.

INTRODUCTION

In the light of its penal laws against the Catholic Church, it is not surprising to find in Carroll's *Report* to Propaganda Fide (1785) the statement that "there are not more than 200 [Catholics] in Virginia who are visited four or five times a year by a priest."[29] These Catholics lived mostly in the northern tier of counties along the Potomac. There are no authentic statistics for the number of Catholic immigrants coming into the United States prior to 1819, but it can safely be stated that Norfolk and Portsmouth had not attracted many of these future citizens of the Republic.[30] Certainly when Father John Dubois arrived at Norfolk in July, 1791, with letters of introduction from Lafayette to Monroe, Patrick Henry, the Randolphs, the Lees and other distinguished Virginians, he found only a few Catholics in the city. During the winter, 1791-92, Father Dubois lived in Richmond and was invited to celebrate Mass in the hall of the House of Delegates.[31] Whether Father Dubois remained in Virginia until 1798, when Dr. Carroll sent Father T. C. Mongrand, is not known with certainty. Apparently the next pastor of Richmond was Father Xavier Miguel, who was appointed in April, 1811. He remained but a short time and applied for admission into the Society of Jesus.[32]

---

29. Guilday, *Carroll*, p. 223.
30. The question of the extent of Catholic immigration into the United States before 1820 has not yet been thoroughly investigated. Bromwell's *History of Immigration to the United States* (New York, 1856) contains suggestions for the period prior to 1820. It was only in this year that official immigration statistics were begun by the government. Maguire's *Irish in America* (New York, 1868), O'Kane Murray's *History of the Catholic Church in the United States* (New York, 1882) and Emmet's *Irish Emigration* (New York, 1899) treat the subject. An attempt at an exhaustive study is Shaughnessy, *A Century of Catholic Growth* (1820-1920)—ms. in the Library of the Catholic University of America. For immigration into Virginia, Cf. G. C. Greer, *Early Immigrants to Virginia* (1623-1666). Richmond, 1912. Linehan's article *Early Irish Settlers in Virginia* in the *Journal of the American-Irish Historical Society*, vol. IV (1904), pp. 30-42, also reveals a number of Catholic settlers in Virginia from the earliest times. Griffin's article, as cited in note 4, is valueless. Numerous references will be found in the Index to the *Researches*, s.v. "Virginia," but they must be carefully controlled.
31. Keiley, *Memoranda of the History of the Catholic Church in Richmond Va.*, p. 5. Norfolk, 1874; references to Father Dubois will be found in Hughes, *op. cit.*, Doc., vol. I, part II, pp. 775, 805, 816, 820, 883. Cf. *The Right Rev. John Dubois, D.D.*, article by Herbermann, in the *Historical Records and Studies*, vol. I, (1900), pp. 281-283.
32. Hughes, *op. cit.*, Doc., vol I, part II, p. 842; Cf. *Records* ACHS, vol. XXIII, p. 197. A biographical sketch of Father Miguel will be found in the Charleston *Miscellany*, vol. VIII, p. 47.

An appeal from the Catholics in Richmond, dated March 25, 1812, is in the Baltimore Cathedral Archives, and evidently refers to the situation caused by Father Miguel's departure:

To the Right Rev. John Carroll, Archbishop of Baltimore, etc.
The following petition is humbly and respectfully submitted by the Catholics of Richmond, State of Virginia:

Right Reverend Father in God:

The Catholics of Richmond, who constitute a small but zealous and faithful portion of the numerous flock entrusted to your apostolic superintendence, have long viewed with deepest anguish their truly deplorable situation in respect to the most important of all concerns, religion. Temptations and dangers surround them on all sides, the foe of salvation incessantly lays snares in their path. Yet they have no spiritual guide, no citadel to which they may fly from the wiles and the violence of a restless foe. They hear not the salutary voice that warns against deviations from the pure doctrine of the true faith; the friendly hand that supports the frail faith and tottering steps of the struggling Christian is not stretched out to them. Their souls thirst in vain after the vivifying influence of the holy sacraments. Their children, too, those interesting pledges of chaste affection, whose eternal as well as temporal welfare it is their bounden duty to promote, their children, alas! are unavoidably surrendered in religious matters to the most fatal dereliction. In that tender age, so favorable to the inculcation of faith, piety and moral principles, they often wander like stray lambs; no careful pastor collects them in the fold of the Lord, nourishes their young minds with the doctrine of Life, develops their nascent virtues, or checks their vices, fortifies them against both present and future perils, in short, gradually inures them to the yoke of Christ and to the ways of salvation. With indescribable sorrow the Catholics of Richmond feel this alarming relaxation of religious and moral ties; they compare themselves to branches lopped from the parent tree, and withering for want of that nutritious supply which alone could refresh and invigorate them.

To you, Reverend Father in God, they look for prompt and efficient relief; they are fully conscious of your apostolic solicitude for the spiritual comfort of all those who compose your flock.

They know that this candid representation of their religious wants will excite your paternal sympathy, that you will extend to them your fostering care.

They request, therefore, earnestly request, a holy minister

of your choice, one who by his exemplary conduct and able discharge of the sacred functions will shine among them a bright and useful luminary; one whose actions will edify whilst his words instruct; and, on account of local circumstances, one acquainted not only with English, but also with the French language. But why minutely delineate the character under consideration? Who better than yourself, Right Reverend Father in God, is able to discern genuine sacerdotal worth? For the support of the clergyman who may eventually be sent us Eight Hundred Dollars per annum have already been obtained by subscription, and this sum will probably be increased, as several Catholics have yet to contribute. We will use every possible exertion to effect the building of a church; a lot has already been presented by a zealous Catholic for that pious purpose. Until the erection of such a church some convenient place shall be provided by us for the celebration of divine worship.

We entreat, Right Reverend Father in God, a favourable answer from you in this momentous subject, either in a direct way to the members of our committee, or through the medium of the Reverend Father DeLacey, whose zeal in promoting the present laudable object and also in bringing as often as it has been in his power so to do the comforts of the true faith and of the holy will of God, we cannot sufficiently acknowledge.

With deepest veneration, and with ardent prayers for the long continuance of your valuable and truly apostolic life, we remain, Right Reverend Father in God,
Your affectionate and faithful children in Christ,

The Committee,

FRANCIS PIATTI
DENIS MCLAUGHLIN
JOHN LAWLOR

Right Reverend Father in God, herewith I enclose a petition signed by the Committee of Roman Catholics in Richmon, to you, and hope it will be in your power to furnish that long wished for felicity which they solicit for in that petition.

With deepest veneration for the long continuance of your truly apostolic life,
Your affectionate and faithful Child in Christ,

JOHN LAWLOR.[33]

---

33. *Researches,* vol. XXV, pp. 53-54; original in the Baltimore Cathedral Archives, Case—8—Nl. These archives are cited through these notes as BCA.

The home of Colonel Fitzgerald, Washington's aide-de-camp and secretary, in Alexandria, was used as a meeting place for the Catholics of that city and vicinity, whenever a priest visited there. Father John Thayer ministered to the Catholics in Alexandria in 1794, and in 1796, Father Francis Neale erected the first Catholic church there. In many of the other towns of Virginia after the close of the War of Independence, Catholics were to be found, but there was no attempt at organized congregations until much later.

In the records of Norfolk Borough, there is an indenture dated December 15, 1794, "between Alexander Moseley of the Borough of Norfolk, and Elenor, his wife, of the one part, and Antonio Wallace and John Spelleman for and in behalf of the trustees of the Roman Catholic society of the Borough of Norfolk of the other part," setting aside one lot or parcel of land for religious purposes. This indenture of bargain and sale was recorded at a hustings court on February 23, 1795.[34] It was about this time, or a year later, that Bishop Carroll sent as pastor of the Norfolk congregation Father James Bushe, who is said to have begun the building of a church there. The Norfolk troubles began with Father Bushe, against whom the trustees sent to Bishop Carroll the serious charge that he did not celebrate Mass according to the rubrics.[35] Shea states that Leonard Neale, the coadjutor Bishop-elect and Vicar-General for the diocese, went to Norfolk to bring about peace in 1799: "He was disquieted by the scenes he witnessed at an election of the trustees and their opposition to their pastor. He urged them earnestly to lay aside all such feelings and to unite heartily in completing the church which they had begun."[36]

Dr. Carroll recalled Father Bushe and sent in his stead (1803) Father Michael Lacy. At a meeting of the Board of Trustees in May, 1804, a series of rules for the permanent government of the Church was adopted and printed. The first part of these rules is concerned with the duties "of the Priest and assistant," and if Father Lacy permitted or was forced to permit this section, he was unwittingly sowing the seed of all the coming trouble. These Rules read: "I. There shall preside over the Church one

---

34. *Letter addressed to the Most Reverend Leonard Neale, Archbishop of Baltimore, by a Member of the Roman Catholic Congregation of Norfolk, in Virginia.* Norfolk, 1816. Cited uniformly as *Letter* (Fernandez).
35. BCA, Case—11—B3.
36. *Op. cit.*, vol. II, p. 493.

Priest, a wise, exemplary and affable man. II. His duties shall be—1st. To celebrate the *Mass.* 2d. To administer the *Sacraments.* 3d. To assist the dying. 4th. To instruct children in the Catechism and the *Christian Morals.* 5th. To inculcate a decent and devout behaviour in his *congregation* during the time of *divine service.* III. He shall represent to the COUNCIL OF TRUSTEES whatever he may deem as necessarily wanted in the *Chapel,* either for the *service of the Altar* or for the administration of the *Sacraments.*"[37] So far as these rules represent a statement of fact, they were passably acceptable, although they are so similar to the parish government of the Established Church that one cannot help suspecting an intimate dependence between them.[38] The restrictions placed by the Catholic trustees on their pastor inevitably led to the assumption of a right the Episcopalian Vestry always possessed: the appointment of the clergyman of their parish. The similarity of the restriction arises from the fact that the pastor was to receive no other compensation for his services than the salary which the trustees should allot to him. All communications between himself and the trustees were to be in writing; and "when the *Priest* chooses to be present at the meetings of the Council, his place shall be at the right hand of the *President.* The *Priest* shall never vote in the Council of Trustees; and shall never address them, unless when information is asked of him by the *President.*" All church revenues were to be collected and administered "under the direction and by order of the Council of Trustees."[39] Among the names of the seven men who formed the Board of Trustees at that date in the Norfolk Church we find those of James Heron, Thomas Moran, John Donaghey, Eugene Higgins, Jasper Moran and the Spanish Consul, Villalobos. These men gained complete financial control of the Norfolk congregation at a meeting held on December 26, 1808, and in spite of all that Archbishops Neale and Maréchal did, retained that control from this time until the coming of Bishop Kelly in 1821. To their body in 1809 was added, in the capacity of Secretary, the Portuguese physician, Dr. John F. Oliveira Fernandez, whose bizarre knowledge of canon law, and of such anti-papal authors as Paolo Sarpi, Edmund Richer, Febronius and other writers, made him a dangerous opponent to episcopal authority.

The Norfolk congregation consisted of forty families at the

---

37. *Letter* (Fernandez), pp. 39-41.
38. Cf. Bruce, *op. cit.,* pp. 62-78.
39. *Letter* (Fernandez), p. 41.

time of Father Lacy's appointment. In a list of pew-holders (January 2, 1809), out of twenty-three names, all but five are Irish. Apparently Father Lacy knew how to deal with these men; and too much credit can hardly be given to him for this knowledge.

The Irish Catholics, cleric and lay, who came to the chief centres during the period previous to 1815, came with certain grim prejudices regarding the administration of the Church here. Father Patrick Smyth's *Present State of the Catholic Missions conducted by the ex-Jesuits in North America* (Dublin, 1788), contained calumnies against Carroll and Neale and the rest of the American clergy which did grave harm to their good name in Ireland.[40] The repetition of the old-time calumnies which had darkened the history of the Church in England during the Secular-Regular controversy, was bound to create animosity between the priests who had borne the burden of the day and the heats for so many years and the bustling and somewhat arrogant type of Irish clergymen who came here to enjoy a liberty and in some sad cases a license which Ireland did not afford. With the coming of the French Sulpicians in 1791, and with their steady progress in the organization of the Church, this feeling of animosity was diverted from the former members of the Society to these French clerics, so many of whom rose to episcopal honors after 1808—Flaget, Du Bourg, Maréchal, David, Chabrat, Dubois and Bruté. For reasons that need not be entered into at this moment but which can be easily surmised, the belief was expressed at the time that the proportion between the number of French priests laboring in our poorer missions was strikingly lower than would warrant such a generous choice from their ranks for episcopal Sees on the part of Propaganda Fide. The Irish clergy did not consider it as blameworthy to promote the idea that the future of the American Church was in danger with so many "foreigners" in the seats of the mighty. It is necessary to accept the Irish clergy of the time at their own estimate of themselves, if we are to judge this first of a series of politico-ecclesiastical tendencies with which the Church in this country is familiar. The Irish clergy estimate of the Irish clergy was that they were *born* Americans. Even John England allowed this sentiment to creep into his first letter to his flock in Charleston (July 13, 1820).[41] The absence of

---

40. A copy of this scarce little pamphlet is in the Library of the University of Notre Dame. Cf. *Records,* vol. XXI, p. 29. For a discussion of the pamphlet, cf. Guilday, *Carroll,* pp. 309-321.
41. BCA, Case—16—P29.

certain failings, social and moral, among the French clergy, placed their priestly lives in striking contrast to that of many of their clerical brethren from the Emerald Isle; but with true Celtic loyalty, this fact had little or no effect upon the groups of Irish laymen in New York, Philadelphia, Norfolk and Charleston. In these centres the anti-French spirit grew stronger as the years went by; and in the case of Norfolk, we will see Jasper Moran, John Donaghey and the others stating bluntly their position in the quarrel between themselves and Neale—they will not have a Frenchman placed over them: any other race will do, but no French priest was welcome.

One of the best expositions of this racial animosity is to be found in one of Father Thomas Carbry's letters to Propaganda, dated New York, July 30, 1817.[42] The Irish Dominican was a keen observer and before coming to America had had a distinguished career both in Rome and in Ireland. He was like all the Irishmen of his day *foncièrement* nationalist; due in large part to the intense feelings aroused by the struggle for Emancipation. Carbry states that the majority of the Catholics here was of the Irish race. They and their children had built the churches, supported the priests and had fought for the Faith; and in some cases had practically impoverished themselves to found the Catholic religion in the young Republic. In spite of all these sacrifices, Father Carbry points out, the administration of the Church in the United States was in the hands of the French clergy. French ecclesiastics, he wrote, were favored over their Irish and American brethren. French bishops ruled every See but one. On no point were the Irish so sensitive as on the exposition of their Faith from the pulpit. It robbed divine service of all attraction for them to hear Catholic doctrine expounded by French priests in a way that amused Protestants and held the Church up to ridicule. Carbry claimed that many Irish priests in Ireland were willing to come to the United States and to devote themselves to the poorer congregations, but they were held back by the fear that the bishops were almost all opposed to their race.[43] Measured by

---

42. Propaganda Archives, *Scritture riferite, America Centrale,* vol. III, fol. 469.
43. That this may be a partisan view of the situation by Father Carbry may need no further proof than the statement made by Bishop John England in 1836. Dr. England's opinion was that the Catholic clergy of England was insufficient at the time to care for its own flocks and was therefore totally unable "to do anything for America. Ireland was in a still worse position; yet the loss of the American

the serious charges made by Archbishops Carroll, Neale and Maréchal in their correspondence with Rome, this anti-Irish sentiment abroad at the time had a firmer basis than mere racial antipathy. This problem need not be discussed here in all its details; but it will become clearer—as the story of the Norfolk Schism develops—that the Irish-French ecclesiastical quarrel here during these years (1815-29) requires more than its American aspect to reach a safe judgment on the merits of the conflict.

From the vantage ground of a score of years later, Bishop John England gives a searching analysis of the feeling between the Irish and the French at this time. "We now arrive," he says, "at another epoch, desolating for Europe, beneficial to America! The machinations of infidelity produced their horrible effects in France! Its religion was proscribed, its clergy was obliged to submit to banishment, to death, or to apostacy; several of its pious laity, escaping with their lives, found asylums in foreign lands, and not a few traversed the Atlantic. That small portion of the clergy that betrayed their holy charge, remained at home, and under the protection of the bad men who ruled, were intruded into desecrated sanctuaries to officiate at polluted altars; their faithful brethren were bathed in their blood, or lurked in hiding-places to serve the few who, at the peril of their lives, adhered to their religion and gave shelter to its ministers; but the great bulk of the holy band was found in exile weeping for the desolation of their country, and beseeching heaven to receive it once more to His mercy. The pious and learned emigrant clergy of France, not only edified several countries by their virtue, but elsewhere they aided greatly to the conversion of Protestants, by their zeal, their prayers, and their example. America had the good for-

---

colonies created in Great Britain a wholesome dread which too far exasperated the plundered population of this ill-treated land. In order to try and secure their attachment, during the war with France and the contest with the revolutionary colonies, the government of Ireland had considerably mitigated the ferocity of its persecution. The Irish Catholics wanted a good many priests and were very insufficiently supplied. As this island had no seminary within her borders, she was dependent upon those which the Catholic nations of Europe, especially France, had allowed to be opened upon their soil for the education of her zealous youth, who, in defiance of the prohibitions of those in power, ventured at the risk of their vengeance, to leave their country by stealth for that purpose, and to return in the face of every peril to serve upon the mission. Little of course could be then done by Ireland for America." *Works* (Reynolds), vol. III, p. 238. This view is corroborated by other writers, among whom may be cited the author of the latest *Life and Work of Mary Aikenhead*, pp. 15-16, 23, 105. London, 1924.

tune to obtain several of them, and they became a very seasonable supply in this moment of her destitution. They made efforts to learn her language, and in many instances they were as successful as could reasonably be expected. There is no language more difficult for a foreigner, and it has its peculiar difficulties for one whose vernacular language is French; it is, therefore, that they who can speak it tolerably in public, are but rare exceptions amidst the great number that acquire it so as to be able to converse with facility. America has been fortunate in possessing a few of those exceptions. She has had two or three excellent men in her pulpits, to whom, even persons of taste and of information could listen with pleasure, and from whom they could derive much instruction, as well as gratification. A number of others were able to make themselves more or less intelligible, but I may say that, with scarcely an exception, all edified with their piety, and preached by their example. It is true that persons who could speak fluently the language of the people, whilst they possessed the learning and the piety of those men, would have been more useful, especially if their habits and customs had better qualified them for mixing with the people, for serving upon the country missions, and for understanding the laws, and the civil and political institutions of the country; but such men could not then be found, and it was a peculiar blessing from heaven, that this seasonable aid was obtained.

"Shortly after this period, the insurrection in St. Domingo [now Haiti], caused great numbers of the colonists of that island to fly with such of their slaves as would accompany them; a few of the clergy came with these emigrants, and they settled principally in the Southern States. Thus, the French portion of the Catholics in the Union was exceedingly well provided with spiritual aid, but it was far otherwise with the Irish, whose number was continually increasing in the seaports, though they went by thousands from these places to the interior, where settlements had already been made, and still farther west, to thin the forest and to subdue the land by cultivation; but in those regions no priest was then to be found.

"Ireland had most of her continental establishments for clerical education destroyed by the French Revolution and by the wars which succeeded, and years elapsed before she could obtain, even under the still greater mitigation which her persecutors granted, houses in which her children could be assembled, professors to teach them, and funds for their support. The devotion of her prelates and of her people having made a commencement, the Irish government gave reluctantly and sparingly a miserable dole, which the economy of those to whose management it had been entrusted, expended to the best account. Still, however, many years elapsed, before she could supply her own churches, and she naturally considered it to be her duty to make provision for them, before she would send any clergymen to those tens of thousands of her children, who having left her shores, were to be found in so many parts of these western regions.

"Thus, though there was an increase of a good clergy by reason of the French Revolution, it was not precisely of the description that was required in the new republic.

"Besides the difficulties arising from the diversity of language and customs, there were some that occasionally arose from difference of political predilections. They who outraged religion and massacred the clergy in France, desecrated the name of liberty by the anarchy and despotism to which they so wickedly and inappropriately gave that appelation; and they moreover rendered the name of republicanism odious through a large portion of the world, by the atrocities which they perpetrated under the semblance of its sanction; and although the clergy of France who had escaped to America were sufficiently aware of the wide distinction between the well-regulated order of American republicanism and licentious and tyrannical infidelity which assumed that name in France, and though several amongst them were gradually becoming attached to American institutions, still, amongst others, unpleasant recollections were excited by the similarity of name, and this could not always exist without an unpleasant influence upon a man who had suffered grievously in the land he loved, for whose ruin he wept, and the memory of which, though dear to his heart, was blent with that of the murder of his cherished companions and devoted friends. It was not, and it could not be in his power always to suppress the exhibition of what he felt. Too often, the thoughtless or the envious, the enthusiastic admirer of liberty or the cool opponent of his religion, made a serious mistake or took an unfair advantage because of this exhibition. Hence, though the cause of religion in the United States gained greatly by this accession, yet it was not free from some disadvantage. And, perhaps, during the twenty years that succeeded the erection of the See of Baltimore, though there was a considerable increase of congregations and of religious opportunities, there was a vast loss to the Church, because there was not a body of clergy sufficiently numerous and perfectly fitted to attend the emigrants that arrived from Germany and from Ireland."[44]

During Father Lacy's pastorate (1803-1815), disagreement in Norfolk was avoided by the fact that he was appointed President of the Board by the trustees themselves. Nevertheless, the trustees kept a strict watch on every aspect of Catholic life except in the actual administration of the Sacraments and the celebration of Mass. Even the sexton was "regulated" in a martinet fashion, one resolution (February 22, 1809) calling his particular attention to the children who came to Mass, "who are to be restrained from making a noise—if infants, their mothers or nurses are to be desired to take them away; likewise, dogs being a great nuisance, are to be prevented from disturbing the congregation or being indelicate." Rules were also drawn up for the discernment of spirits in case it was uncertain whether a dead person should be buried in the Catholic graveyard. Mr. Edward Toole, the sexton, was solemnly suspended by the trustees on September 15, 1809, and Mr. Coggin was installed in his place at a salary of twenty-five dollars a year. The praise heaped on Father Lacy after his death by the trustees suffers from the fact that they were continually haggling during his life-time over the six hundred dollars they had allotted to him.

IV

The remote beginning of the Norfolk Schism dates from the meeting of December 26, 1809, when the evil tendency of self-perpetuation was first displayed. A public notice of the meeting had been given, but "no one attended except the present year Trustees," and they resolved that "despairing of collecting together the congregation, and unwilling to abandon to chance the preservation and prosperity of the Church," they would "remain for the present in the exercise" of their functions. The next statement is worthy of notice—"it being our wish to engage the talents and patronage of other worthy members of the congregation, *we do hereby nominate and appoint* as member of our body Doctor Fernandez." Father Lacy soon realized that he could not depend upon the trustees for adequate support in completing the church. He visited Baltimore and other cities, taking up a collection in the churches for this object. As the work proceeded, the trustees became alarmed about their property rights; and at a meeting held on March 22, 1810, they forced the pastor to acknowl-

---

44. *Works* (Reynolds), vol. III, pp. 240-241.

edge that the new brick church being erected with the money collected outside the city of Norfolk would in no way be considered his personal property but would be placed under their jurisdiction. Lacy signed a "solemn declaration that he relinquished all right and title whatsoever to the Catholic Church in this place, except such as belong to him as the incumbent clergyman for the time being."[45] Father Lacy evidently was intent on keeping the peace with these headstrong leaders of his flock. We have no letters for the years 1810-15 to tell us how that peace was kept, but if we are to trust the correspondence of his successor, Rev. James Lucas, many sad mortifications were heaped upon Lacy, in spite of his conciliatory spirit, up to the time of his death in 1815.

The day after Father Lacy's death (February 24, 1815), Jasper Moran wrote to Archbishop Carroll:

> It is with deep and painful regret, and the liveliest sensibility of heart, I have to announce to you, Most Reverend Sir, the loss which our Church has sustained by the death of our truly pious and venerable Pastor, the Reverend Mr. Lacy, which occurred last night between 9 and 10 o'clock, after a short and severe attack of a pleurisy.
>
> On Tuesday last he prepared to celebrate the Mass, but found himself unable to proceed from the sudden and violent approach of his disease, which hourly increased with inflammatory and alarming symptoms, until his last moments!
>
> Aware of his approaching dissolution, he supported his afflictions with all the fortitude and composure of a truly pious man; who from the whole tenor of a long life, devoted and consecrated to real and pure charity and piety, could calmly enjoy the most religious hope and confidence in the Mercy of his God!!!
>
> In the full collection and possession of all his mental faculties, on the very *eve* his sainted soul was about to take its flight to heaven! he executed a *Will;* by which he appointed the Rev. Mr. Tessier (with another gentleman) to carry it into execution.—As that Clergyman has been addressed to-day upon the subject we may anticipate his arrival here in a few days.
>
> From this very unexpected and grievous *calamity* you will, no doubt, Most Reverend Sir, perceive the propriety of early providing a suitable character to supply the *vacancy.*—From your own knowledge of the increasing population and importance of Norfolk, I need not impress upon your mind the important advantages, in every point of view, to result from

---

45. *Letter* (Fernandez), p. 23.

the selection of a *Pastor,* not only distinguished for true zeal and piety, but likewise gifted with a very respectable portion of eloquence and information in the liturgy.

Our beloved country being again restored to the blessings of peace, and our Church being now in need of no extraordinary expenditures, I may confidently affirm that such a character would meet with adequate and ample support from this Congregation; while he would confer, by his talents and piety, equal dignity upon the Church, and his flock, in leading them in peace and harmony to the Temple of their God!

I beg leave further to remark, in addition to what I have already suggested, relative to the qualifications of the Clergyman whom you may think proper to appoint at this place, that my suggestions on that head, were more *dictated from a view of our society generally,* than from a particular regard to the members of our immediate communion, which of course will not be diminished by the absence of talent, while real piety exists in the Pastor. Knowing too that a number of very valuable members of that *general society,* who are religiously disposed, but without any fixed principle or understanding of Religion; and who through the happy influence sent forth through the eloquence, precepts and example of such a character as I have before described, might be *confirmed* in our doctrine, and *rendered* a highly *important acquisition* to our Congregation.

I have to add, my Dear Sir, that from the mortality now prevailing generally throughout the country, a successor to Mr. Lacy will be looked for with much anxiety and solicitude, by the members of this now distressed Congregation, from that calamitous stroke of death to our ever to be revered and lamented pious Pastor!

In the hope that my observations will be received in the same spirit in which they were conceived and intended, accept my sincere prayers to the Almighty for the preservation of every earthly blessing towards you; for the prosperity and happiness of that Church over which you have with exemplary dignity and mildness so long presided; and when it shall please the Almighty to close that happy life, may you obtain at His merciful hands the blessed reward of all your virtues and useful labors![46]

Dr. Carroll's answer (March 7, 1815) shows that he was cognizant of the temper of the trustees:

Your highly esteemed, though sorrowful letter of the 25th of February, was received yesterday, and excited those pain-

---

46. Moran, *Vindicatory Address etc.,* p. 55. Norfolk, 1818.

ful sensations, which must of necessity result from the tidings it bore, and the prospect it opened to my view. The death of such a respectable Clergyman as Mr. Lacy, the father, the example, the guide of his flock; whose whole study was to lead them to perfect obedience to the maxims of real religion, and, with his best abilities, to instruct them in the doctrines of truth, is at all times, and in all places a heavy loss. But, it is in the present instance, much more grevious by the difficulty of procuring a successor, considering *the great diminution of Clergymen in* this diocess, *of so much zeal and such indefatigable industry to promote their sanctification,* who are to be committed to his pastoral charge.—A life such as his, could not fail of being rewarded by a death full of hope and tranquility. The Rev. Mr. Tessier, superior of the seminary of Baltimore, will be the bearer of this, whom I do most earnestly recommend as one of the most eminent of our Clergy, to your special civilities, and those of our Catholic brethren during his stay at Norfolk.—After paying [*honor*] to the revered memory of Mr. Lacy, by celebrating his funeral, I requested him to confer with you, and learn from you the present state of the Church of Norfolk, and the congregation, which probably has suffered and been considerably diminished during the late calamitous times.—Before I select your future Pastor and solicit him to undertake the charge, I should be instructed to inform him what will be the certain amount of his means of subsistence.

It has happened too often, that relying too easily on the assurances given by some Congregations, I have appointed certain of my reverend brethren to undertake the care of souls, which they were soon compelled to abandon, through absolute failure of the assurances previously given.—Wishing earnestly to appoint a Priest at Norfolk, of very respectable talents and zeal, I must earnestly request you to afford Mr. Tessier the information necessary on this subject.—Be please to assure Mrs. Moran, Mr. and Mrs. Herron and all my respected friends, and be yourself assured, of the esteem and respect of, Dear Sir, &c. &c.[47]

Evidently, Father Tessier, Vicar-General of the diocese, went shortly afterwards to Norfolk to settle up the affairs of Father Lacy, taking with him Dr. Carroll's answer. Tessier's report on the condition of affairs in the city gave Dr. Carroll an intimate knowledge of the situation. On March 21, 1815, the trustees sent a satisfactory reply to Dr. Carroll; and on April 18, the Archbishop announced to them that he had appointed the Rev. Dr. Matthew O'Brien as pastor of their congregation.

---

47. *Ibid.*, p. 57.

Few Irish clergymen in the country bore a higher reputation than the Dominican Dr. O'Brien, and his gift of eloquence made him a desirable pastor to any Irish congregation, especially since such groups often measured a priest's spiritual value from the standpoint of his ability to preach. Dr. O'Brien's career in New York City (1799-1815) had been a notable one. He was, as Carroll says in his letter to the Norfolk Trustees (April 18), "a gentleman of pleasing manners, a very considerable stock of literature, not only on sacred but general subjects, and who has enjoyed a distinguished character for preaching; and though years may have impaired in some degree his talents in that respect, yet they are still superior to many who are heard with pleasure." It was in St. Peter's Church in New York City in March 1805, that Father O'Brien received Elizabeth Ann Seton into the fold; and he might have been elected first Bishop of New York had Carroll nominated him for that post. Dr. O'Brien's health was failing in 1815, when he accepted the Norfolk charge, and Carroll asked "one of the gentlemen now residing at the seminary, though not yet a priest, to accompany and reside with the Doctor, taking on himself the principal share of teaching and explaining the catechism." This seminarian, one of the interesting characters of the day, was Samuel Cooper, who was born in Norfolk in 1769. Neither of them remained more than a few months in Norfolk. In a letter from Father Tessier to Eugene Higgins (August 18, 1815), there is mention of Dr. O'Brien's return to Baltimore, and of his inability to take up the charge at Norfolk, since he was then seriously ill; "Your worthy pastor is sometimes better, sometimes worse; his distemper is a kind of dropsy, in the state of beginning; it may be cured, but with difficulty."[48]

Carroll's last illness and death prevented further action on the pastorate at Norfolk, and the appointment of the French secular priest, Father James Lucas, by Archbishop Neale, was the occasion for the first outbreak against the spiritual authority of the See of Baltimore by a part of the Norfolk congregation, with Jasper Moran as its leader.

---

48. Dr. O'Brien died at Baltimore, Oct. 15, 1816. Cf. Moran, *l.c.*, Appendix S.

THE CATHOLIC CHURCH IN VIRGINIA
1815-1822

CHAPTER I

THE CATHOLIC CHURCH IN VIRGINIA
UNDER ARCHBISHOP NEALE

The second Archbishop of Baltimore, Leonard Neale, was in his seventieth year when he took up the task of guiding the American Church.

Leonard Neale was a native of Maryland, and was born near Port Tobacco, in Charles County, on October 15, 1746, eleven years after the birth of John Carroll.[1] His father was descended

---

1. "William and Anne (Brooke) Neale of Portobacco, had seven sons, of whom six entered the Society or applied for admission after their studies at St. Omer's, Bruges, or Liège:—William Chandler, a Jesuit priest in England; Joseph, who died when in the class of Rhetoric, and took simple vows of devotion on his death-bed; Oswald (Roswell), who was in the class of Grammar, and died too young to be granted his desire for the same privilege; Raphael, who married, but died soon; Leonard,............; Charles, who had not quite finished his two years' novitiate, when the Suppression occurred; finally, Francis Neale, born 3 June, 1756, and therefore only seventeen years of age at the moment of the Suppression. Of six daughters, one, Ann, became a Poor Clare at Aire in Artois; two died in their infancy; Mary was the mother of the Rev. William Matthews; Clare, who married a Brent and a Slye, was the mother of Chandler Brent; Eleanor married a Holmes and a Boarman. Father Francis Dzierozynski, Superior of the Maryland Mission, sent to the General an extensive biographical note about the family, on the occasion of Father Charles Neale's death (27 Apr., 1823), saying that a notice of this family should be entered in the records of the Society of Jesus: *Notitia domus hujus sane meretur, ut in fastis Societatis suum locum inveniat.*" Hughes, *op. cit.* Doc., vol. 1, part II, p. 221 note; cf. M. S. Pine, *A Glory of Maryland*, p. 71, Phila., 1917.

from Captain James Neale and Anne Gill, his wife (a maid of honor to Queen Henrietta Maria), who emigrated to Maryland in 1642. William Neale, a great-grandson of the Captain was Leonard's father, and his mother was Anne Brooke, of the Maryland family of that name. Leonard attended Bohemia Manor Academy as a boy; and at the age of twelve was sent to St. Omer College, France, for his collegiate studies.[2] After finishing his course in philosophy and theology, he was ordained to the priesthood, probably in the year 1767.[3] Six years later when the Suppression of the Society of Jesus was decreed by the Holy See, Leonard Neale went to England and labored as a secular priest in the English missions. In the archives of the English Province of the Society of Jesus, his name is found in a list of *Catholic Chaplaincies in the North during the Eighteenth Century*, as living "at Hardwick, with Mr. Rose, from about 1773 to 1777."[4]

Father Neale's life during the next three years is uncertain. The traditional account says that in the following year (1778) he volunteered for the English missions of Demerara, British Guiana.[5] Hughes, however, hints at his presence in Bruges during these three years and speaks of his "experiences" there prior to his offering himself for these South American missions, no doubt referring to the treatment being accorded to the British ex-Jesuits then in the Low Countries. The few letters found so far do not throw much light on this period of his life.[6] On June 13, 1780, Maggiora, the auditor of the Belgian Nuncio, wrote to Cardinal Antonelli, that Neale had come to Brussels from Liège and that he had accepted the Demerara congregation. Neale was then thirty-four years old, had been a Jesuit for five years at the time of the Suppression and had not made his solemn profession. Maggiora wrote again on July 11, 1780, from Brussels, saying that he had given to Neale the faculties sent by Propaganda. There is also a letter (July 16) written with Neale's characteristic humility, accepting the arduous post.[7] He was probably then residing as temporary chaplain at the convent of the English

---

2. For the history of these two schools, cf. Guilday, *Carroll*, p. 14ss.
3. Hughes, *op. cit.*, Text, vol ii, p. 700.
4. Catholic Record Society Publications, *Miscellanea*, vol. iv. p. 248. London, 1907, cf., Foley, *Records, S.J.*, vol. vii, pt. II, p. 537.
5. Hughes, *op. cit.*, Doc., vol. i, pt. ii, p. 710 note.
6. The Bruges Episcopal Archives were searched in the summer of 1923 for letters on this incident, but nothing was found to shed any light on it.
7. Prop Arch., *Scritt. rifer., Amer. Cent.*, vol. 2, f. 118.

Canonesses at Bruges.[8] In all likelihood, Father Neale went to Demerara about this time. Bishop Galton, S.J., of Georgetown, British Guiana, wrote to the writer on February 5, 1923, in regard to Neale's short stay in that colony, and sending a translation of a passage in the *Litterae Annuae,* which was printed in pamphlet form for private circulation, some time after 1857:

> The next Missioner after Father Chamberlain was Father Leonard Neale of Maryland, who with two brothers entered the Society in Belgium, and did good service in it. About four years after the Suppression of the Society he had a small mission in England, but after seven years landed alone in Demerara or Stabroek. The Dutch at that time possessed Guiana and had built two towns, one Stabroek the capital, and the other New Amsterdam or Barbica. When he could do nothing among the Dutch colonists, nor get leave to build a chapel, he betook himself to the natives, who had retired to the woods on the occupation of the country by the Europeans, and there did for some time good missionary work. A sick child whom he had baptized having been restored to health, he converted the father with some four others. At last, broken in health by the climate, he bade farewell to a perverse nation. His account was sent to Rome; as is said, about the year 1782. Father Neale landed in Maryland, from which he had been absent thirty-seven years, in the month of January 1783, though he was captured on the way by the English on the seas. After some years of meritorious service, in which he nearly fell a victim in attending the sick, during an epidemic, he was sent as Superior to the College at Georgetown, and in the year 1800, made Bishop of Gortyna, and coadjutor with the right of succession.

This is the sole record of Neale's residence in the colony. "It seems to me," Bishop Galton writes, "that he must have come here during the year 1780, as on December 20, 1780, war broke out between England and the Netherlands, and in February, 1781, an English fleet blockaded the Demerara River, and later took possession of the Colony which, however, in January, 1782, was conquered by the French, who kept possession of it for about a year. It would seem that Father Neale had left while the Dutch were still in peaceful possession, but after the war had begun with the Netherlands, as he was captured by an English ship." There is a letter from Neale in the Propaganda Archives, under

---

8. Cf. Guilday, *English Catholic Refugees on the Continent,* p. 385. London, 1914.

date of 1782, in which "he bitterly laments the blindness and corruption of the inhabitants, and announces his determination to quit a people, among whom his labors are so fruitless, and where the difficulties of his mission are almost insuperable. The prejudice of the settlers would allow him no church for Catholic worship, and, owing to the inclemency of the climate, the severity of his labours, and the meanness of his comforts, his health was greatly impaired." [9] He left Demerara in January, 1783, and after an absence from the United States of twenty-five years, reached his native State, in April of that year. His first mission was at St. Thomas' Manor, near Port Tobacco.

Sometime after his arrival in Maryland, Neale sent a report on the Demerara missions to Propaganda, and on January 20, 1787, a reply came from Rome acknowledging his interest in the congregation he had been obliged to leave on account of ill health. He was asked to propose a suitable missionary for British Guiana, and also to give to the Sacred Congregation the proper information about the missions nearest to Demerara, to which recourse might be had by Popaganda for spiritual care.[10]

Neale remained at St. Thomas' Manor, taking an active part in the deliberations of the Corporation of the Clergy until 1793, when Bishop Carroll sent him to Philadelphia to fill the place of Bishop-elect Lawrence Graessl, who had died during the yellow fever epidemic that year.[11] On March 23, 1795, at a general congregation of Propaganda, Leonard Neale was appointed in place of the late Bishop-elect Graessl, and on March 26, the Secretary of Briefs, Cardinal Braschi, was requested to forward the official papers of Neale's appointment. Pius VI confirmed the selection of Leonard Neale, and on April 17, 1795, the bulls were sent to Bishop Carroll, Neale being named Bishop of Gortyna and coadjutor to Carroll.[12]

Owing to the disturbed conditions of affairs in Europe, consequent to the French Revolution, the documents necessary for Neale's consecration did not reach Baltimore until the summer of 1800. Bishop-elect Neale remained in Philadelphia until 1799,

---

9. Propaganda Archives, *l.c.*, vol. 2 f. 119 Cf. *United States Catholic Magazine*, vol. iii, p. 507 (Biography of Archbishop Neale).
10. Propaganda Archives, *Lettere*, vol. 250, f. 555.
11. Hughes, *op. cit.*, Doc., vol. i, pt. ii, p. 661 note (Carroll to Plowden, December 22, 1791).
12. Prop. Arch., *Lettere,* vol. 265, p. 87; cf. *Researches,* vol. ix, p. 66; vol. xxi, p. 69.

when he was appointed President of Georgetown College. His consecration on December 7, 1800, in Baltimore, was the first ceremony of its kind to be held within the borders of the United States. Bishop Neale announced his consecration to Propaganda on January 12, 1801, in a letter in which the spiritual outlook of his new dignity dominates so completely that not a single word regarding conditions around and about him found its way into his message.[13] He continued to act as President of Georgetown College until 1806, when that important post was conferred upon Father Robert Molyneux, who became Superior of the restored Society. From 1806 until the death of Carroll, Bishop Neale made his home near the Visitation Convent, Georgetown. It was there that he died on June 18, 1817, and he lies buried in the crypt of the Visitation Chapel.[14]

During the two years that he was Archbishop of Baltimore, he was continually harassed by ill health. The malarial fever contracted as a missionary in Demerara rendered him a ready subject to the yellow fever epidemics in Philadelphia from 1793 to 1799; and his succession to the See of Baltimore found him a broken, infirm man, physically unprepared for the burdensome legacy Carroll had bequeathed. Among the tasks which confronted him, that of Church discipline was the heaviest and the most difficult.

One evil stalked step-by-step with the progress of the Faith in the United States during the first half-century of its organized canonical life—lay trusteeship of ecclesiastical property. From the time of his appointment as Prefect-Apostolic (1784) to his death (1815), Archbishop Carroll had witnessed serious conflicts between the episcopal authority of the Church and certain groups of laymen who possessed the legal power of trusteeship. It is not necessary to enter deeply here into the origin of the evil side of trusteeism. Various causes contributed to bring about disorder. The country was new. Canon law was not known to the various State legislatures. The Catholics, then a minority in all the States, sought to protect their ecclesiastical property by the legal means then in vogue. Many of those who composed the Catholic congregations in the centres disturbed by trusteeism, were enjoying for the first time political liberty of action in their religious worship and were carried away with the new freedom. They were,

---

13. Prop. Arch., *Scritt. rifer., Amer. Cent.*, vol. 3, f. 120.
14. Cf. Lathrop, *A Story of Courage*, pp. 185-192. Cambridge, 1895.

moreover, influenced by the vestry system of the Protestant churches.[15]

The problem of controlling the right and equable administration of church property could not at the time be dealt with in a national way; local regulations had to be resorted to, in order to protect ecclesiastical holdings. The civil law at the time, with the exception of Virginia, gave the right of possessing such holdings to the congregation, on the condition that they be administered by a board of trustees duly elected by the members of each congregation.[16] There was in this system nothing essentially at variance with the Catholic discipline, and for protection's sake, Bishop Carroll sanctioned it. "That the system was dangerous and liable to great abuses, is patent to the most casual observer of the Church's development in the United States. Scandals and schisms were the outgrowth of the system."[17]

But the origin of these scandals and schisms is not found in the system itself, but in the pretensions set up by the trustees who employed their legal power to force upon the bishops the acceptance of the right of patronage.

Bishop England, who conquered the evils in trusteeism, had no fault to find with the system of American church property incorporation. "I do not know," he writes, "any system more favorable to the security of religious rights and of church property than that of the American law. I have consulted eminent jurists upon the subject. I have closely studied it, and have acted according to its provisions in various circumstances, favorable and unfavorable, during several years, and in many of the details and as a whole, I prefer it to the law of almost every Catholic country with which I am acquainted. I think, with the exception of one, perhaps two States, that it is a more honest, fair, and liberal system. Like any other, it is liable to be abused and sometimes the prejudices of the individual will accompany him to the bench or to the jury-box but this is not the fault of the system."[18]

In some instances, however, Catholic laymen of that day carried over into the trustee system the policy and the regulations of non-Catholic American congregations, and gradually the fatal tendency of regarding their priests as "servants to perform religious

---

15. Cf. *The Evils of Trusteeism,* by G. C. Treacy, S.J., in the *Historical Records and Studies,* vol. viii (1915), pp. 136-156.
16. Zollmann, *op. cit.,* p. 25.
17. Treacy, *ut supra,* p. 137.
18. *Works* (Reynolds), vol. iii, p. 241.

services" became apparent in their attitude. There was, moreover, the belief present among many laymen that the clergy should be relieved of all the worries and anxieties attendant upon the temporal management of church affairs, and having excluded the priests from this material attention, they gradually excluded them from all control of the property incorporated in the name of the congregation. Once this right was claimed, as legally it could be in the courts, the trustees arrogated the further power of dismissing any priest who attacked the system and of selecting clergymen who were amenable to dictation from themselves. In this way, unworthy priests were intruded into congregations, and when episcopal authority for the good of religion attempted to exercise a restraining and pruning hand upon such restrictions, attack, rebellion, and schism were the inevitable result. "No persons," writes Dr. England," were more ready than were the 'Catholic Atheists' to be in the foremost ground to protect their rights, to aid religion, and to preserve liberty, by opposing the bishop, by humbling the priest, and by teaching the whole body of the clergy the proper mode of governing the Catholic Church!" Dr. England does not exculpate entirely some of the clergy of the day, who forgot "the boundary of their sphere and endeavored to encroach upon that of the laity."[19]

The trustee system was ill-regulated, and as such it became during these earliest decades of our organized Church "a source of great disaster, of many scandals, and of several schisms," estranging great numbers from the Church, "by disgusting many respectable and peaceable members, by driving many of the schismatics into heresy, and by fomenting not only a spirit of disorder, of anarchy, and of contempt for discipline, but an estrangement from religious practices, an absence from the sacraments, and a distraction of the spirit of piety, in comparison to which the gross mismanagement of funds and other temporal losses are a mere insignificant trifle."[20] There were, moreover, hazy notions about the *jus patronatus*, and Neale had been forced to send an open letter to the schismatics of Philadelphia in 1796, telling them, as he later told the rebellious trustees of Norfolk and of Charleston, that the right of patronage did not exist in this land. Carroll had given the keynote of the Church's stand on the matter in a letter to Neale (October 11, 1796) in which he said:

---

19. *Ibid.*, p. 243.
20. *Ibid.*

"Their pretended *jus patronatus* must be resolutely resisted, and is absolutely untenable."[21]

It would be quite easy to solve the problem of the evils of trusteeism with the statement that rebillious laymen, with here and there priests as their abettors, were upholding a principle which involved a very delicate point in canon law. But such a solution is not actually in accord with the facts. There was something more serious at the root of the quarrel than the bare question of financial ownership of church property. In reality the trustee trouble arose only when the issue was that of accepting the pastor appointed by the bishop to a particular congregation. The evil mainly consisted of this: that the trustees wished not only to control these appointments, but also to be invested with the power of dismissing their pastors at will. There was a legitimate interpretation of the *jus patronatus* which could have been accepted by Archbishop Neale, but the trustees went far beyond the canonical import of the privilege. Racial feeling also ran high here during the first quarter of the nineteenth century, and the appointment by Archbishop Neale of the Rev. James Lucas, a French secular priest, to Norfolk, a congregation largely Irish and inclined to be anti-French, is one example of the origin of these scandals. The appointment of Father Clorivière to Charleston, also an Irish congregation, caused the same difficulty there. The New York, Philadelphia and New Orleans schisms were, it is true, caused by priests who made use of the trustees to strengthen their disobedience to episcopal authority. In the case of Norfolk and Charleston, however, the theory of the *jus patronatus* came apparently as a last resort, when it was evident that Archbishop Neale would not yield to the trustees' demand that Lucas and Clorivière be removed.

Various antipathies were alive, at the time. Poterie's little diatribe, *The Resurrection of Laurent Ricci*,[22] and Smyth's *Present State of the Catholic Missions, etc.*, though hard to find today, were read rather widely during the last two decades of the eighteenth century, and were the cause of considerable feeling against Carroll and Neale as ex-members of the suppressed Society of Jesus. This feeling found voice in criticism against the Clergy

---

21. BCA, Case—11—V3. For Neale's letter of December 8, 1796, see Guilday, *Carroll*, pp. 650-653.
22. Through a search in various Jesuit libraries instituted by the Rev. John J. Wynne, S.J., a copy of this scarce booklet was discovered and a photograph copy made for the writer's use.

Corporation which had formulated rather strict rules for the administration of the ex-Jesuit property and likewise stringent regulations regarding the admission into the Corporation of secular priests coming to the American missions from abroad. A feeling akin to the old Secular-Regular controversy in the English Catholic Church was created by the criticism of men like the Harolds and Ryan, who had returned to Europe; and it may be safely asserted that many of the priests coming from Ireland to the United States after 1815, were imbued with this anti-Jesuit prejudice. The fact that some of the most prominent Irish priests were members of the Dominican Order would give an apparent anti-Jesuit coloring to the struggle against the authority of Carroll and Neale, but this is modified by the fact that Maréchal, a Sulpician, was equally the object of their attack. An important factor is that among the rank and file of the Irish Catholics in the country at the time, there was a distinct political antipathy to all things French. This is evident in the case of Fathers Lucas and Clorivière, and of Bishop Dubois of New York (1826-42). The First Provincial Council of Baltimore (1829), as we have seen, while not recognizing the problem of trusteeism from the standpoint of these racial antipathies, legislated that no ecclesiastical patronage existed in the country, and the bishops were urged to interdict any church where the congregation through its trustees or others, retained any priest not approved in the regular canonical manner or whose faculties had been revoked or who was suspended, or where the duly-appointed priest was prevented from officiating or deprived of his income.[23] This wise legislation was reënacted in the Provincial Councils of 1837, 1840 and 1843. In 1837, a decree (IV) urged the bishops to secure all ecclesiastical property by the best means the civil laws of the different States afforded. In 1840, a decree (VIII) ordered bishops to control ecclesiastical property in their own name and not to permit priests to do so. Between the Council of 1840 and the first Plenary Council of Baltimore in 1852, trusteeism was brought to a definite close by the energetic John Hughes of New York.[24] This brief summary will serve as a background for the story of the Norfolk Schism.

The Norfolk pastorate remained vacant from August to December 1815, owing to Carroll's last illness. On December 12,

---

23. *Concilia Baltimori habita etc.*, p. 36. Cf. Hughes, *Works*, vol. ii, p. 551.
24. *Works*, vol. ii, pp. 549-632.

1815, Tessier wrote to Higgins as follows: "I feel a great pleasure to see at last a priest sent to reside in Norfolk, who will, after some time, I hope, fulfil all your desires and surpass your expectations. He is young yet, but has already served three years in the holy ministry in France; he is now learning English very fast; and once he has preached in our church with real success for his composition and pronunciation. He is a decent, pious, and learned clergyman; and I hope that he will succeed very well in Norfolk, both for the French and the Irish."[25]

This worthy young priest, the Rev. James Lucas, was to be the storm-centre of one of the most serious conflicts between episcopal authority and lay-trusteeism in the American Church.[26] The appointment of Lucas was the first made by Archbishop Neale, who wrote to the Norfolk Trustees on December 13, 1815: "You have, no doubt, been informed how it has pleased heaven to deprive the See of Baltimore of its most Rev. and justly lamented Archbishop Carroll, who, for many years had filled the Sacred Post of Prelate, with such dignity, Prudence and integrity, as to command the esteem, respect and veneration of all that knew him. His labors are now at an end. . . . He has merited our grateful memory. Since his departure, the weighty burden rests on me of unequal force and ability. But as God has imposed the necessity, so, I trust, He will supply my deficiency. Hence being informed of your being destitute of a Pastor, and having promised one of your community to send one as soon as it were in my power, I feel happy that Providence has so opportunely supplied me with the means of complying with my promise. I have appointed for your pastor the Rev. Mr. James Lucas, who is the bearer of this, which I have directed him to read to the assembled congregation from the pulpit or from the Altar. He is a gentleman in whom I have entire confidence, and considering the respectability of character you bear in the eyes of all your acquaintances I have conversed with, I confide you will receive him with every mark of kindness and attention and will dispose everything so as to render him happy and comfortable among you."[27]

On his arrival in Norfolk (December 18, 1815), Father Lucas was received rather coldly by the trustees, one of whom was

---

25. In Appendix T. of Moran's *Vindicatory Address*.
26. Prop. Arch., *Scritt. rifer., Amer. Cent.*, vol. 3, f. 361. Neale to Prop., February 4, 1816: "Alterum presbyterum nuper huc advectum de Gallia, ubi officium pastoris laudabiliter et fructuose—per tres annos."
27. Shea, *op. cit.*, vol. iii, p. 26.

suspicious that he was not the person mentioned in the Archbishop's letter. The following Sunday, Lucas read Neale's message from the altar. Some days later (December 28), the trustees held a meeting to which Lucas was not invited. Another meeting, held two days later at the house of Dr. Fernandez, was attended by Lucas, although uninvited. "I was not invited to that assembly," he wrote to Neale on February 8, 1816, "but desiring to know how they would proceed, I went to the Doctor's, who has a very proper building for such assemblies. At my first entrance, he told me that I was not requested, and that I ought to go out; and he spoke in French, in order not to be understood by the Irish who were present. I answered in English with calm: 'Doctor, you are not polite in your own house; I come only as a spectator; let me see how you proceed; I am curious to see.' And I staid—some moments after, the deliberations began."[28] Lucas was then offered the chairmanship of the meeting, but declined, "on account of my ignorance of the language." The Spanish Consul also refused the chairmanship, and Fernandez was then elected. Owing to his imperfect knowledge of English, Lucas' earlier letters are considerably confused in diction. It is evident, however, from this letter of February 8, that the Portuguese had decided to declare war on Lucas and Archbishop Neale: "The Doctor, who had the intention to exclude the pastor of every administration of the Church, and to take on himself all the right, said that . . . the priest ought to take care of the spiritual only; that the Popes had no right in the temporal, therefore nor the priests; that the trustees and the congregation had been deceived by Mr. Lacy, etc., etc. It is impossible to give you an exact account of all his impoliteness. He added that the trustees had the right to refuse a priest sent by the Bishop, if they judged him not suitable for their Church, etc. He proposed one of the trustees to be the President [*of the Board*]. Almost all said that the Pastor ought to be President, and they elected me." Fernandez then offered his resignation from the Board; Lucas tried to dissuade him, but the resignation was accepted. "The Doctor is an enemy to me and has some partisans. The other Trustees are not better for me. They seem to be zealous for their Church, but they will have the priest entirely dependent on them, even for his preaching."[29]

This letter contains the first statement of the conflict which

---

28. BCA, Case—12A—G5.
29. BCA, Case—12A—G6.

was to grow in bitterness and violence up to the erection of the See of Richmond in July, 1820. The appointment of Lucas from the standpoint of tact may have been a mistake, as also that of Father Clorivière in Charleston at this same time; but once appointed, no bishop would have recalled them while principles such as those enunciated by Fernandez were accepted by the leaders of the congregation. Archbishop Neale could not abrogate the canonical right his office as Ordinary entailed, and the conflict which followed, unique in many respects in American Church annals, was inevitable. It would be too tedious to follow every move made by both parties from this time until the Jansenist "Independent Catholick Church of the United States" was projected by the malcontented trustees of the South.

Lucas clashed first with the trustees over a collection taken up among the ladies of the congregation to purchase new vestments. This was rudely resented by the Board, and Lucas wrote to the Archbishop that "one of them told me that they will write to you, and that they have the right to make [*you*] move a priest who is not suitable to [*them*] : 'Say a priest who refuses to give you an entire administration of the Church.' " Lucas was also informed by the trustees that he could not celebrate Mass or preach in any other place without their consent. There were neglected congregations in Richmond, Fredericksburg and Portsmouth at the time, but the trustees held that his faculties existed only within the borders of the Norfolk parish. "They look upon me as a journeyman. I told them that I despised their money and that I could go where I am pleased without their consent. I know now from a good hand that Mr. Lacy had the greatest contradictions with them and was very much persecuted. I hope that these difficulties will have an end soon, when they see that I have the best intentions for this Church."[30]

Had he realized it, these difficulties were but in their infancy. In reply to the letter quoted above, Archbishop Neale wrote from Georgetown on March 6, 1816: "Your uncouth reception and treatment from the trustees are nothing but harsh mementoes of the impropriety of laytrusteeship which I have always been inimical to, and henceforward as far as I can prevent that pernicious system, I shall not fail to do it, *as I stand firmly convinced that great evils must eventually flow from it, wherever it is established* . . . . Their pretended right of choosing their Priest or

---

30. BCA, Case—12A—G7.

Missionary Pastor is perfectly unfounded; for they are not Patrons of the Church according to the language of the Council of Trent, who alone have a right of choosing their Pastor. In the See of Baltimore, none but the Archbishop can place or remove a Priest: and that he can do at will, as there are no parishes established here, no benefices conferred, and no collations made and no powers granted but what are merely missionary, revocable at will. Hence the trustees can claim no jurisdiction over their Priest, nor prevent his missionary functions, which, with my full permission, you may extend beyond the limits of Norfolk, as you shall see the good of religion requires."[31]

The Archbishop urged him to have courage in the face of the insubordinate spirit he found about him and prudently to overcome the relaxed and negligent part of his congregation by his own spiritual life and mildness. "You say," he wrote, "that you and the trustees are still friendly; so much the better. Those little bickerings must not discompose you. Turn all to advantage. Never let them discover in you unbecoming warmth of temper; but proceeding with cool deliberateness, stick close to your conscientious duty with steadiness and dignity."[32] Father Lucas did his best to follow the advice of his venerable superior, but his temperament was not a prudent one, and his temper at times was not mild. He had one serious disadvantage in the conflict with these older heads, the disadvantage of youth and of youth's impetuous attitude towards the integrity of a principle. His opponents were Irishmen with the Irishman's cleverness in debate. It must be remembered also that Neale, upon whom he had to depend for guidance, was a day's journey away and unable physically for such a matching of wits.

"I am an old man of seventy," he had written to Propaganda Fide on February 4, 1816, "and my strength is exhausted by reason of the forty years I have spent in missionary labors. Hence, not wishing to excuse myself, for I desire to be sacrificed wholly in the *opus Dei,* I am compelled to ask for a coadjutor who will sustain me in my old age and be my aid in this great work."[33] Either Cheverus of Boston or Maréchal was his choice, and he begged the Holy See to act quickly. The Norfolk troubles, the Charleston difficulties, the quarrels in New York and in Philadelphia, all bore the outward appearance of an inward disease which

---
31. BCA, Case—12—R2.
32. *Ibid.*
33. Prop. Arch., *Scritt. rifer., Amer. Cent.,* vol. 3, f. 361-362.

threatened the very existence of authority and discipline; and certainly in perusing the numerous letters sent to Neale by Lucas, we cannot help sympathizing with the saintly successor to Carroll in his request to Rome for assistance.

On March 12, 1816, Lucas wrote that he had found by that date very few practising Catholics in his congregation. Fernandez bore a shady reputation, and Edward Higgins who aided the recalcitrants, had studied for the priesthood in Ireland and was supposed to have received some of the minor orders.[34] The church was rather large, with forty-eight pews, five persons sitting in each pew: "The greatest part of the congregation is *bad* French; they come to church on Sunday; [*there are*] eight or ten families, Irish or American, and distinguished by their wealth, not by *piety*." At the last meeting of the board, Lucas found the trustees more polite and more willing to make changes in their resolutions. It is characteristic of Lucas to find him insisting upon a change from the phrase; "the Revd. Mr. Lucas *shall be paid*," to "the *fees* of Revd. Mr. Lucas shall be." But the ill-feeling aroused at the outset by the stand Father Lucas felt obliged to take, would not cease. The situation became acute when he threatened to denounce the trustees from the altar. Spiritually, he had made progress in the parish. He had a trained choir of young ladies to sing the Plain Chant of the Mass and of Vespers. Every Sunday he preached in French and English, and during Lent he held services every Tuesday and Friday, and explained the ceremonies of the Church. These services were ended with the Benediction of the Blessed Sacrament and with night prayers. The contention of Lucas was that as pastor, he was, "the first trustee" and to him, therefore, belonged the administration of the parish revenues. Against this the trustees set themselves as a stone wall, and Lucas asked the Archbishop (April 10, 1816) for authority to abolish the board publicly. The French portion of the congregation gradually gathered around him, many of them being dissatisfied because the trustees (all Irish) were controlling parish affairs. Lucas knew enough of the Irish temperament to realize that his greatest threat over them was "to read them publicly from the altar." His courage increased and he defined to them their duties: "First to help me in what I can not do myself, and to follow the directions I will give, or to propose to me their views, and if I approve, to put them into execution."[35] He then asked

---

34. BCA, Case—12A—G6.
35. BCA, Case—12A—G7.

the Archbishop to give him an open letter to the congregation declaring the power of the trustees null and void:—"I beseech you to authorize me to act without any of them, and the revenues of the church will not diminish. . . . I hope you will seaze the good opportunity to pull them down entirely. It is the best part to take."[36]

Neale's answer (April 19, 1816) contains a definite statement of the whole controversy and places the control of the trusteeship in Lucas' hands:

> I am sorry to hear that those whom you call Trustees, continue to give you uneasiness. What you have said about pewholders appointing them, leads me to think that they have no legal authority to act, but to collect the pew-rents for you, because the Church belongs not to the pews, but the pews belong to the Church, and were instituted to provide means for the Pastor's support and the necessary arrangement for Divine Service in the Church, which properly speaking belongs to the Clergyman under his Bishop to whom he is amenable for his administration.
>
> The Presbiterian system puts the Vestrymen over the Clergyman, but the Catholic system places the Clergyman over the Vestrymen *whom he appoints and dismisses at will*. Because they are taken into their office to assist the Pastor in temporal matters, as in the primitive Church, Deacons were appointed to assist the Apostles in the administration of temporalities. Surely there are no Catholics to be found who would not condemn those Deacons had they presumed an authority over the Apostles whom they were appointed to assist.
>
> Therefore no *Vestryman* ought to presume to control the Pastor, whom he is appointed to assist, not to oppose.
>
> Great evils have flowed in upon the Church in this Country wherever Trustees have been appointed by an act of the civil law, because the Trustees have availed themselves of the civil law to lord it over their Pastor, instead of assisting him.
>
> This evil I would wish to avoid, and the congregation of Norfolk should wish the same, if they mean to be respectable and happy. To effect this, I recommend the following system, viz: The Pastor will from time to time, choose a certain number of his Congregation, whom he may think the best calculated to assist him in the management of the temporal concerns of the Church, and by whom he may be helped by sound advice, to meet the various emergencies of the place. He will, by this

---

36. *Ibid.*

system be enabled to manage all things in peace and great respectability.[37]

Father Lucas made known the Archbishop's decision to the trustees privately, and on May 6, he received the following communication from the Board:

> The Trustees of the Church have to regret that, notwithstanding their most anxious wishes and their best endeavors to preserve a good understanding with their Pastor, so far from succeeding in this object, they observe that instances of unpleasant irritation are frequently occurring and as they wish to avoid every thing of this nature, especially with their Pastor, they must decline attending any meeting at present. They say that they were very much surprised at the communication from the Altar for it is their most decided belief that such a course of proceeding would have the unhappy tendency of producing schism in our Church. The Trustees beg leave to call to the recollection of Rev. Mr. Lucas the arrangements which were made at their first meeting. It was then distinctly understood that the Trustees were to have charge of the revenue of the Church, that it was their duty to make the disbursements for altering and repairing the Church, and that in conjunction with the Pastor, they were to decide what was proper to be done. The Trustees, at this time, passed a resolution requesting the Pastor to provide such things as he considered necessary *for the use of the Altar,* and present the account monthly to the Trustees for payment. This, they believe, is the practice of the Roman Catholic Churches throughout the United States, and particularly at the Church at Baltimore, over which our late Right Reverend Archbishop Carroll so long presided. This mode of proceeding is in the opinion of the Trustees, the only one that can be pursued, to promote the welfare and advancement of our Church, and as that is their *sole object,* they hope the Rev. Mr. Lucas will view it in the same light that they do. *We are, Rev. Sir, very respectfully, your obedient servants,* James Herron, Thos. Moran, Eugene Higgins, Bernard Mulhollan, John Donaghey.[38]

The challenge thus given was courageously taken up by Lucas who replied: "The Pastor of the Roman Catholic Church in Norfolk, in the name of the Archbishop and in his own, declares to MM. J. Herron, Th. Moran, Eug. Higgins, B. Mulhollan and J. Donaghey that they are Trustees no more; and that if this private admonition is not sufficient they will receive a public one, as he is authorized to do so. That the Archbishop does not view such

---

37. BCA, Case—12—R3.
38. BCA, Case—12—Y7.

a dissolution in the same light as the Trustees, since he tells me: *stick close to your consciencious duty with steadiness and dignity,* and what will be the result? Hear the Archbishop: *This will put malice at defiance and stem the torrent of depravity; and whilst it becomes the terror of vice, it will yield support and joy to the faithful and virtuous.* . . . I shall require publicly, if you refuse to listen to a private request: 1st. The register of the resolutions of the trustees. . . . 2ndly. All the notes of the pew-holders, the whole of the money of the Church and the accounts in good order. . . .[39]

This authorized abolition of the Board was met with sullen obstinacy. James Herron, to whom Lucas addressed his private admonition, replied that he had heard from Luke Tiernan of Baltimore who gave him "a different account of the rights of the Trustees even in the Church of the Archbishop."[40] Donaghey insulted Lucas publicly in the street. The same day (May 8) Herron and Thomas Moran came to Lucas and asked him to recall the letter—"I refused, and told them if they refused to communicate it to the other trustees, I would read it publicly. They consented to communicate it."[41] A meeting of the trustees and other prominent Irish members of the congregation was held on May 9, and it was decided to appeal directly to the Archbishop against Father Lucas.

By this time the bickerings had become public gossip. One of the trustees foolishly remarked that Father Lucas should not be allowed even to write to Archbishop Neale without the written consent of the Board. Another member of the Irish faction said that pastoral rights were ancient "bigotry, good for the Church in France, but not in the United States." Another claimed that since Archbishop Carroll had addressed the "Board of Trustees of the Roman Catholic Church in Norfolk," he had implicitly recognized their authority in administering the church. All this Lucas included in his letter to Neale, of May 10-11, 1816. An hour or so after he had posted this long communication, he received this message from the trustees:

> The Trustees have taken into consideration the letter which you addressed to them on the 7th of this month, and as they cannot comply with the demands contained in that letter, they hope Mr. Lucas will not make any communication from the

---

39. BCA, Case—12A—G5.
40. Cf. *Researches*, vol. xii, pp. 189, 192.
41. BCA, Case—12—Y7.

Altar relative to any matters of difference that exist between him and the trustees.

They assure Mr. Lucas at the same time, that this request does not arise from any regard to their own particular situations, but from their conviction that such a course of proceeding will be attended with the most unhappy consequences, as it regards our Church. Under this impression, the trustees are persuaded that Mr. Lucas will not adopt a measure that is pregnant with the most lamentable consequences.

We are very respectfully, Revd. Sir, your obedt. sevts. for the Board of Trustees.   Signed, JAMES HERRON, *Secy.*[42]

On the following Sunday, Father Lucas did not say anything from the altar concerning the trustees, but at the end of the service, he asked Donaghey, Higgins, Mulhollan, Thomas Moran and Herron "to stay in Church after the rest of the Congregation," as he had an important communication to make to them. He explained to them the discipline of the Church in the matter of pastoral rights and duties. The trustees soon became violent in their protestations against his and the Archbishop's authority: "They left the Church very unsatisfied. I told them that their opinions were entirely heretical. . . . I told them that I was disposed to sustain the discipline of the Catholic Church even till *death.*"[43] Meanwhile, the trustees had drafted an appeal to the Archbishop, dated May 10, 1816:

The Trustees of the Roman Catholic Church of Norfolk ever solicitous in common with the rest of their brethren of the congregation, for its welfare and respectability in providing an adequate support for our Pastor, and in conjunction with him in procuring everything necessary, compatible with our means, for the greater order and decency of Divine Worship, could, not without extreme pain, discover for some time past on the part of the Rev. Mr. Lucas a disposition to take to himself the entire control and direction of the Revenue of the Church and to deprive the Congregation, or their Trustees, of any Agency or authority in their distribution—contrary to the established rules and regulations which have existed since the first establishment of a Church here, sanctioned too by our late and ever to be revered Prelate Archbishop Carroll, and acquiesced in and approved by all our former Pastors, and by the Rev. Mr. Lucas himself upon entering upon his pastoral duties—All concurring we believe in the opinion that by a proper union and harmony

---

42. BCA, Case—12A—G5.
43. *Ibid.*

between Pastor and Trustees, the Revenues would be enhanced, greater economy be perceived in their disposition and the objects of Religion generally amongst us best be promoted.—Our regret was rendered the most poignant upon the manifestation of such an intention from the respect and esteem with which we regarded the Rev. Mr. Lucas's zeal, piety, and talents.—What was our grief and astonishment upon receiving a letter a few days ago from our Pastor to find, most Reverend Sir, that you have not only given your sanction to such proceedings but have under circumstances the most painful authorized him to dissolve our Body, accompanied with these extraordinary expressions—"This will put malice at defiance and stem the torrent of depravity, and whilst it becomes the terror of vice, it will yield support and joy to the faithful and virtuous."

Any person, Most Reverend Sir, in the least acquainted with our characters, motives, or conduct could not probably apply them to us.—& if founded upon any representations made to you by the Rev. Mr. Lucas, he has certainly mistaken our motives and done us most serious injustice.—We concur in the opinion, Most Rev. Sir, that where malice and depravity prevail, a firm and conscientious opposition is the surest means of arresting their progress. But if the Rev. Mr. Lucas will unfortunately take up mistaken views and conceptions of our conduct, and magnify every vague and loose expression of every individual into Acts or opinions of our body, and still more unfortunately impress them upon your mind, we cannot, Most Reverend Sir, be accountable for the consequences.—Notwithstanding that we enjoy the consolation of being always guided by the purest motives, in our conduct as Trustees, language cannot express the deep sense of regret and mortification which we feel upon the existing state of things.—We are disposed to make every allowance for the Rev. Mr. Lucas being as yet in a great degree unacquainted with our language, manners and customs, which united to a quickness and warmth of temper may often lead him to erroneous opinions.—At all the meetings of the Trustees the Pastor presided, and all questions upon temporal affairs are decided by a majority of votes. Without any interference being made, in the smallest degree, with his spiritual functions, which we should disclaim as heretical & corresponding with the practice of Schismatics.—Everything necessary for the support of the Altar has hitherto been left to the discretion of Rev. Mr. Lucas and the expenses paid monthly from the general fund.—While we withhold our assent to yielding up everything to the Rev. Mr. Lucas, from a sense of the duty we owe to ourselves and the Congregation, and while at the same time we view your sanction of the measure, Most Reverend Sir, as founded upon opinions erroneously formed by our Pastor, as to our motives, We ardently and sincerely hope and believe that after a mature and candid review of all the circumstances of this very unpleasant affair, you will have the goodness to request the Rev. Mr. Lucas to recall his letter containing those painful expressions as applied to our body.—This we most humbly beg of you, most Reverend Sir, being the only excuse, as we apprehend, that is calculated to restore that harmony and confidence that should always exist between the Pastor and the members of the Congregation.

Once we submit it to you, Most Rev. Sir, to decide how far public denunciations delivered from the Altar, against the Trustees, or other Members of our Church, are calculated to preserve harmony, and the due respect which we should have for our Pastor.—We most ardently hope that those awful and serious consequences which we apprehend from such a system, will be averted by the benign influence of your authority, guided by your best reflections, enlightened wisdom, and experience.—To enable you to judge fully upon this subject we send you a copy of a letter from the Trustees to the Reverend Mr. Lucas with his answer to them, and extracts from the proceedings of the Board of Trustees, accompanied with such remarks as were considered important!:—

"The Trustees of the Roman Catholic Church of Norfolk beg leave most respectfully to represent to the Right Rev. Archbishop Neale, that some differences of opinion have existed between themselves and their pastor as to their duties respecting the temporal concerns of the Church, they will state these differences. I pray the Right Rev. Archbishop for instructions how they should proceed."

The Rev. Mr. Lucas presented his letters of appointment to the Trustees on the 19th December, 1815, and was received by them as Pastor of the Church.

The Trustees met on the 27 December to fix the rate of compensation for the Clergyman, and agreed that it should be settled at Eight Hundred Dollars per annum. At this meeting the Pastor was not present.

A meeting of the Congregation was held on the 30th December for the purpose of electing Trustees for the ensuing year—the Trustees were elected in the usual manner by the Congregation, the Pastor being present.

At the first monthly meeting of the Trustees in January, they elected their Treasurer and Secretary, and adopted sundry resolutions respecting the temporal concerns of the Church. A resolution was passed in the following words: "Resolved that the Rev. Mr. Lucas be requested to provide everything necessary for the use of the Altar and present his account of expenditures once a month to the Treasurer for payment." In all these proceedings the Pastor acquiesced, and the Trustees were much gratified to find that from the good dispositions of the Congregation the Revenue of the Church was so much increased, that they should be enabled during the present year to make considerable improvements to the Church.

The number of the pew-holders are Forty-eight, and the pew rents as they stand on our books amount to *Twelve Hundred and Eighty Dollars per annum.* The Sunday collections may be estimated at One Hundred and Fifty Dollars per annum.

This is intended to show that in proportion to the numbers that compose our congregation, no Church can be better supported. It was not until the meeting of the Trustees in the month of April that the Rev. Mr. Lucas gave them to understand that the whole of the Revenue of the Church must be under his control. This was so contrary to the practice hitherto pursued that the Trustees informed him they could not conform to it.

Unwilling, however to adopt their own opinions in opposition to that of their Pastor, one of our members wrote to Baltimore for information as to the practice that prevailed there. The information obtained was from a gentleman who has been a Trustee of the Church for near twenty years and we found that our practice was in conformity with that of the Church of Baltimore—this authority was of such weight that we were confirmed in the rectitude of our proceedings.

This will be presented to you by our much esteemed friend Colonel Freeman who has been for some years past a member and supporter of our Church.

We would beg leave to refer you to him for such further information as may enable you to form a more correct opinion upon the important subject which we here humbly submit to your judgment. Hoping you will receive our remarks upon it, in the same spirit in which they are conceived and intended. We beg to assure you of the high esteem and veneration with which we are, Most Reverend Father,

Your Very Obedient and Faithful Servants, James Herron, Eugene Higgins, Thomas Moran, Bernard Mulhollan, John Donaghey.[44]

More than two months passed before Archbishop Neale answered the letter of May 10-11, from Father Lucas, and the appeal of the Trustees of May 18, 1816. To Father Lucas he wrote on July 6:

I should have answered your esteemed favor of the 10th of May last, had not Divine Providence disposed of things other-

---
44. BCA, Case—12—Y4.

wise. About the same time as I received yours, I also received a joint letter from your Vestrymen, nearly of the same purport as yours; an answer to which you have herein inclosed, that you may see what I have written to them. After you shall have read it, you will seal it and transmit it to its address. But be cautious not to let them know that you have seen it.

Your proceedings with these gentlemen taken in general, meet with my approbation, and I hope, will produce their desired effect.

The system I wish should be established respecting Vestrymen, is traced out in my inclosed letter, to which I refer you to avoid a repetition of the same in this.

How the title of the land may be secured without legislative interference, I do not clearly see: or how the overbearing power of the Trustees may be averted, should resort be made to the Legislative body. The counsel of a friendly Civilian well acquainted with the Virginian Laws, is necessary on the occasion.

Be prudently mild in treating with your people about this subject matter: but do not lose sight of the system alluded to above.

If a considerable majority can be induced in a friendly way to join you, the business may be done both peaceable and solidly.

At present, considering the expressions of the conveyance of the Lot to the purchasers, viz: *for and in behalf of the Trustees of the Roman Catholic Society of the Borough of Norfolk*, it appears to me doubtful whether the title to said Lot be not rendered nul, as neither the names of the Trustees are mentioned, neither were there then, or since that period, have there been appointed any *legal Trustees* to inherit the property in trust for the Roman Catholic Society of Norfolk. Thus things stand in a very delicate situation, and it may be necessary to procure an act of the Legislature to supply the deficiency of title. If this be done, caution must be had that the Trustees appointed under the Law, be declared merely titulary men, who only have a power to prevent the said lot from being ever alienated from the use of Divine worship as practised by the Catholic Congregation of Norfolk, or from being responsible for debts of the Pastor who may be occasionally appointed to officiate there by the Bishop. So that the Pastor be left free to choose his Vestrymen to assist him in the management of all improvements of the Church thereon established and all other temporal concerns which may regard the place and Divine worship.

In the above plan, the legislative would appoint the number of Trustees and the term of their duration and the mode of their Election.

However, I leave you perfectly free to proceed in the whole business according to the advice of sound and prudent friends.

He adds:

> May the Almighty give a blessing to all your exertions. May he establish among you a system which will secure peace and harmony and promote the essential interests of his Holy Church. Be steady and firm in complying with your pastoral duty; and let your whole conduct be stamped with temperate mildness and prudence. *Estote prudentes sicut serpentes et simplices sicut columbae.*[45]

To the trustees Archbishop Neale penned (July 5, 1816) this admirable letter:

> Your polite letter of the 16th of May last came safe to hand, and would long since have been answered, had I not been prevented by most weighty and urgent affairs which intervened and even forced me from home. I hope, therefore, you will admit of my apology, especially as I can assure you, that it was not through slight or disrespect of your persons that my answer was delayed.
>
> I am sorry that my letter to the Rev. Mr. Lucas has given rise to disturbance and uneasiness among you.
>
> It is my earnest desire ever to promote peace and harmony; I even avow myself an open enemy to anything that is calculated to produce confusion and schism in any congregation. This being my avowed principle, which you in your joint letter also acknowledge to be your's, you must naturally conclude that I feel myself solidly bottomed on the said principle, when I differ in opinion from you relative to lay trusteeship, as you understand it, viz:—That I consider this kind of lay trusteeship as calculated fully to produce confusion and schism in the congregation.
>
> This, my conviction, is founded on experience as well as the nature of things; and, as I hope you will hold yourself open to conviction, I will here sketch down some observations which go to prove the solidity of my opinion.
>
> 1st. Lay Trustees chosen by the Congregation, and established with power to transact all the temporal concerns of the Church by a majority of votes, have it in their power from their number to frustrate the most genuine views of the Pastor on all occasions. This appears to me unjust, and a fair inversion of the order of nature, which forbids the head to become the tail.
>
> Neither will it avail anything to suppose that the congregation will choose for Trustees, characters of such respectability as would scorn to take such an advantage over the Pastor; for though that prudent caution might, for a certain length of time,

---

45 BCA, Case—12—R2.

be followed by the choosing congregation, yet the time must be expected to come, when prejudice or party spirit, so unavoidable among poor weak mortals, will produce a choice of characters of quite a different cast; and then Adieu to order, peace and harmony.

This truth has been clearly evinced in the German Church of Philadelphia; in St. Mary's Church of the same city, in the German Church of Baltimore, and the Catholic Church of Charleston, South Carolina; in all which places the most scandalous disturbances, ruptures and schisms, have most shamefully delacerated the seamless garment of the Church of Christ. It is needless to remark, that all those dreadful evils proceeded from the system of the lay trusteeships.

2ndly. It has been notoriously observable, that in most places where lay Trustees have been appointed with power, and authority has been assumed by them, which goes to subject the pastor to their decisions, to cramp him in the exercise of his duty, and to render him most unpleasantly dependent on them, contrary to the spirit and practice of the Catholic Church—nay, which goes to oppose even the episcopal authority in the appointment of pastors, pretending a right to choose their own pastors, and to admit and reject whom they please. This kind of power is not granted to the laity by the Catholic Church, and will ever be opposed as pregnant with the greatest of evils, viz: the subversion of the authority of Christ's Church.

I remember that immediately after the late Bishop's death, I was informed by some one who had been at Norfolk, that there were some among you gentlemen, who pretended to the right of choosing your own Pastor, and of admitting or rejecting any one who might be sent in that capacity, &c., &c., &c., and indeed from your own letter you appear to be under some such impression, for you remark that "The Rev. Mr. Lucas presented his letter of appointment to the Trustees on the 19th December, 1815, and was received by them as Pastor of the Church." The Rev. Gentleman did not seek your approbation by shewing you my letter, as he knew the directions he had received from me, respecting the mode of communicating the said letter to the congregation. I directed him to read the letter from the pulpit to the assembled congregation, that all might know that I had appointed him Pastor among them.

In the Catholic Church none but Bishops have the power of appointing or removing subordinate pastors within their respective dioceses, and whatever goes to contradict that, goes to subvert episcopal authority, and to establish a system which must eventually deluge the public with confusion and disorder.

Hence I conclude, that the trustees and vestrymen in the Catholic congregations of this diocess should only be such as are appointed by the pastor to assist him in the administration of temporal concerns, not to suppose him amenable to their authority with degradation to his character as to their appointed pastor, who is solely amenable to his bishop.

But you seem to think that it would be degrading for you to serve in that capacity. How you can deem yourselves degraded by being under the guidance and direction of your pastor, I do not conceive!

In all Catholic countries, where the true spirit of the faith reigns, the marguilliers or vestrymen are held in honor before the whole congregation; they have a place appointed them next the sanctuary, or if convenient, even in the sanctuary, where none else are admitted; they receive holy communion before all others, and are respected by all. This is real becoming dignity, which establishes harmony and peace, and represents the comely proceedings of well regulated members under a dignified head, both mutually reflecting honor and respectability on each other. Such trustees as these only, were craved by the Reverend Mr. Lacy, the founder of your church, as to the building—such only, were acknowledged at Norfolk by my worthy predecessor; and such only, am I willing to admit, as best calculated to establish and support peace and harmony among you.

The apprehension which seems to haunt your minds, of your being unfavorably represented to me by the Rev. Mr. Lucas is unfounded. He has done no such thing, nay, several among you have been eulogized by that gentleman, in his different letters addressed to me; neither does your idea appear correct, when you fancy that he applied to you personally, those expressions he cited from my letter, which you are pleased to term "extraordinary." He evidently applied them to those only, who, under the influence of incorrect principles, might endeavor to excite disturbances and schisms in the congregation.

Neither could those expressions as they stand in my letter, bear any application to you; they related to the general management of the congregation, and were applicable in my meaning, to such members of the congregation only, as might eventually be found to act against the true spirit of religion through malice and depravity of heart. Now my dear gentlemen, as from the favorable representations made to me of your private characters, I could not consider you to be of that number, so it is evident that I did not mean to apply them to you. However, I am really sorry that your feelings should have been so sensibly affected on the occasion, though through mistake; but, as you now see, that you stand possessed of my good opinion and esteem, I trust all uneasiness will subside, and that from your goodness of disposition, you will cheerfully concur in the establishment of a system, which, under the influence of the Divine

Spirit, I judge to be the only one which will make you perseveringly happy, and render you respectable in the eyes of all denominations.

May the light of Heaven shine on you—may the plenitude of its blessings be imparted to you—and may the Divine Spirit diffuse through your hearts, and those of all my dear children of Norfolk, the inestimable gift of peace and Divine charity. With all due regard, dear gentlemen, *I remain, etc.* [46]

The Archbishop's answer was sent to Lucas and was received on July 12. It was transmitted to the trustees the same day; after a fortnight's deliberation, they replied (July 25) to Lucas in these evasive terms:

> The Trustees have had under their consideration the letter which was addressed to them by the R. R. Arch. Neale. No circumstance could possibly have occurred in our church that could have given the Trustees more serious concern, than the differences which have existed for some months past. The Trustees have taken much pains to place the revenue of the Church upon a respectable footing, and their endeavors have been crowned with success.—Under the arrangements made by the Trustees the income of the Church for the present year, would have been 1500 dollars.—They had contemplated such improvements to the Church as their surplus funds (aided by private contributions which were promised them), would admit; and to have gone on progressively from year to year, to make such improvements as were deemed necessary.— Amongst which their intention would have been very early called to the erection of a Dwelling house for the Clergyman.—In all these measures, it was their most anxious wish to harmonize and concur with the pastor.—Believing that by this mode of proceeding the great objects of their religion would be best promoted.
>
> Your acquiescence, Rev. Sir, in the mode of their election, and in the course pursued in the early proceedings, left them no room to doubt but they were pursuing the most regular and proper course.—It is therefore with the most serious concern they discover that a different system is now thought necessary. The election of the Trustees by the pew-holders having been declared irregular, their acts and engagements cannot be binding. The pew-holders therefore will in all probability consider themselves as absolved from any engagements made with them. —They cannot help expressing their fears that the revenue of the Church will be materially diminished. We therefore request you, Rev. Sir, to convene the pew-holders upon such week day

---

46. *Letter* (Fernandez), Appendix V, pp. 36-37.

as you may think most proper, in order to ascertain their sentiments relative to the payment of the notes which they have granted.—And that you may be able to restore that good understanding and cordiality, which should always exist between the latter and his Congregation, is our most ardent wish. We are respectfully, Rev. Sir, *your ob. Servants.*

J. Herron, Thos. Moran, E. Higgins, Dan Mulhollan. [47]

This message was forwarded to Archbishop Neale by Father Lucas on August 1, 1816, and his letter closes with the significant remark: "I have a dreadful enemy in Dr. Fernandez."[48] On August 16, Lucas wrote again: "Our disturbances are not at an end. The principal cause is Dr. Fernandez. He will have a priest of his [*own country?*]. He says: 'In a free country, every man is independent. The priest is independent of the bishop.' He is united to the other trustees now, and I would not be astonished, if they had a priest here, to see him officiate in the church, in spite of all."[49] Fernandez was even then at work upon his *Letter Addressed to the Most Reverend Leonard Neale.*

Meanwhile (October 2, 1816), Father Lucas had informed the Archbishop that he had extended his missionary activity to Richmond where he has found some Catholics, mostly Irish, who longed to have a Priest among them. "I pray you to send a Priest there the soonest possible. The Irishmen who are numerous and poor will pay the sum they have subscribed, —— if they have an American or Irish Priest." [50]

---

47. BCA, Case—12A—H1.
48. *Ibid.*
49. BCA, Case—12A—H2.
50. BCA, Case—12A—H3.

CHAPTER II

THE "LETTER TO ARCHBISHOP NEALE"

The answer of the trustees to Neale's letter of July 5, is a printed pamphlet of forty-four pages, with a documentary appendix of forty-eight additional pages, published at Norfolk sometime between November 30, 1816, and the beginning of the following year. The appendix contains some of the correspondence we have thus far quoted from the originals in the Baltimore Cathedral Archives.[1] The whole *Letter* is the work of Fernandez; and when one recalls the comparatively few libraries in Virginia at that time, the *Letter* is undoubtedly one of the remarkable literary productions in American Catholic history.[2] It takes its place with other anti-papal documents of the eighteenth and early nineteenth centuries. Few of the members of the Cisalpine Club in its palmier period could have penned a more cogent and plausible attack upon papal and episcopal prerogatives. If Fernandez wrote the whole of it without aid, he knew his Febronius better than any of the Hoganites in the next decade. The anti-Jesuit phrases in the *Letter* are redolent of the days when Pombalism was at its height in Portugal, whence Fernandez hailed. The sources used in the *Letter* are: Febronius, Gerson, Mosheim, Paolo Sarpi (translation of Le Courayer), and others. Febronius (*De Statu Ecclesiae et legitima potestate Romani Pontificis*) and Paolo Sarpi (*Istoria del Concilio Tridentino*) dominate in the *Letter,* which consists of fifty numbered paragraphs, the first of which is a declaration of faith:

"In the first place, I most solemnly declare and avow, that I am a Catholic, Apostolic Orthodox, Roman Christian; and that being perfectly acquainted as well with my Christian duties, as with my natural and political rights, I have been, and will ever be ready, for the devout and pious performance of the former; and no less so, for the maintaining in a lawful and decorous manner, my claim as just and indisputable to the free performance of the latter."

The members of the Norfolk congregation, he told the Arch-

---

1. BCA, Case—12A—H4 (Lucas to Neale, December 18, 1816).
2. An original copy of the letter is in the Baltimore Cathedral Archives, Case—12—U8.

bishop, grounded their rights for independence in administering their church "on the precepts of Our Saviour, of the Apostles, and of the Holy Fathers; on the Canons (not the spurious and apocryphal ones of Gratian; or the false Decretals of Isidorus Mercator; Clementines, etc., etc., etc.), but the genuine ones of the ancient, sacred, oecumenic Councils, in the first centuries of our primitive Church—as well as on the Right of Nations; on the Canonic Right, and finally upon experience and the nature of things."

Upon this bombastic and garbled statement from Gerson, the Portuguese bases his entire pamphlet. Paragraphs VII-XXIII contain a specious attack upon the authority of the Holy See in all temporal matters. Quoting liberally in footnotes from Febronius and Mosheim, he repeats the main arguments of the Gallician theory of Church government, and states as a conclusion the Febronian principle that "by ignorance and superstition, both in the Emperors and Kings, as well as in the people, by ruinous wars in Palestine, such as crusades, by the creation of different monastic orders, and above all, by an *uninterrupted system of Machiavelic politics in the Roman Curia,* the rights of both the people and of the Princes, were altogether insulted and trampled upon." This is, of course, a new descant upon an old record, and makes tiresome reading nowadays; but it must be remembered that the reading public of Fernandez' day, especially in Virginia, could hardly avoid being deeply impressed with the showy learning of the Doctor. Placed in the setting of its times, the *Letter* could do only incalculable harm to the fair name of the Church. The conclusion of his first part (VII-XXIII) is obvious: princes and people (through their public authorities) have a sovereign right over the temporal affairs of the nation and the inherent right "to control any ecclesiastical disposition, which, either directly or indirectly, may be in any way against the said public authority." Besides this sovereign right, "there is another which a certain class of Laymen, not Princes but private persons, enjoy in the Ecclesiastic concerns; these, in Canonic right, are called Rights of Patronage—*Jura Patronatus.*"

With this declaration we reach the end of the tentative efforts on the part of the trustees to assume spiritual as well as temporal control of the Norfolk church, and the beginning of the larger conflict between episcopal authority and the trustee system which was to embrace all the malcontented groups from New York to Savannah and to end in what was perilously close to the schismatic "Independent Catholick Church in the United States."

Fernandez gave the trustees their platform in the following (XXIV-XXVI) paragraphs:

Jura Patronatus. One of these, is that of becoming Collators of the Benefices, either Pastoral or Simple, for the Churches they support and maintain; and this, from very ancient times, always respected by the Sovereigns, by the Oecumenic Councils, by the Popes and the Bishops. It is needless, in this letter, to alledge extensive authorities; however, any doubts on this subject, will be easily removed by the perusal of Z. B. Van Espen, as well as by the Council of Trent, where (Sec. 7, Can. 13) you will observe that "To the Clergyman presented for the Benefices, by the Ecclesiastic Patrons, whosoever they may be, possession will not be given but after being examined by the Ordinary; unless appointed by the Universities."

This Canon does not mention anything about the power of the Lay Patrons, because it is a practice adopted and indisputable; consequently a matter of course, clearly explained in the note to the said Canon by the very learned Peter Francis Le Courayer.

Agreeable to the ordinances at Orleans and at Moulins (says he) the Clergymen appointed by the Universities are not exempt from examination, as well as the others in France. N.B. "even those (who are appointed by the Lay Patrons) to serve any pastoral benefice are included in the rule, as well as those appointed by the Ecclesiastic Patrons."

This leads any one to conclude that the Lay Patrons have the indispensable right to appoint worthy Pastors for the Churches they support and protect, and without being examined by the Ordinary, except at Orleans and Moulins, in France.

If you acknowledge as applicable the axiom of right, that "Cujus est instituere, ejus est ablegare," they enjoy the right of dismissing them, whenever their public behaviour, as Pastors, becomes improper or notoriously scandalous.[3]

Upon those principles: the supremacy of the State over the Church; the right of the prince or public authority to protect the temporal affairs of the Church from ecclesiastical interference; the indisputable right of lay patrons to appoint or to dismiss pastors, the author of the *Letter* proceeds by applying them to Norfolk, in order to establish the claims of the rebels to the enjoyment of lay patronage. "There are, most Reverend Sir," he writes (XXIX) "three ways by which any person may acquire domain—

---

3. *Letter* (Fernandez), pp. 19-22.

Dominium in rebus, viz.—1st. Natural Right. 2nd. Civil Right, and 3d. Lawful Contract between individuals. On which of these are grounded your Ecclesiastic pretensions, to regulate the temporal affairs of our Congregation? Who has granted them? Or in what code of laws is that which invests you with the power for so acting? I beg the favor of your information."

The rest of the pamphlet is devoted to a belittling of the memory of Father Lacy and to a vicious assault upon the reputation of Father Lucas. The trustees, according to Fernandez, charge Lucas with only one aim—"to take good care of the income of the Church." His preaching, far from doing any good "excited diversion and nausea. He is not eloquent, nor is his knowledge of the English language such, as to enable him to preach with propriety; even his Sermons delivered in French are rather low diatribes than pastoral Homilies." Fernandez advises him (in a footnote) to study "our excellent classic preachers, to avoid the roughness, the disagreeableness, and the coldness of his few sermons—delivered (as St. Augustine says) *obtuse, deformiter, frigide.*"

By this time the argument of the *Letter* has brought the reader skilfully into the hazy borderland of schism, if not of heresy; and with paragraph XXXVIII, the suggestion is first made that episcopal authority in the temporal affairs of the church is in contradiction to "our National Constitution." A footnote throws considerable light upon the spirit of the *Letter*: "The revival of the ecclesiastic [*sic*] political authority (after the fall of the Emperor Napoleon) always increasing and developing itself, in the direct ratio of the ignorance, superstition, and despotism of the kings, appears to have intoxicated the heads of some Clergymen in the United States, where, in all probability, arbitrary acts of the kind, will never be *climatised*—for, it is altogether impossible, that while our government will be animated by a philosophical, and philanthropic spirit; and mindful of the horrors inflicted on suffering humanity by Ecclesiastic tyranny, Ecclesiastics will ever have to meddle with the temporal concerns of the Religious Tenets—much less so, over the Roman Catholic Congregations, where the auricular confession is observed and held as Sacrament; an Institution really useful, when well conducted; but also an engine the most powerful and destructive of the social happiness and order, when exercised by arrogant, wicked, or ambitious Priests, upon weak, supersitious, or ignorant persons!!!"

The concluding paragraphs (XXXIX-L) of the *Letter* contain

a declaration of independence from the Holy See, from the Archbishop of Baltimore, and from the authority of any pastor not directly chosen by the trustees themselves. The general theme is that from "the very cradle of our Religion, Ecclesiastics have been protected by, and subordinate to, the civil authority." The conclusion is obvious—"the Norfolk Roman Catholic Congregation does enjoy the incontrovertible Right of Patronage."

Lucas must go, such is the intent and purpose of the *Letter.* "From the very first day of his admission to the meeting of the Trustees, he has developed a Jesuitical System of despotic command; as far from the maxims of the Gospels as darkness from light." Consequently, "guided neither by blind prejudice or stupid superstition, but with an eye on the Gospel and another on our *political free Constitution,*" they have determined to "oppose and frustrate." On Neale's abolition of the Board of Trustees—"it is therefore useless to speak of or command servitude to Citizens of a free nation—Our Church is, *at present,* a branch, but by no means a slave, or tributarian of yours."

Father Lucas did not need to wait for the publication of the *Letter* to Neale to be cognizant that he was dealing with a thorough-going schism. On December 18, 1816, he wrote to the Archbishop to announce that he had appointed during Mass on the previous Sunday a new Board of Trustees, and that one of the old Board had attempted to start a disturbance during the service. Within a week, the old Board gave Lucas warning that they would shut up the church and dismiss him from the pastorate. On December 21, 1816, there appeared a printed *Address to the Members of the Roman Catholic Congregation of Norfolk, or a Short Exposition of the Rights, as well as of the facts (which have taken place from the last of December, 1815, to the present date), aiming at the total and full usurpation of the same, by the Revd. J. Lucas, appointed Pastor by the Most Revd. L. Neale, Archbishop of Baltimore, presented to, and approved of, by the Trustees of the Same Congregation, at their meeting in December, 1815, held at the house of E. Higgins, Esqr:; Treasurer of the Board. By the Actual Remaining Trustees, lawfully appointed by the Congregation.*[4]

These "actual remaining Trustees," as we learn from a note written by the Archbishop on his own copy of the *Address,* were Donaghey, Mulhollan, Higgins and Jasper Moran. The *Address*

---

4. Copy in the BCA, Case—12—U3.

was written by Fernandez and though short in length was a covert appeal for non-Catholic influence, since the views of Lucas (and, therefore, of the Archbishop) were declared to be "in full opposition and contrariety to our free Constitution and State Laws." As the "Lawful Trustees (because appointed and elected by the Congregation)," they deemed it their duty to inform the pew-holders that "we are under the necessity of appealing to the protection of the Laws of our Country, against the tyrannical usurpation of the Rev. Mr. Lucas . . . We ask him where does he exist? in Turkey, or on the *free soil of the United States?*" Advertisements began to make their appearance in the newspapers of Norfolk and Portsmouth of meetings called by the rejected Board, and the little Virginia cities were rife with news about the dissensions among the Catholics. On December 28, the trustees asked for the keys of the church, and being refused by Lucas, they barred and bolted the doors and windows, and a chain was locked about the gate of the churchyard.

The stage was now set for one of the singularly dramatic episodes in American Catholic history. Father Lucas turned a large room in his house into a chapel and those who were faithful to him came there to hear Mass and to receive the Sacraments. The rebellious trustees secured from the court an injunction against the use of the church by Lucas or his followers. On December 26, 1816, the pew-holders met and issued an open letter to the "remaining trustees," and expressed their "most pointed disapprobation" of the printed *Address* of December 21.[5] Among the signatures are those of James Herron, Thomas Moran, Walter Herron, some thirty French men and women and fourteen Irish men and women. They considered the "style and tenor of this pamphlet as highly indecorous," and those who were responsible for it "as highly censurable." They could not see "with indifference the circulation of a pamphlet casting such foul and calumnious aspersions upon our Pastor, the Reverd. Mr. Lucas, whose ability, zeal, and piety in the exercise of his clerical functions are entitled to our highest commendations." Two days later, Fernandez, as chairman of the Board, called a meeting of the trustees and the following resolutions were passed: "1. *Resolved*: That the *Civil Power* of our Roman Catholic Congregation resides in all those members who support our Church . . . 3. *Resolved:* That it being a fact, that the *Prelates of the Church* as well as

---

5. BCA, Case—12A—D4.

the *pastors* or *any other clergyman* or *clergymen invested with ecclesiastical dignity have no other* but *spiritual authority* and by no means *upon the temporal concerns* of the Church, any order from the Most Rev. Archbishop either directly or indirectly through the Rev. Jas. Lucas, is *null and void.*"

Apparently Neale was unable to answer any of Lucas' letters during the rest of the year. All the correspondence that passed between the Archbishop and himself was copied by Lucas about the end of January, 1817, and there is no letter from Neale between July 6, 1816, and January 14, 1817; nor does Neale's correspondence with Rome for these same months contain any reference to the Norfolk Schism. This silence on the part of the Archbishop can be explained by two facts: first, there was a schism in Charleston which had grown in strength *pari passu* with that of Norfolk and was considered even more dangerous because it was led by priests; and secondly, because the Archbishop's mind was preoccupied with the far more important question of the succession to the See of Baltimore. Owing to his state of ill health, and anxious that the diocese might have a duly appointed leader before death should overtake him, Archbishop Neale believed it more prudent to secure a successor who could cope with the schismatic movement in the Southland rather than to take action upon a problem which was beyond his physical powers.

As we have already seen, Neale wrote to the Congregation de Propaganda Fide on February 4, 1816, telling the Cardinal-Prefect that it was the unanimous opinion of the bishops and priests that Cheverus should be immediately appointed coadjutor of Baltimore. As an alternative, Neale proposed Ambrose Maréchal, who was then a professor of theology in St. Mary's Seminary, Baltimore. He had been recommended in 1814 for the vacant See of New York. This burden he successfully avoided, but on July 3, 1816, the Bulls appointing him to the See of Philadelphia as successor to Bishop Egan reached him. Again he succeeded in escaping the honor the Holy See had conferred on him. On August 17, 1816, Propaganda Fide informed Neale that his request for Maréchal was accepted,[6] and on September 10, Maréchal wrote to Whitfield, then at Crosby Hall in England: *Le malheur que je redoutais tant, m'a frappé.*[7] He still had hopes however of being permitted to decline the coadjutorship, for we find him writing

---

6. Propaganda Archives, *Lettere,* vol. 297, f. 200.
7. BCA, Case—12—R3.

to Propaganda Fide on December 1, 1816, that the good of the Church in America demanded the appointment of Cheverus to Baltimore. Boston, he believed, could easily be taken care of in the meantime, and Maréchal asked to be allowed to remain quietly where he was as professor of theology and a member of the Society of St. Sulpice.[8] On December 20, 1816, Neale wrote to Propaganda stating that Dr. Cheverus had conferred the pallium on him (November 19) at Georgetown, because he was too feeble to make the journey to Baltimore. Neale's purpose was to have Cheverus appointed coadjutor to Baltimore *cum jure successionis*, but with the understanding that he need not leave Boston until Neale's death. When Cheverus declined the promotion, Neale asked again for Maréchal. It is significant of Neale's attitude that in this letter, one of the last he wrote to Rome, there is no mention of the Norfolk Schism, though much space is given to the troubles in Charleston. Maréchal's appointment as coadjutor post-dates Neale's death by several weeks, the Bulls having been issued on July 4, 1817. They reached Baltimore on November 14, 1817, and on December 14, he was consecrated Archbishop of Baltimore in St. Peter's pro-Cathedral by Bishops Cheverus and Connolly.

To provide for any vacancy which might occur on account of his own death, Archbishop Neale had appointed Dr. Maréchal Vicar-General "to govern and administer the diocese of Baltimore,"[9] and from that day onwards, the burden of guiding the diocese through the serious disorders of Norfolk and Charleston largely fell to him.

Lucas had written to the Archbishop (December 30, 1816) asking for direction "in the difficult situation in which I am." He had abandoned the little church to avoid conflict with the legal injunction upon the building, and when the rebel trustees saw that he meant to fight the question of ecclesiastical authority to the end, they secretly offered him a salary of twelve hundred dollars a year if he would agree to their *Resolutions*. This letter Archbishop Neale answered on January 14, 1817:

> I acknowledge the rect. of your two letters and the concomitant papers inclosed from which I discern the smart trial God has been pleased to send you. Despond not; but support yourself by a lively confidence in His infinite goodness, Who wisely disposes all matters and sweetly terminates all trials. I should

---

8. Prop. Arch., *Scritt. rifer., Amer. Cent.*, vol. 3, f. 395.
9. Shea, *op. cit.*, vol. iii, p. 32.

have answered you sooner, had I not been too closely engaged in expediting my dispatches for Rome.

I have the happiness of informing you that our bountiful God has severed the Head from the Schismatical body at Charleston, by reclaiming Dr. Gallagher, who has submitted to my authority, and is gone on to New York, never more to return to Charleston. I hope the same bountiful God will do away the schism excited by Fernandez in Norfolk.

The situation of the property, say the Church, and attached premises at Norfolk, is just what I supposed it to be, and of which I spoke to you, when you called to see me. I told you then that I considered the title of said premises as nul, because the conveyance in favor of the Trustees could never reach its legal object, unless there were Trustees appointed by Law; for how could they be legally conveyed to those who did not legally exist. The Premises, in my opinion, are in the legal right of those to whom they were conveyed in favor of the Trustees or their Heirs; If no such Heirs are to be found, the premises become escheatable, a circumstance which you must be cautious of publishing, for fear of the adverse party taking the advantage of circumstances. If you can find the heirs, immediate application should be made to induce them, to convey them to *me* for the use and behoof of the R. Catholics in Norfolk and its vicinity. If this be obtained, all matters would be settled.

I hope you have not given up the keys to Fernandez and his party; but if you have, and they be in possession of the Church and premises, I hereby interdict the same, forbidding Mass to be celebrated, Sacraments to be received, or any religious ceremonies to be performed therein.

This interdict is not intended to comprehend the premises which are external to the Church, and this interdict is to remain in its full force, till the Church be delivered up to the lawful Pastor, as independent of Trustees, and amenable to the Archbishop for the administration thereof, according to the system which I shall sketch below.

You say that they have reduced the whole question to this point: viz:

Has the Bishop authority to change an usage existing since 20 or 25 years without the consent of the Congregation?

Respondeo. He is fully authorized to do it. Nay I will say that he be bound in conscience so to do, especially as the good of religion requires it. The extravagant pretensions of Fernandez and his party to Patronage are truly absurd, as they do not possess even one single point of the requisites to establish patronage. No such title is established in this Diocese, where there are no Benefices, no collations granted, but all things are merely of a missionary nature, there being no established Parishes, but mere congregations.

You mention that you told them you would excommunicate them. Probably you will find most of them freemasons, whom I consider as already excommunicated. Pope Clement 12th issued an excommunication against them, 1738, April 28, and Pope Benedict 14th confirmed the same, 1761, May 17, and in our meeting of the Bishops at Baltimore, when our number amounted to five, it was determined that none of our Pastors or Priests were allowed to impart absolution to freemasons, unless on their repenting and quitting their Society.

Fernandez and party are to be considered *Schismatics*.

I am truly rejoiced that the majority of the Congregation both as to number and respectability are faithful to you and their Church. I feel a warm heart towards them, and most cordially send them my Apostolical Benediction; most certainly exhorting them to stand firm, and remain immovable on the ground they have chosen.

You say that you have abandoned the Church for fear of scandal and conflict of parties. I applaud your motive.

Should you get peaceable possession and use of the Church, a particular system must be adopted for the proper administration of the Church Concerns of which I here give a short sketch, that the Catholics of the Congregation may be convinced that I have nothing else in view but to attend particularly to their interest.

First, I have to observe that a more glaring proof they could not have of fatal disorder being the necessary sequel of Lay trusteeship than the present occurrence, where a few disorderly characters are sufficient to convulse the whole Congregation.

Wherefore, to preserve peace and regularity in the Congregation, I would control the following system: Viz:

1. The administration of the Church fabric and annexed property be under control of the Archbishop of Baltimore.

2. That the Pastor lawfully appointed, to be the Archbishop's agent in the aforesaid administration.

3. That aforesaid Pastor choose two or three regular and respectable gentlemen of the Congregation to assist him in the said administration, who are always to have a particular seat in the Church by way of preëminence.

4. That the salary of the Pastor never exceed 8 hundred dollars, but may be less according to circumstances.

5. That all the residue of the money be held Sacred and solely be appropriated to the repairs and improvements of the Church and premises.

6. That every year, during the second week after Easter

an accurate and fair statement of the Administration of the preceeding 12 months, signed by the Pastor and his two or three assistants be forwarded to the Archbishop, by one of the assistants who shall deliver the same to him in person and give him a detailed account of all that shall have been done.

This system will preserve peace, and the Congregation will enjoy the full advantage of all they may contribute.

In great haste I send you and all my children my Blessing and remain, etc.[10]

Father Lucas had not received this letter with its threat of interdict on the church when he despatched to Neale three days later (January 17, 1817) a long letter in which he says that having inadvertently failed to comply with the laws of Virginia requiring marriage functions, the trustees were hoping to be able to make him leave the State on that score.

Fernandez was setting out that week for Georgetown to see the Archbishop in person—"with all the deception, *la ruse, la souplesse d'un hérétique,* [*he*] will endeavor to persuade you of his innocence, or perhaps show to you the power the Laws of Virginia give to him." Lucas began his letter with the statement: "I want consolation and advice—so destitute as I am, not having a single one good true friend among the Irish."

There is little wonder that, in writing to Maréchal on January 24, 1817, to acquaint him with the fact that his nomination to the coadjutorship was on the way to Rome, Neale should tell him that in such a post he would be *damnatus ad bestias*.[11]

The next letter from Norfolk, dated February 28, 1817, records the first public breach between Lucas and the schismatics at the burial of the father-in-law of Edward Higgins. Father Lucas was unwilling to preside at the ceremony; in order to induce him to be present, Jasper Moran came to his house, and, as Lucas alleged, "proposed to me the best allowances, if I would go to the house" of Higgins. Lucas was highly indignant at the apparent bribe, and spoke of it to some of his parishioners. The following Sunday (February 23), Moran appeared in church, and towards the end of the Mass, created a scene at the altar by accusing Lucas of lying. The affair caused considerable stir in the city and Moran added to the confusion by an impassioned attack upon the pastor, in a printed pamphlet of seventy-four pages, entitled: *A Vindicatory Address, or an Appeal to the calm feelings and*

---

10. BCA, Case—12—R2.
11. BCA, Case—21—P8.

unbiased judgments of the Roman Catholics of Norfolk, Portsmouth and their Vicinities, respecting the foul charges alledged against the writer, in presence of the Congregation of Norfolk, on the 23d of February, 1817, by the Rev. James Lucas, with an Enquiry into the Causes of the Abuses which have for some time past prevailed in the Affairs of the Church.[12]

Written in a grandiloquent style and with occasional flights of eloquence that do credit to a man who was, as he claims, "self-taught, without any experience in the art of composition," Moran's pamphlet assails Lucas with such epithets as "hypocrite; adept at chicanery; young in years but gray in iniquity; a stripling of yesterday, etc." Moran announced his pamphlet to Archbishop Neale on April 8, 1817, threatening its publication unless Lucas were instantly removed. The venerable prelate was unable to follow the controversy, his last illness then being upon him. Moran proposed to the Archbishop "the propriety of your coming immediately to Norfolk, assembling here likewise all the Clergy that could be conveniently spared and could arrive here in time." Lucas was to be "tried" before this assemblage "in our brick church, which should be put in mourning for the occasion." Both Neale and Maréchal ignored this letter, and on April 28, Moran wrote again in his own frenzied way to a friend in Baltimore that Neale had not deigned to make a reply, and that "this work." therefore, "will get publicity in a few days, and will, I think, confound and astonish even Mr. Lucas's opponents, to say nothing of his deluded followers and supporters." By this time, Moran appears to have become somewhat unbalanced in mind, for he fully believed that his *Address* would inaugurate "a new era in Church affairs, not only in America, but also in Europe, and from which may possibly arise the promised millenium for the universal happiness of mankind."

In our chronicle of the events leading up to the attempt to create the "Independent Catholick Church in the United States," mention has been made that the Norfolk schismatics were not alone in the project. A situation similar to that in which Father Lucas found himself existed at Charleston with Fathers Robert Browne, O.S.A., and Simon Felix Gallagher as the leaders of the schismatic group determined to oust Father Clorivière from the pastorate in that city. The Charleston *affaire* is even a sadder one than that of Norfolk. From the end of the year 1817, however, the

---

12. BCA, Case—12—U9.

two centres of disorder can be treated to a certain extent as one. The opposition to Neale's authority and later to that of Maréchal in Norfolk and Charleston met in the person of Browne, who was sent to Rome in the summer of 1816 to appeal to Propaganda. He laid "a mass of false and garbled statements before Propaganda, and returned with a peremptory letter from Cardinal Litta, in which Gallagher and Browne were represented as men of the most eminent piety and exemplary life whom the Archbishop had unjustly deprived of their charge in order to place there a French priest."[13] The Cardinal-Prefect ordered the reinstatement of the two priests *causa pendente,* and if Neale *should refuse, then they were reinstated ipso facto* by the Holy See.

This letter of October 5, 1816, one of the most extraordinary acts of Propaganda in the whole history of its supervision of the American Church, would have been the death-knell of all episcopal authority in the Catholic Church here, if the venerable Archbishop had not immediately foreseen its grave consequences. Cardinal Litta undoubtedly believed the version of the schismatic outbreaks in the diocese as given to him by Browne who, as Gallagher's agent, caused Litta to be highly timorous lest the rebels should mbrace the Protestant faith. Gallagher, who had submitted to Neale's authority before the close of 1816, handed Litta's letter to Neale in person, and the Archbishop at once (March 6, 1817) wrote directly to the Supreme Pontiff, Pius VII, a letter in which he accused the Roman authorities of blindly aiding and abetting he schismatics.[14]

Shea sums up this remarkable letter:

> The Archbishop at once addressed Pope Pius VII, stating that Gallagher had been suspended by his predecessor for gross and notorious intemperance; and that he himself had been compelled to pursue the same course by his continued misconduct; that after suspension he returned to Charleston, drove Rev. Mr. Clorivière from the church, and held it with Browne, who had abandoned his own mission at Augusta and gone to Charleston without any authority, and in defiance of the Archbishop. That the chapel used by Rev. Mr. Clorivière was attended by all Catholics attached to their religion, and who approached the sacraments, while Gallagher had few, not one in ten of whom ever received Holy Communion. He told of Gallagher's repentance and submission, and how when scandal had at last been removed, Cardinal Litta's letter arrived. "Most Holy

---

13. Shea, *op. cit.,* vol. iii, p. 32.
14. BCA, Case—12—R16.

Father," he continued, "is it thus the faith is propagated? Is this the way to treat archbishops who in penury, amid countless difficulties and miseries, labor for the faith and salvation of souls even to decrepit age, and who sink under the bitter burthen? I can scarcely believe that such an order emanated from the Holy See, or surely if it did emanate, it must have been obtained surreptitiously: for by this course, the door is open to every rebellion in this distant country, and means are given, as I think, for the destruction of religion, for the children of this world are more prudent than the children of light. Before truth can reach Rome deceit and falsehood have already occupied the ground, and because they are supported by the testimony of faithless men, they find credit and advocates, my declarations being neglected because they are not upheld by the number and zeal of men without faith, or because my poverty does not permit me to have a procurator or a defender at Rome, for I and my brethren, bishops of this country, are much poorer than the rest of the clergy. . . . Would that your Holiness had leisure to examine my letters and documents forwarded to the Sacred Congregation; I might hope for a prompt remedy to our evils."[15]

This opened the eyes of the authorities in Rome, and they saw how grossly they had been imposed upon.

We know now the startling effect Neale's letter had on Pius VII and upon the Roman Curia. It was answered shortly after it was received, by the Holy Father himself, on July 9, 1817, in a letter which proved beyond doubt a sympathetic understanding between Rome and Baltimore. To a large extent, Neale had himself to blame for Browne's success in influencing the officials at Rome. In a letter from Propaganda to Du Bourg, who was then at Paris (June 7, 1817), the Cardinal-Prefect justly complains that the recalcitrants of the Southland had presented a mass of documents to the Holy See, that Propaganda decided in their favor *ad cautelam*, because of the grave fear that the Catholics there would secede from the Church, and that Archbishop Neale had not written a word of all this trouble to Propaganda (*tamen, quod miror, nihil unquam S. Congregationi hac de re scripsit*).

Neale was dead when the Pope's letter of July 9, 1817, reached Baltimore.

Meanwhile, March 12, 1817, Edward Higgins wrote from Norfolk, giving the Archbishop a detailed account of the public quarrel between Father Lucas and Jasper Moran. The differences be-

---

15. *Op. cit.*, vol. iii, pp. 33-34.

tween Lucas and the trustees, as Higgins saw them, were brought on "by his most overbearing conduct and . . . contemptuous manner . . . but . . . above all his most irritable temper and implacable disposition. To these, his unhappy failings, I sincerely say may be attributed all the scandal and disgrace which happened to our holy religion since his arrival in this place to the present time."

The aged prelate was conscious at this time that the heavy burden of his office would not long remain upon his shoulders, and his last letter to Father Lucas is dated March 26, 1817. Neale's sense of defeat was pathetic. He knew that Maréchal was still unwilling to accept the coadjutorship, and he saw no hope of inducing Cheverus to leave Boston for the higher post of Baltimore. Maréchal had indeed written on March 15, 1817, to Propaganda Fide making a last appeal against his appointment to the See. Without any doubt, he declared, "the future condition of the American Church, next to God, depends absolutely upon the choice which shall be made of Neale's successor. If a worthy ecclesiastic be elected to the See, all will be peaceful and religion will flourish; if not, then the confusion that will reign will be deplorable."[16] The Holy See had decided by this time that Ambrose Maréchal was, to use his own words . . . *"summo hoc officio dignus vir eligendus";* and certain it was, that once Maréchal assumed the reins of spiritual power, trustees in rebellion at Norfolk and clerics recalcitrant at Charleston, soon learned that the day of opposition to spiritual authority was past.

Neale's letter of March 26, contains the admission that Lucas had been imprudent in his action with Jasper Moran. He had proposed already to Lucas that the new church, being built there, be conveyed by deed to the Archbishop of Baltimore and to his successors. This, he adds, "is no new system; it is what has been followed all along throughout the State of Maryland, with the exception of a very few places. It was adopted to prevent disturbances and has fully answered its end . . . No disturbances have ever arisen or can arise from such a system. All our disturbances have exclusively arisen from the system of lay trusteeship, which carries with it the seed of disturbances."[17]

From this time onward the situation became worse in the two centres of turbulence. One letter from Father John Grassi, S.J.,

---

16. Prop. Arch., *Scritt. rifer., Amer. Cent.,* vol. 3, ff. 419-422.
17. BCA, Case—12—R2.

to Maréchal (February 2, 1817) is so carefully worded that it may be not wrong to infer from it that the leaders of the diocese had discussed seriously the wisdom of Neale's resigning the Archbishopric.[18] Neale had suggested to Grassi a journey to Rome to fight the baneful influence of Browne and Gallagher there, but Grassi declined on the score that the presence of a Jesuit in the quarrel might be misunderstood.[19] Grassi did, however, go to Rome in May of that year, and was of much service to the American Church during the first years of Maréchal's regime.[20] The publication of Moran's *Vindicatory Address* caused intense feeling and many letters were sent to Archbishop Neale by the rebellious trustees in support of their stand. Higgins wrote on April 8, 1817;[21] and that same day, Moran wrote a bitter attack upon Lucas to the Archbishop;[22] and yet we find Neale writing to Propaganda Fide on April 11, 1817, regarding the publication of the decree of the Council of Trent on matrimony, with no word of the serious trouble all about him. Cheverus wrote from Bristol, Rhode Island, on May 1, 1817, to Maréchal, that he had despatched a letter to Rome in Neale's defence.[23]

On May 4, Lucas wrote to Neale stating that the rebels at Norfolk had at last joined the rebellious trustees of Charleston, with the hope of securing a priest through Browne and Gallagher.[24] Clorivière had written to Lucas that the coalition was in course of formation. That same day (May 4), Bishop Du Bourg wrote from Paris to Cardinal Litta, warning him that Propaganda's favorable attitude to Browne and Gallagher would ruin all order and discipline in the American Church. After asserting that he would resign immediately the heavy burden of New Orleans in case a similar action were taken with the trouble-makers there; he adds: *Et certes, Eminence, j'ose le dire de tous mes Collègues dans l'Episcopat, qu'il n'est pas un qui ne supliât Sa Saintéte de consentir à leur retraite, si leur autorité dans leurs Diocèses est exposée à se voir sacrifiée aux intrigues de laiques rebelles.*[25] Du Bourg received his information about the state of affairs in Charleston and Norfolk from Father Clorivière, the Jesuit Pro-

---

18. BCA, Case—17—G8.
19. BCA, Case—17—G9.
20. BCA, Case—17—G10.
21. BCA, Case—12A—G2.
22. BCA, Case—12H—H1.
23. Prop. Arch., *Scritt. rifer., Amer. Cent.*, vol. 3, f. 427.
24. BCA, Case—12—Y6.
25. Prop. Arch., *Scritt. rifer., Amer. Cent.*, vol. 5, f. 84.

vincial in France, an uncle of the Father Clorivière, of Charleston. It was in reply to this letter that Propaganda rather briskly called the New Orleans prelate's attention to the fact that very little information about the schism in the Southland had reached Rome from Neale. And it is characteristic of Neale that, writing what is actually his last letter to Propaganda Fide, on May 9, 1817, dealing wholly with a marriage case, he adds a postscript in his own hand asking for Maréchal's immediate (*quantocius*) appointment.

It is a curious thing that even Maréchal who wrote the body of the letter for the venerable old man to sign, did not suggest a word about the schism, which by that time was being discussed in every Catholic centre in the United States.

CHAPTER III

THE APPEAL TO THE HOLY SEE

The Norfolk trustees had now decided to carry their case to Rome. Browne had been very successful the previous year in his personal appeal to Propaganda Fide for the malcontents at Charleston against the decision of the Archbishop in his own and in Dr. Gallagher's case; and he may be largely responsible for this next serious move on the part of the Norfolk rebels. The documents prepared for this appeal were written by Fernandez, and are dated May 31-June 1, 1817. The first of these documents is a printed *Petition to the Holy See,* setting forth the claim of the trustees for the right of patronage; it merits insertion in full:

WE

The Vestrymen of the ROMAN CATHOLIC APOSTOLIC CHRISTIAN CONGREGATION, established in the Borough of Norfolk, duly and unanimously elected by all the Members of the Congregation, publickly and lawfully convoked and assembled, with the assistance of the first Magistrate, the Mayor of the Borough, WILLIAM B. LAMB, Esq., in our own name and in the name and behalf of the good Roman Catholic Christians, inhabitants of this State of Virginia, consulted on the occasion, residents in the towns of Portsmouth, Petersburg, Winchester, Richmond, (the City Capital of this State) Staunton, Lynchburg, Fredericksburg, Falmouth and others. . . . At a full meeting on the 26th of the month of February, of this present year, to consider the best means for redressing the grievances, under which they suffer, unanimously agreed to forward the following Petition to HIS HOLINESS THE POPE.

THE PETITION

Of the Roman Catholics of this State of Virginia, in North America, to HIS HOLINESS THE POPE PIUS THE SEVENTH,
HUMBLY SHEWETH.

1st. That in consequence of the distance from the Arch-Episcopal See of Baltimore, we are subject to many weighty inconveniences and serious hardships, with respect to our Religion and Spiritual concerns.

2d. That during upwards of twenty-two years, neither this Church nor Congregation has been visited by their Chief Prelates, contrary to the determination of the OECUMENIC COUNCILS of the UNIVERSAL CHURCH, and during all that time our offspring has been deprived of the Holy Sacrament of Confirmation, and of the presence of our supreme Pastor, to watch over the discipline of our Churches, and to heal the wounds it might have received, from the weaknesses and imperfections of man; as well as to remove those little bitternesses that are unavoidable from the peculiarity of our situations.

3d. That since the death of our honest and charitable Pastor, the Reverend Michael Lacy, who first co-operated to rally this Congregation, as well as of our much lamented Reverend Doctor O'Bryan; to whose example of virtue and eloquence, this Congregation has been increased by some very respectable Proselytes; we have been deprived of a Shepherd, whose language we could understand, and whose manners were congenial and agreeable to our own, and to that of our country which we have adopted, and of which we are now citizens.

4th. That the natural consequence of this order of things, was a deviation from the laws and customs of this country by foreign Priests, whose opinions instead of conforming to the local circumstances peculiar to these United States, were modelled and governed by those of the country from which they came, in opposition to the advice of very learned and holy Pontiffs.

5th. That this has been productive of much mischief, both to the Spiritual welfare of the people and to the temporal interest of our Churches, whose revenues or rather voluntary donations they wish to appropriate to themselves, to amass sums of money and again retire to their own countries, and deliver up the faithful to new comers, who would follow the steps of their predecessors; and which we have great reason to apprehend, will indispose the people to continue their contributions, and thus eventually ruin our Churches, and disable us from supporting the Ministers of our Religion.

6th. That the great body of Roman Catholics in this State, as well as in all the other States of this country are Irish or their descendants; that they alone (with small assistance of a few members, Spanish, Portuguese and French) have built all the Churches, save one in Philadelphia.

7th. That almost all the Church property in Maryland, is the result of their pious zeal, (although now appropriated, God knows by what Bulls, rights or permissions, by a religious order, not remarkable for a spirit of disinterestedness; and already conspicuous here, as formerly at China, Ouraguay and Paraguay, for the disobedience of the Holy See); and that all, are now supported by their largesses together with their Clergy; except in those provinces which formerly belonged to France or to Spain.

8th. That they feel it inconvenient, nay unreasonable, not to say intolerable, to be refused a Clergy of their own nation and Nomination, acquainted with their characters and dispositions; for nobody can dispute or deny, that they themselves being the sole co-operators, contributors and supporters, both for the purchase of the ground for the building of their Church, and for the support of their Pastors, should be deprived of that RIGHT OF PATRONAGE; much more so in these United States, where, without their zeal and assiduity in promoting the respect due to Religion, our Roman Catholic Congregations would be merely nominal, and insignificant; and notwithstanding all this, the heterogeneous introduction of foreign (French) Clergymen with mercenary character, causes many of the rising generations to quit the Religion of their Forefathers and pass over to other Sects, or to become unbelievers altogether.

9th. That we are satisfied HIS HOLINESS must feel conscious of the evils that would result to our Holy Religion, were Germans, or French or Spaniards, to be exclusively Bishops and Pastors in Italy, or Italians, English or Irish, to occupy these offices in their countries.

10th. That from such a preposterous system, conversions are very rare; that when one sometimes occurs, the French through an unparalleled effrontery, assume the whole merit to themselves, and make such a parade about it, as might be blameless in those Countries, where the Government is Catholic; but which gives much offence here to the other Sects, where prudence ought to dictate to them to let those things remain private, and not to irritate the prejudices that have grown up in this Country with the growth of its population; whilst they are silent about the numbers of Catholic Children, that annually abandon the Faith through the want of those Ministers of the Gospel, who from being born in Countries resembling this, are best calculated for the Ministry here, from the prudence which experience teaches them in the examples which they saw in their own Country.

11th. That although we do not feel disposed to add to the uneasiness of HIS HOLINESS by our complaints, which indeed are many and weighty for years past; yet, our grievances of late, have become so intolerable, that we are unable to bear them any longer, and we are firmly determined rather to trust our destiny to a merciful Providence, than to submit to such pitiless and cruel vexations as we have experienced since the death of the Most Reverend Archbishop John Carroll, our late Chief Pastor.

12th. That we have heard with the deepest sorrow, the

troubles and distractions introduced among our Catholic Brethren in the West India Islands, and in our neighboring States, by the wild extravagance and incorrigible obstinacy of the present Archbishop of Baltimore, and that their lamentations and complaints have pierced even to the Foot of the Throne of GOD'S VICE-GERENT on Earth, and we are now unable, any longer to restrain our own afflictions and bitterness from swelling the tide of universal complaint.

13th. That we have bought ground for our Churches and Burying places, by our own contributions we have built our Churches; and with our annual donations, we have supported our Pastors, and everything necessary to the performance of Divine Service; we therefore enjoy fully the RIGHTS OF PATRONAGE; to assail them, it will be at once to throw dismay and despondence on the Religious sentiments of the Christians, and cut up by the root the enthusiasm, the laudable enthusiasm, of doing good in our own dictates, and generous deeds.

These RIGHTS OF DOMINION AND PATRONAGE have been invaded, and our property has been seized under the colour of Religion, by the sanction of the Archbishop's authority; and were it not, for our profound respect and veneration for the honour of our Holy Religion, we could by the law of this Country, inflict direful vengeance upon the infatuated young French priest (James Lucas), who presumed to execute his illegal mandate. Our mild remonstrance and our temperate resistance to those outrages have been answered with contumely, and insulted with the misplaced interdict of our Church; the refusal of Baptism to our infants; of the last rights of our Faith to the dying, and of the suffrages and prayers for the deceased; in fine, we have been treated in every respect as if guilty of the most atrocious crimes against Heaven and Earth; unless we blindly submitted to such illegal and unjust decisions. Our wives and families have been insulted for visiting the tombs of our deceased relatives and friends, to offer their Prayers to Heaven for the repose of their Souls; and altho' we have purchased, as above said, those repositories for the dead with our own money, and they are *our real property,* according to the laws of this Country; yet Mr. Lucas, an incendiary French Clergyman, has presumed to appropriate them to himself, by the orders of Archbishop Neale, for the purpose of levying such fees as might satisfy his unbounded avarice. He has thus forced us to the painful necessity of taking them out of his hands; wounded the profound respect, which we entertain for the sacerdotal character, and shed a gloom on the veneration, which fills our hearts for the honor of our Holy Religion.

14th. That such proceedings now become public and

notorious to the Members of different Sects; impress on their minds the most unfavorable notions of our *Religion* and Ecclesiastical Government; and must shake and impair even the Faith of our weak Brethren, who confound frail and imperfect men with the precepts of our Faith, and the laws and regulations that guide and govern the authority and power of our Church.

15th. That the only remedy which occurs to us for these numberless evils, which we might swell to a volume, and that now aggravate the bitterness of our hearts, is to beseech and implore the *General Father of the Faithful,* through the love and mercy of our Common REDEEMER, to grant us a BISHOP; to be near us, to soothe our afflictions; to relieve our anxiety; to strengthen our Faith and to restore to us the blessings of peace and the comforts of our Holy *Religion.*

16th. That while we are deprived of a seminary of Priests, (American born) under the care and superintendence of the *Bishop* of the States of Virginia and North Carolina, or of the State of Virginia alone, which we hope *His Holiness,* animated with the Apostolic zeal to promote the *Religion,* pure and orthodoxal, will be willing to create; WE the *Managers* and *Vestrymen* of the *Roman Catholic Congregation* of *Norfolk,* lawfully, publicly and regularly assembled in our own name and in behalf of all our Roman Catholic Brethren, living all over the territory of the State of Virginia, after the most minute and dispassionate enquiry into the characters and qualifications of the *Clergy* of these *United States* of North America, as *Patrons* of our Churches, supporters and sole contributors for the congruous sustentation of our Pastors, and maintenance of all the needful, for the performance and the rites and ceremonies of our *Holy Religion,* we have fixed our wishes and beg leave to present to HIS HOLINESS the Reverend Thomas Carbry, of the order of the St. Dominick, now residing in the City of New York; and we do not cease to offer to the ALMIGHTY BESTOWER of all gifts, our most ardent prayers that he may vouchsafe to inspire our *Holy Father,* to confirm him our *Bishop* and *Spiritual Head,* to the States of Virginia and North Carolina, in North America, (or of the State of Virginia alone) with the title and dignity of Bishop of Norfolk; this being the most numerously inhabited, and where there is always a great concourse of foreigners. We have learned that he has studied in the Convent of *Minerva at Rome,* where his character stands recorded on the Books of the College; that he has been the fellow student of Father Chiesa, now procurator general of his order; and who possibly may remember him and inform His Holiness of his qualifications; that he has served the Missions in Ireland for many years, under the immediate inspection of the Most *Reverend Doctor Troy,* now *Archbishop of Dublin;*

that while *Bishop* of Ossory he acted as one of his Vicars, and that afterwards in Dublin, he appointed him one of the administrators of the Parish commonly called *Rosemary Lane,* of which Doctor Murphy, (who called himself Jackson while student in the Roman College, for some private reasons) who lost his reason, was Parish Priest.

17th. That we intend writing to the most Reverend *Archbishop of Dublin,* to send recommendation of him to *His Holiness,* which we doubt not he will cheerfully do, and that we will procure other recommendations of him here from persons well known in Rome.

We therefore flatter ourselves to find in him all, that can contribute to calm our disquietudes, to restore to us the consolation of our Faith and to promote our Spiritual welfare; whilst the Holy See will be sure to meet in him a person steadfastly attached to it, from the early impressions of his education which he received, we may say, in its bosom.

18th. That we will strenuously co-operate with him in all things for the diffusion of our *Holy Faith;* for the establishment of a Diocesan Priesthood, Children of the Catholics of this State, who will be dear to them by the ties of blood, and agreeable to the other Sects, by the relations of birth, of neighborhood and of social intercourse, and pleasing to all, by being educated among our people and habituated to their manners.

19th. That we will exert every means for the establishment of Schools, for the instruction of our Youth, and a seminary for the education of those destined for the sacred Ministry, the want of which is now so severely felt, and which we hope may become in due season an Auxiliary to other Dioceses; that all attempts of this kind either directed by the French, unacquainted with the genius, the manners and the language of those Countries, have but very imperfectly succeeded, and can never be effected; owing to a general dislike to them, (particularly Jesuits) even by the foreigners who come from other nations of Europe, on account of their principles and intrigueing dispositions; nor are the faults of that Religious Society more likely to meet with success from some of the same causes, but more especially from the apprehensions of our National Government, which we have reason to believe from the *highest authority,* only waits for a pretext to get rid of it altogether.

20th. That we have not consulted the *Archbishop of Baltimore,* on account of the strangeness and extravagance of his character; and because he has so much aggravated our old grievances by his unwarrantable attacks on our property and our unalienable *rights of patronage;* because we have reason to believe that he and the body to which he belongs, wish to make the Southern States of this Region, hereditary to the See of

Baltimore, (which it will always contrive to govern) on account of their being naturally richer and more fertile than the rest.

Nor have we thought proper to consult the French, which this nation regrets to see filling the Episcopal Sees here, because they are all creatures of the Archbishop and of his Body, and will, right or wrong, adhere to them, because they act upon the same principles with them, and wish to reserve the Southern States for them, and for such Priests as occasionally come from France, who are the fittest tools to them and to their *subterraneous* views; although nearly useless in this Country, unless to accumulate money, of which they are beyond all measure, avaricious and greedy; and (what is to be bitterly lamented) in dishonor to the character of our Roman Catholic Religion in this Country; because they are extremely zealous, cunning and intriguing, and will never agree to anything that will not suit and promote their own individual interest, which they understand and cultivate better than any other people; because the Catholics of this Country, who are almost all Irish, or their descendants, and the few Portuguese, Spaniards and Italians, who are here, are more attached to the Irish than to the French Clergy, on account of the openness and candour of their character, which is contemplated with a jealous and invidious eye by the Bishops of that nation, who are established here; and we are convinced that this consideration alone, exclusive even of all other motives, would influence them to oppose our wishes, and the appointment of any Bishop pleasing to us; and that they would misrepresent and calumniate any Clergyman, whose *canonic institution* we might beg of *His Holiness,* unless he was of their own Country and principles; and we beg to assure His Holiness before hand, that if they by any means hear of our determination, (and they are extremely vigilant to discover everything that tends, even in the most distant manner, to interfere with their views, they will not fail to have recourse to all the arts of misrepresentation and calumny, to counteract our wishes and even to traduce the Clergyman, who is the object of our *most sincere desire,* and Christian Choice; although to all who have the opportunity to be acquainted with him, he is above the reach of their malicious artifices; and we would wish to impress in the strongest manner on the mind of *His Holiness,* that the Country of his birth can be the only source of their dislike to him, if they should entertain any, (for they are not acquainted with him) and that he and all his Countrymen are alike objectionable to them on the same account; because they know that we do not approve of the low spirit of intrigue, of cunning and of avarice, that marks the character of almost all of the Clergy of that nation, who resort to this Country, almost on every occurrence, and turn of their conduct here among us; because they know that we would not receive them in any manner, could we find other Clergymen especially of our own Country, and that the dislike to them is becoming so general, that the Catholics of these states (it is apprehended) will come to a resolution, to remain without a Clergy altogether and trust to the merciful Providence of God, rather than to be harrassed and tormented with the intrigues, the schemes and the avarice of such Ecclesiastics. The Catholics of St. Croix, have already come to that determination; those of Charleston and Virginia *were much disposed to follow the example,* when that Heavenly decree, which seems to be dictated to *the Supreme Head of our Church* by the HOLY GHOST, furnished a timely balm to assuage the bitterness, to allay the indignation of the Catholics of Carolina, and to inspire a hope to the Catholics of Virginia, that the *Tender Father of the Faithful* will hear their lamentations and relieve their distresses. The boldness and arrogance of those wandering Priests, are becoming daily more insolent and unsufferable, since the death of the Archbishop John Carroll, whose mild disposition was a check upon their petulance and audacity, and it is well known that they prevailed on that Prelate, in the weak moments of his decline, to endeavour to *poison the mind* of the *Court of Rome,* against Irish Clergymen; hoping that the Sees of those estates being filled by the Bishops of their nation and Rome, being averse to the sending of any Bishops of the Irish nation to this Country, they might suck at their pleasure the substance of the Irish, Spanish, Portuguese and German Catholics of the United States of America. This rapid view of the State of the Catholic Religion and of its votaries in this Country, and our own particular grievances we trust will not prove disagreeable or uninteresting to the *Holy See,* and our own first and last prayer, is to let us have a Clergy of our own nation, but if that cannot be applied, that we may have the choice of *Italians, Portuguese or Spaniards,* but *never French Bishops or Priests,* for we foresee that *we must sooner or later drive them away.*

After having thus fairly and candidly represented our situation, and the only remedy that we conceive adequate to redress the grievances and hardships of which we have so much reason to complain, *unless we apply to the laws of this Country,* which, through respect and veneration for the honor of our *Holy Religion* we would wish to avoid, though certain of the most successful result, we are flattered with hope, that the sighs and tears of the afflicted Catholics of Virginia will excite a sentiment of commiseration in the bosom of our *Holy Father;* that the true interest of our *Holy Religion* in this country, (if not misrepresented to the *Holy See,*) and that if genuine zeal for the Salvation of the Sheepfold of *Christ our Lord,* animates, as we are convinced it does, unless mislead, the *Supreme Moderators* of our *Holy Religion,* that our statement of the sufferings and wrongs we endure, however superficial and imperfect, will induce them to attend to this our representation, and influence them to grant to us the object of our most sanguine hopes and of our ardent vows; and that *we will not be compelled to have recourse to lay and unorthodox tribunals for redress, which in the last extremity we must do,* if we fail in our expectations.

But by granting to us the Bishop of *our affections and choice,* (the Reverend Thomas Carbry) this evil and its consequences will be prevented; the anguish of our Souls will be mitigated; our sorrows will be changed into exultations, and the charity and peace that have fled from amongst us, will come back to us, accompanied with unceasing gratitude to our *Holy Father,* and with daily prayers and vows for his earthly prosperity and endless enjoyment in a world of everlasting happiness and glory.

Written in the Borough of Norfolk, on this thirty-first of May, of the year of our Lord Jesus Christ one thousand eight hundred and seventeen.

>THOMAS REILLY, *President pro temp.,*
>JOHN DONAGHEY,
>EUGENE HIGGINS,
>BERNARD MULHOLLAN,
>JASPER MORAN,
>JOHN F. OLIVEIRA FERNANDEZ, *Med. Doctor, Secretary to the Board of Trustees.*[1]

The second of these documents, written also on May 31, 1817, is an explanation or *Instructio* to Messrs. Donaghey and Moran, who had volunteered to go to Rome to present the above Petition:

Gentlemen:

If we consider with reflection and impartiality the events which we have observed, during the period of the Reverend Mr. James Lucas' admission to the Pastorship of this Church and Congregation; and at the same time, the resolutions adopted, as well as the circumstances, which, apparently by chance, have taken place, we cannot help thinking that the occult hand of the Divine Providence has, most unquestionably, guided and conducted us through so many difficulties and perplexities. We saw, no doubt, our Rights invaded; and the management of our property, taken from our hands, we have observed, also, without any efforts on our parts, the false Pastor abandoning to us, the Church; and by creating himself, the Chief of an unconsti-

---

1. From a printed copy in the Prop. Arch., *Scritt. rifer., Amer. Cent.* vol. 3, ff. 406-409.

tutional Congregation, to declare himself, although indirectly, an improper organ for the transmission of the Divine word.

By that neglect, we took lawful possession of our Church; and nobody has attempted since, to dispute to us our rights.

We have had an uncharitable, anti-Christian Archbishop against us; but amidst our perplexity and distresses, Providence gave us resignation and courage, and by an unexpected accident, a man most suitable to soothe our afflictions has appeared, and, like the column of fire in former times, has guided us through darkness and difficulties, and accepted the Supreme Pastorship of the Churches of our State.

Notwithstanding all that, we were under the uncertainty how to direct our humble representations to the Holy See, and how to arrange our business in Rome; and behold! the Divine Providence has inspired two of our most respectable members, to quit families, business and commodities of life, without the least request or persuasion, guided by the invisible Hand of Almighty God, resolved to hazard, (like the intrepid Apostle St. Paul) dangers at home, dangers at sea, dangers abroad, and perhaps dangers with false Brothers!

Let us, then for a moment, adore with Divine Providence and implore the continuation of the protection, to have the pleasure of your return (which we augur and foresee, to be quick and happy) our most sincere thanks to the Almighty Dispenser who so visibly has directed and conducted us through the paths of rectitude in promoting his own cause.

This Board having considered the magnitude of your sacrifice, in the cause of God and of men, has not but sincere thanks to offer to you at present, however, animated with sentiments of the purest gratitude, they will not forget on your return, to offer you an everlasting proof of their most Religious and most grateful feelings. However, as it is but natural that the Holy See will condescend to our just and Catholic representations: We do hereby promise to you in our own name and in the name of our Congregation and in the name of all our good Roman Christian Brethren who, now, or in future, will enjoy the benefits from your efforts, to indemnify you of all the expense and all purchase of the [*ms. mutilated*] for which sum, you are at liberty to draw on us, thoroughly convinced and persuaded that your draft will meet due honour!

Both of you will find very serviceable to your health the trip by water, as well as by land, in a good season through a delicious climate, abounding with every comfort of life; of course persuaded of your arrival in full vigour of health; you will proceed to Rome, without delay; after having arranged your correspondence with us, either by way of Marseilles, Leghorn, or London.

Should you proceed to Rome by way of Leghorne you will see Mr. Antonio Felichi; who, agreeable to correct information, is a gentleman who bears good character, as merchant and correspondent.

Arrived at Rome, you will see a gentleman (we presume) of Law; who, we are informed, is a man of uprightness and activity, his name is John Joseph Argenti; resides at the Strada Rassella. To this gentleman, you will communicate your business and the grounds of our RIGHT OF PATRONAGE which you, *in no case whatsoever* will give up; viz:

1st. The members of this congregation are the sole owners of the grounds both of Church and burying place; by real purchase, as per documents.

2nd. That our Norfolk Church, was built, out of our own contributions and of our Christian Brethren in different towns of the Union.

3d. That we are the sole regular though *voluntary contributors* for the congruous sustentation of our Pastors, as per documents, as well as for every article needful to the performance of divine service, consequently that [*ms. mutilated*]. We the Roman Catholic Apostolic Christians of the State of Virginia lawfully represented by our Trustees appointed annually by, and from amongst ourselves enjoy *the right of Patronage,* to determine and decide *finally,* on any temporal concerns of our Congregation; in consequence of which right, we have framed the following regulations for the Ecclesiastic establishment of our Church.

Temporal Power of The Congregation.

1st. The power of every Congregation resides in their Trustees annually elected in full meeting of the Congregation lawfully and publickly convoked and assembled.

2d. The TRUSTEES assembled in their regular meetings will decide without opposition, on all the temporal concerns of their respective Churches.

3d. In their meetings, the Pastor has no seat *by right,* but will have one at the right side of the President, whenever invited by his desire, by the secretary of the Board, to be consulted therein.

4th. The Trustees shall superintend on the moral and official character of the Pastor, whenever his publick behaviour, as Pastor, becomes suspect or scandalous.

5th. The Bishop in case of repetition of representations is in duty bound to dismiss the Pastor, if such is the wish of the Majority of the Congregation, convoked by the Trustees expressly for the case.

6th. The Bishop will have no authority to remove a Pastor or introduce another without representation or consent of the Trustees; with whom the Bishop will correspond; but never with the Pastor, but on matters purely spiritual; for in any other of mixed character the Trustees must be consulted.

7th. The orders of the Bishop to the Pastors will not be executed without the "PLACET" of the Trustees, if not previously consulted on the case.

8th. As well as the Trustees with the Pastor of any Congregation represent a particular congregation and Church; so two deputies and the Pastor of each Congregation assembled together with the Bishop will form the *Supreme Ecclesiastical Synodus* of the State.

9th. The Ecclesiastical Synodus of the State will decide on all the general affairs of the Church establishments, viz: the system of revenues, its collection, and compatibility—the foundation of Churches in parts where there are not numerous Christians—the congruous sustentations of the Pastors—the increase of Curates and their salaries—the support of the Episcopal Seminary—Schools—Professors of different sciences—matters to be teached by them—salaries—Degrees and Premiums.

10th. There will be always two Presidents in the Ecclesiastical Synodus, viz., a Layman the most aged amongst the deputies and the most Reverend Bishop of this State, and in case of absence, or death, the eldest Pastor.

11th. To avoid intrigues in the Church-administration of our State we will *HIS* HOLINESS to approve of this our economic plan, viz:

In consequence of our unalienable right of Patronage our first Bishop will be elected by us, Trustees, of this Congregation from amongst the best informed prudent and wise Clergymen in these United States and His Holiness after approving of the election will grant to him the CANONIC INSTITUTION.

[*Ms. mutilated*]

After his death it will be for the Bishop, the most aged amongst our Virginia Pastors—altho' it is in the power of the Congregation as a particle of their Right of Patronage to appoint and collate their own Pastor still none shall be elected in future after the approbation of the present system, but having the following qualifications: viz.:

1st. A residence of three years in this State or at least in these United States.

2d. Certificate of his character, virtue and science to perform the functions of a Pastor.

Episcopal Seminary.

The expenses for the establishment of our Episcopal Seminary will be supported by all the congregations of this State.

The expenses for the support for each particular Church, its Pastor and all the needful, for the said Church, shall be paid by the proper congregation, if able; else the needful balance to be taken from the Treasury of State Church.

The Episcopal See, and Seminary will be at Norfolk.

The Most Reverend Bishop will have under his own roof the assistant priests, Presbyters and Preacher, named first and second assistants.

There will be also two young gentlemen Aspirants also named first and second aspirants; who after producing certificates

[*Ms. mutilated*]

of the church established of the State.

The Most Reverend Bishop, the two assistant priests, and the Pastor of the Norfolk Congregation will be professors of the Episcopal Seminary, of which the Most Reverend Bishop will be the President—the first assistant Priest will be the prefect and the second assistant Priest the Secretary thereof.

The doctrine to be teached in the Episcopal Seminary, will be as follows, divided into three classes, viz:

3d. Class—Eloquence; Logic, Metaphysic, and Moral Philosophy.

2d. Class—Ecclesiastic History; Canonic Institutions; Scriptures.

1st Class—Moral Theology; Dogmatic Theology; Liturgy.

N.B.—The Greek language will be teached and examination made of, before the students may be admitted to the first Class. There will be in every year two courses of studies of four months, each, viz:

1st Course from the 1st of October to the last of January.

2d Course from the 1st of April to the last of July. The months of February and March and August and September will be spent in Episcopal Visits to the different Towns of this State, where the Most Reverend Bishop and his assistants will Preach and confer the sacraments with solemnity.

He will be accompanied by one or two members of the Congregation appointed by the Board of the managers of the Church established who will receive the collections and gratuitous donations from the members or Prosselytes for the benefit of the said Establishment, which collections will be deposited by them in the General Treasury Establishment at the Episcopal See Town, with the declaration of the quantities and persons and places, from whom, and where, they have been collected.

The Most Reverend Bishop will admit, with the consent of

the Managers of the general Board, of the Church Establishment as many pupils as he may approve of, to attend the lectures at the Seminary who will keep their antiquity after the day of their admission, in order to obtain places of access; according to their character, studies, and morality; for instance: Whenever a Church becomes vacant, either by appointment of the Pastor, or by death; the first assistant Priest will be the Pastor of that vacant Church.

The second assistant Priest will become the first assistant.

The first Aspirant (9 being already ordained) will have the place of second assistant Priest.

The second Aspirant will be the first, and the eldest of the Pupils in the order of the entry, or matriculation if deserving, if not the next to him shall be admitted to the place of the second Aspirant each individual receiving a Sallary, attached to the place they are promoted to.

The actual situation, to which the present confusion has reduced our Congregation, prevents us from offering larger compensations than those which follow.

Congruous Sustentations.

For the Most Reverend Bishop	$1000
Annuity to assist his table expense	200
For the Norfolk Pastor	480
Annuity in case of being one of the Teachers	120
For the Pastor of Richmond	480
For each Pastor the same amount	
For the first assistant Priest	300
For the second assistant Priest	240
For the first Aspirant	120
For the second Aspirant	96
For the assistant or Pupil bookkeeper of the Seminary	50
For a servant to wait on the most Reverent Bishop and keep the School Rooms of Seminary in order	50
Besides these Sallaries there will be three Premiums each	50

To be conferred annually in the Celebration of the anniversary of the Creation of the Bishoprick of this State by the Holy See, on three of the pupils, one in each class; after a public examination. The distribution of these premiums in case of equality of Talents shall be given in preference to those who will excell in moral character.

These, gentlemen, are the outlines of our intended plan. By it, you will perceive that our intention is directed altogether.

1st. To have constitutional Priests, knowing and executing

the laws of these U. States with full submission to the constituted authority of our Country.

2d. To avoid the intrigues, generally consequencial to the introduction of foreign habits, manners and discipline.

3d. To have a Clergy, wise, charitable, prudent and educated with the pure maxims of the Gospell.

4th. That in so doing we may call by prudent and wise measures, to the Bosom of our Roman Catholic Religion immense quantity of individuals who willing to worship God, are led astray by ignorant mercenary leaders (called themselves Ministers of the Gospel) without any knowledge or even the least idea of the commencement of our Religion, and of the causes which have unfortunately produced so many Schisms in Religion and horrors in Society.

These truths are too palpable to be not perceived, at the very first glance of His Holiness and His Counsellors. It being evident that without a great and sincere desire on our part to promote the progress of our Holy Religion, pure and unstained, in these Countries, we were at liberty to act in a very different way without the least censure to public reproach. We beg also of you to inform His Holiness the Pope, that ourselves being left altogether without spiritual comfort whatsoever, we are firmly resolved to engage the very first Priest lawfully ordained, coming from Europe, (French or Jesuit excepted) to celebrate Mass in our Church and to administer the Sacraments in any case of necessity.

Leaving the balance to be decided to your sound judgment, we remain, Gentlemen, Your sincere Brothers in Christ and most obt. Servants.

THOMAS REILLY, *President pro tem.*
EUGENE HIGGINS,
BERNARD MULHOLLAN,
JOHN F. OLIVEIRA FERNANDEZ, *Med. Doct., Secretary to the Board of Trustees.*[2]

The high point of the discussion is manifest in these letters —the "inconvenient, unreasonable, intolerable" system of refusing the Irish Catholics of Norfolk a priest of their own nation. The issue was now clear: it was the anti-French feeling of years crystallized into a policy which demanded release from subjection to a pro-French Archbishop in Baltimore, and the creation of a separate Diocese for Virginia with an Irish bishop. And it was this policy which formed the link between each group of fighting trustees from New York to Savannah. It is hardly necessary to call the

---

2. *Ibid.*, ff. 442-447. The photostat copy in my possession has faded at the places marked, "*ms. mutilated.*"

reader's attention to the obvious fact that the racial feeling was not one-sided. The anti-Irish sentiment was as old in the Church here as the Diocese of Baltimore. The second fact in the documents is the mention of Father Thomas Carbry. The trustees presented him to the Holy See as their choice for the Bishopric of Virginia.

Father Thomas Carbry was a boyhood friend of Dr. Connolly, the second Bishop of New York. His life before coming to America was one spent in distinguished services for the Order of Friars Preacher, to which he belonged. Whether Bishop Connolly asked him to precede him to America is not certain, but he was one of the four priests the Bishop found in New York on his arrival on November 24, 1815. The trustee evil had been given an opportunity to implant itself in the New York Church during the five years' interim between the death of Dr. Concanen and the coming of Dr. Connolly; and during the four years that Carbry resided in New York, priests and people were gradually assuming opposite views on the problem of lay trusteeship. With the Bishop were Carbry and Charles Ffrench, all three Dominicans. Opposed to them were Father William Taylor and Father Peter Malou, S.J.[3] The story of this remarkable group of men belongs to the history of the New York Diocese, but their names will be found in many of the documents in the Norfolk-Charleston Schism from this time to the creation of the two Dioceses of Richmond and Charleston in 1820.

With the belief that the mere proposal of Carbry as Bishop of Virginia would be agreeably received at Rome, Fernandez wrote on June 1, 1817, to Cardinal Litta:

Most Reverend and most Eminent Sir,

As Prefect of the Congregation of "de propaganda Fide" I beg leave to address to your Eminency, as Secretary of the Board of Trustees or Managers of the Roman Catholic Congregation of this Borough, both in their Name, as well as in the Name and in behalf of all the good Roman Catholics, now living in this extensive State of Virginia; requesting of your Eminency your particular attention to the humble Representation of our Rights unjustly assailed by those very persons, who, (should they be possessed of the true spirit of their pastoral duty); would have acted in a very different manner towards us.

---

3. J. Talbot Smith, *History of the Catholic Church in New York*, vol. i, pp. 56-58. New York, 1905.

This representation, (copy of which I beg leave to enclose) will be presented to the foot of the Throne of His Holiness by two Gentlemen of the first respectability amongst us; who most devoutedly, have offered their services, in benefice of the cause of our Religion, as well as, for the temporal tranquility and harmony of our Congregation; and whom, the Trustees beg leave to recommend to your Eminency's paternal care and Pastoral kindness.

In these circumstances, I deem it necessary to convey to your Eminency's mind, that, should it not be our decided intention to worship God, agreeably to the precepts of our Holy Roman Catholic Religion, we were at full liberty, to act altogether differently; but, as it is our firm Resolution to live, and to die Roman Catholic Christians, as we were born; so it is our determination to keep, to transmit and to cause to be transmitted our Religion, *pure* or *orthodox* and free from any yoke but that of the Holy Scriptures; precepts of the Holy Fathers and Canons of the Oecumenic Councils of the Church.

Permit, then, most Eminent Sir, that our Religion be teached and preached by word and example of men, endowed with Apostolic virtue; and not of Pharisaic character; by men devoted to the salvation of our Souls, and not to the greedy pursuit of riches; acquired by improper, shameful and unlawful means; and (unfortunately for the propagation of our Religion) practised among Protestants and Heretics of all denominations, who in order to keep on, and cause their Tenets to be kept and adopted, lose no opportunity to cast ridiculous observations and sharp sarcasms on the wild and avaracious behaviour of some of our Priests.

Our two Brethren, John Donaghey and Jasper Moran, Esqrs., will have the honour of informing your Eminency of the long series of our sufferings; of our mild but lawful resistance; of our vain redress to the most Reverend Archbishop of Baltimore; of our useless application to the most Reverd. Bishop of New York; to provide us, with spiritual food; and finally of our determination to engage, the first, regularly ordained, Clergyman, that the Divine Providence may bring to our shores; and trust to him the care of our Souls; meanwhile we wait both patiently and confidently the Paternal Decision of our Universal Father in Christ, whom we most fervently deprecate to inspire your Eminency, to favour us, with your high protection, that the Roman Catholics of this State may obtain from the Holy See, the confirmation of a Bishop for the two States of Virginia and North Carolina; or of the State of Virginia alone; as it may please better, the Religious intentions of His Holiness.

Permit me, most Reverend and most Eminent Sir, to subscribe myself with sincere sentiments of the most profound respect and filial devotion, etc.[4]

Neale lay dying at Georgetown while this dismemberment of his diocese was planned. He had performed his last episcopal act on May 31, 1817, when he ordained to the priesthood Fathers Roger Baxter and John McElroy of the Society of Jesus and the Reverends John Franklin and Timothy Ryan, seculars.[5] On June 16, after finishing the celebration of Mass in the Visitation Chapel, he remarked to the Superior that he felt the end very near. That same day he was overtaken with a coma, and Father John Grassi, who had administered the last rites to Archbishop Carroll, was called to Neale's bedside to perform the same sad ceremony.[6]

Leonard Neale died early on the morning of June 18, 1817. He was buried the following day in the crypt beneath the chapel of the Visitation Convent.

The earliest biography of Neale, written at the time when traditions were still vibrant with his memory, tells us that "though the highest dignitary in the Church of the United States, he lived in the silence of retirement which charity only or the duties of his station could induce him to interrupt. He was never unoccupied. If the duties of the ministry left him a leisure moment, he had recourse to prayer which, even in his intercourse with others, he did not entirely abandon. His attention always fixed on God, imparted to his words a spirit of piety which was a source of edification to all. Whatever related to the interests of religion, was a matter of deep concern for Archbishop Neale, who, like the illustrious founder of his Order, proposed to himself the Glory of God, as the principal end of all his actions."[7] Neale's sanctity was generally recognized at the time. Maréchal had been summoned from Baltimore, but he reached Georgetown some hours after Neale died. Father Tessier, the Superior of St. Mary's Seminary, as Vicar-General of the Diocese, announced Neale's death to Propaganda on June 18, and added that his ardent wish was to see the succession provided for immediately.

---

4. Prop. Arch., *Scritt. rifer., Amer. Cent.*, vol. 3, ff. 448-449.
5. Shea, *op. cit.*, vol. iii, p. 35.
6. Cf. USCM., vol. iii, pp. 510-512.
7. *Catholic Almanack*, 1838.

CHAPTER IV

Archbishop Maréchal and the Norfolk Schism

The Norfolk troubles followed Neale beyond the grave. At the time of his burial in Georgetown, Lucas wrote from Williamsburg (June 18, 1817), about the libelous pamphlet of Moran, who had publicly declared: "Mr. Lucas will leave Norfolk or I shall perish in the attempt!" Some were beginning to say openly that Moran was insane. This letter is an important one on account of the marginal comments made by Maréchal. As administrator *pro tempore,* it came to him for answer. Lucas wrote that Donaghey had sailed from Norfolk for Marseilles on June 5, carrying with him the documents prepared by Fernandez: "Jasr. Moran had had an idea of going with him, and put all his provisions on board, but he got them out and is now at home, afraid, as some say, of being burnt alive at Rome, but rather on account of some misunderstanding which took place between them. All the rebels will bear the expenses in common, if the messenger succeed; if not, he himself will bear them. They say they want a bishop, His Holiness might be deceived, as it seems he has been by the deputies from Charleston." One of Maréchal's marginal notes runs: *No fear! H. H. is or shall be soon informed!* The calumnies in Moran's *Vindicatory Address* were hotly resented by those who remained faithful to Lucas, and they urged him to reply in kind. Maréchal's note *Silence, Moderation, Charity,* gives us the key to his own policy towards the recalcitrants. Before his departure Donaghey had personally distributed Moran's diatribe among all the Protestant ministers of Norfolk and vicinity. "I pray you," Lucas adds, "not to forget poor Virginia and me." Maréchal answered this letter on June 29, advising Lucas to stand firm, but to avoid all contentions.

On June 20, 1817, Maréchal addressed this circular to the clergy of the diocese announcing the death of the Archbishop:

> Although the habitual sanctity of the Most Rev. Prelate and loving Father, whose loss we now deplore, leaves no room to doubt, but that his Soul is now in possession of the everlasting bliss, which his eminent virtues have merited; yet, in conformity with the constant and immemorial practice of the Church of

God, and in order to afford the Faithful committed to your pastoral solicitude, an occasion of publicly paying the tribute of gratitude and veneration due to his memory, I request you to have a funeral service celebrated, and if this be not possible, at least Mass said, as soon as convenient, for the repose of his soul, to which you will be pleased to invite all the members of your congregation. It is likewise my wish, that you recommend to all the pious Catholics under your spiritual direction, to approach the sacred table, on the day of the funeral ceremony, and to partake of the adorable victim, which you will offer to Almighty God for the repose of our venerable and deceased Pastor.

The See of Baltimore is now vacant and will remain so, until the Sovereign Pontiff appoint a Successor. You are well aware how important it is for the prosperity of Religion in the United States, that the choice, which His Holiness is about to make, may fall upon a person adorned with all the eminent virtues, which the sublime and awful office requires. In the primitive ages of Christianity, days of fasting and public prayers were appointed to obtain from the Divine mercy, the most important blessing. In compliance with this spirit of the Church, it is my earnest desire, that on every Sunday after the reading of the Gospel, you will recite at the head of your congregation, the psalm 120: *Levavi oculos meos in montes,* the Hymn, *Veni Creator Spiritus,* with the following prayers: *Deus qui corda fidelium,* and *Concede, quaesumus,* to the Holy Mother of God, Patroness of this Diocese, until the appointment of the Apostolic See be known.[1]

Within the week (June 25, 1817), Maréchal wrote officially as Administrator to Cardinal Litta of the death of Neale. During a half century, he says, this excellent shepherd continually rendered services of the most important nature to the Church. On all sides one heard of his beautiful piety, of his spirit of retirement from the world, of the vigorous constancy of his zeal, and above all of his tender love for Jesus Christ. Shortly after Maréchal's arrival at Georgetown, Neale's secretary handed him in the presence of witnesses a document appointing him Vicar-General and Administrator of the Diocese of Baltimore during the vacancy of the See: *Ainsi me voilà lancé en pleine mer; Dieu seul sçait combien elle me paroit terrible!* Again Maréchal appealed to Propaganda against his own nomination as Neale's successor. If the Holy See should persist in promoting him, he wrote, he feared very much for the future of the seminary

---
1. *Researches,* vol. xxi, p. 22.

to which he was wedded: *Car aussitôt que je serai consacré, il me faudra necessairement en sortir tout de suite et il n'y a personne pour me remplacer.* He then accused Du Bourg of interfering in the selection for the succession made by the American Bishops, namely that of Cheverus, for Baltimore: *Mr. Cheverus est une lumière actuellement cachée sous le boisseau. Tout le monde ici gémit de voir cet excellent Prélat à la tête d'une petite Paroisse.* The Diocese of Boston had at the time only fifteen hundred souls and Maréchal believed that they could be governed by a Vicar-General. Maréchal adds that all Catholics in the State, bishops, priests, and people, were unanimous in the selection of Cheverus for Baltimore. If the Sacred Congregation would only heed the *voeux unanimes de l'église des Etats-Unis,* then Cheverus should be sent to Baltimore, and David should be appointed to the See of Philadelphia; and thus the Church here would be rescued from its present state of disorder.

Proceeding to diocesan affairs, Maréchal warned Cardinal Litta that twice Propaganda had been deceived by Dr. Gallagher, once in Archbishop Carroll's time and once during the régime of Archbishop Neale. The success of Browne in these negotiations had given necessarily a false courage to the malcontents of Norfolk who had fallen into schism: *Ce n'est pas dans un pays tel que les Etats Unis ou MM. les Evêques puissent jamais exercer une authorité despotique. Leur grand malheur est d'être forcé, pour éviter de plus grands maux, de tolérer plusieurs mauvais Prêtres qui en Europe n'exerceroient point le St. Ministère.*[2]

On June 27, 1817, Maréchal wrote to one of the Cardinals in Rome (Dugnani), reminding him that he had the honor of making his acquaintance in France, and that he was presuming on this fact to ask him to hasten Propaganda's action on the state of the American Church.[3] He repeated practically the same arguments against his own nomination to Baltimore; adding that there was no doubt that if he be elected, the seminary, his *maison chérie,* would be ruined. Again he pleads for the *pieux, zélé, savant et très éloquent Cheverus.*

Before these letters reached Rome Maréchal had been selected by the Holy See (July 4, 1817) for the Archbishopric of Baltimore. The Bulls did not reach him, however, until the following November. Maréchal did not allow the delay to interfere with his

---

2. Prop. Arch., *Scritt. rifer., Amer. Cent.,* vol 3, ff. 459-462.
3. *Ibid.,* ff. 463-464.

bounden duty as Administrator of the Diocese. His letter to Eugene Higgins, of Norfolk, dated Baltimore, July 2, 1817, is a good example of his policy in approaching an amelioration of the disorders of the diocese:

> You directed your letter to me, as if I were actually Archbishop of Baltimore. This is a mistake which is, however, common to you with the many other persons at a considerable distance from the place where I reside. No! I am not raised to that awful dignity and I hope, through the mercy of God, I never shall be. I am only appointed administrator of the Diocese till the Holy See shall have nominated a Successor to our late and venerable Archbishop, Dr. Neale.
>
> Since long indeed, I have heard of the many afflicting scenes which a part of the congregation of Norfolk has exhibited to the rest of their Catholic Brethren in the United States. The simple recital of them, although under some respects foreign to me, filled my soul with the deepest grief and I frequently lamented that our Holy Religion, which under the free and happy government of this Country, could so rapidly extend her heavenly and mild Empire over thousands of our fellow citizens should be violently agitated in some cities, by internal and convulsive dissentions, which cannot prove but eminently detrimental to her propagation.
>
> The present lamentable state of your congregation shall be most certainly a considerable object of my solicitude and I am resolved not to omit any means consistent with the sacred principles of the Catholic Church, to bring it again to the happy state of peace and tranquillity it formerly enjoyed. But, sir, I am not as yet fully or sufficiently acquainted with the sad history of your differences to pronounce whether the man you propose can be admitted with justice or even with propriety.
>
> But if it be now out of my power to settle definitely the existing dissentions, I hope you will do all in your power to enable me to obtain that desirable end by your moderation, your respect for the gentleman who is now your Pastor and above all by a punctual attendance to all the various duties incumbent on every sincere and true member of the Church of God.[4]

Late in August or sometime early in September, Maréchal received the letter of Pius VII, dated at Rome, July 9, 1817, rescinding absolutely the previous action taken by the Holy See in the case of Browne and Gallagher. This letter was addressed to Archbishop Neale and it was a vindication of Neale's interpre-

---

4. *Ibid.*, ff. 465-466.

tation of the obnoxious mandate. Neale had written early in 1817 (probably to Bishop Connolly): "His Holyness mandate I have considered as nul, being subreptitiously obtained, and shall, if possible, send a priest [*Father John Grassi, S.J.*] to Rome, to urge the cause and support the episcopal authority in the United States against refractory priests, who have in the present instance been patronized by the Propaganda. The coarse and rude way they have treated me in favor of Messers. Gallagher and Browne, both notoriously refractory, plainly shows, unless effectual opposition be made in the present instance, our authority or the government of the unruly will be reduced to inanity."[5] The answer of Pius VII was therefore the strongest weapon the Holy See could place in the hands of the spiritual head of the diocese for the complete restoration of episcopal authority. The original letter says:

Pius PP.VII

Venerabilis Frater Salutem et Apostolicam Benedictionem. Litteras Tuas diei decimae tertiae Aprilis hujus anni celerrime accepimus, sexagesima quinta scilicet die postquam fuerant datae. Et quamquam eo tempore adversa valetudine (qua nunc optima, favente Deo, utimur) premeremur, negotium tamen de quo in iis agebatur, pro rei gravitate, proque studio in Te nostro, diligenter nullaque mora interposita considerandum suscepimus. Mox Venerabili Fratre Laurentio S.R.E. Cardinali Litta, Episcopo Sabinensi, et Congregationis de Propaganda Fide Praefecto ad nos vocato, cum eo totam rem accurate studioseque perpendimus. Nec multis opus fuit ad eam conficiendam: ex plurimis enim litteris quae isthic advenerant, Congregatio ipsa plene jam constare cognoverat de gravibus publicisque Presbyteri Felicis Simeonis Gallagher excessibus, deque intoleranda ejus pertinacia, qua non modo sese prorsus incorrigibilem multorum annorum spatio praebuit, sed etiam malis artibus semel atque iterum praefatae Congregationi insidias paravit, ut ex litteris bo. mem. Cardinalis Borgia iam satis apparet. Quare et ex Congregationis sententia et judicio nostro causa appellationis omnino finita est, Tuque, Venerabilis Frater, contra ipsum Gallagher, ejusque socium Robertum Browne pleno liberoque jure procedere poteris: Nos enim omnia quaecumque gesseris rata ac firma habenda esse decernimus. Sapientiae vero tuae erit considerare, utrum Sacerdos Gallus Cloriviere Pastoris officium in civitate Carolopoleos retinere debeat, an potius expediat, alium ei ex Anglicana Natione Presbyterum suffici, qui ob faciliorem linguae usum fidelibus illius Congregationis esse

---
5. Hughes, *op. cit.*, Doc., vol. i, pt. i, p. 573.

fortasse possit acceptior. Nihil tamen hac de re Tibi neque praecipere, neque ex animi nostri sententia intendimus insinuare: in tua enim prudentia conscientiam nostram exonerantes, integrum plane Tibi esse volumus id decernere, quod magis in Domino ad animarum utilitatem Catholicaeque fidei praesidium opportunum judicabis. Plura ad Te a Congregatione ipsa de toto hoc negotio scribentur; voluimus tamen et Nos haec tibi significare, ut intelligas quanti Te faciamus, quantique ponderis apud Nos tuae fuerint expostulationes. Quod ad reliquum vero tempus pertinet, omnem quidem tui, Congregatio de Propaganda Fide, caeterorumque Americae Episcoporum, ut par est, rationem habebit, quin tamen *Sacrorum et antiquorum Canonum Statuta* circa appellationes, quae Consilium ipsum Tridentinum *illibata persistere* voluit, abrogentur. Interea cum peculiaribus benevolentiae in Te Nostrae significationibus Apostolicam Benedictionem Tibi gregique tuo peramanter impertimur.

Datum Romae apud S. Mariam Majorem die nona Julii, Anni 1817, Pontificatus Nostri Anno XVIII.[6]

It was an encouraging sign of the new relations between Rome and Baltimore to find the Cardinal-Prefect writing on the following day (July 10) in full accord with the action taken by the Pope.[7] About this time Father John Grassi had yielded to Maréchal's solicitations and had departed for Rome to present the Norfolk and Charleston schismatic churches in their true light to Propaganda.[8] Cardinal Litta followed up his letter of July 10, with another (July 12) explaining the reason for Propaganda's original attitude towards the schismatics, namely, the danger of perversion of the whole congregation—*nisi periculum, quod impendere putabatur, Catholicae illius Congregationis perversionis.*[9] On July 16, Litta wrote again to Neale, intimating that the Roman officials felt keenly the situation created by their action, but warning the deceased Archbishop that such actions would always be liable to occur unless the Holy See were supplied with the necessary documentary material beforehand.

Maréchal probably learned of his appointment to Baltimore from Du Bourg, who was then at Bordeaux. In reply to Du Bourg's statement that Propaganda was wrecking the American Church, Litta had written (July, 19): "No one knows better than

---

6. The original is in BCA—Special Case B—P4. The Brief, with several minor changes, will be found in De Martinis, *Juris Pontificii de Propaganda Fide* etc., vol. iv., pp. 557-558. Rome 1892.
7. BCA—Case—12—S2.
8. Hughes, *op. cit.*, Doc., vol. i, pt. i, p. 573.
9. Prop. Arch., *Lettere,* vol. 292, f. 401.

Your Lordship," the letter runs, "that the Sacred Congregation has never protected lay trustees of ecclesiastical property against the authority of the bishops." But that did not mean that the Holy See would refuse to listen to appeals made directly to itself, since the decrees of the Council of Trent on such an important aspect of Church discipline could not be abrogated.[10] Propaganda's official announcement to the then deceased Archbishop that Maréchal was appointed his successor is dated July 21, 1817. In this letter Cardinal Litta again refers to the schismatic movement in the Southland. As Propaganda saw the situation the choice lay between the vast number of documents from the trustees, all of which proved imminent danger of perversion, and Neale's silence —*Miror autem Amplitudinem Tuam nihil unquam ea de re S. Congregationi scripsisse*.[11] This same sentiment is expressed in a letter to Neale from Propaganda the following week (July 26, 1817): "If you had immediately instructed us concerning the case [*of Gallagher, etc.*], and had sent us sooner these documents which have lately arrived, we would not have feared the perversion of the congregation or suspended your decision in the case."[12]

Letters continued to come from Norfolk during the interim after Neale's death. In July and in August, Maréchal received several messages containing the same decision on the part of the trustees: namely, that Father Lucas must be recalled.[13] On August 9, 1817, Maréchal wrote in triplicate to Cardinal Litta a detailed account of the Norfolk schism up to that date. Propaganda's action, he said, in the case of the Charleston trustees had given a dangerous leverage to the discontented groups in other parts of the country, particularly in Norfolk, where, six "pseudo-Catholics" with the help of the civil authorities had obtained possession of the church and were upholding their alleged right of accepting or rejecting the pastor sent to them. They had joined forces with the disturbers of the peace in Charleston who were being led by Browne and Gallagher, and they had recently sent an emissary to Rome. Maréchal begged Propaganda not to accept the statements of Donaghey until they were first sent to him for reply. If unhappily a second time, the Sacred Congregation has incau-

---

10. Propaganda to Bishop Du Bourg, July 19, 1817 (*Lettere*, vol. 298, ff. 23-26).
11. *Ibid.*, f. 354.
12. *Ibid.*, f. 424.
13. BCA, Case—17—T1.

tiously agreed with Donaghey, then *plane actum erit in Americae ecclesia de bonis moribus atque disciplina*.[14]

A few days later, Maréchal was informed by Fernandez (August 11) that the schismatics had secured a priest, the Rev. Manuel Vincent Figueira, who was then exercising the ministry in Portsmouth: "This Reverend Gentleman, offering to me his kind services, has celebrated Mass once a week, some time once in a fortnight, as he pleased." It looks, however, as if Fernandez had not sent for this particular clergyman, since he was "in the expectation of a clergyman duly and legally authorized to perform all the Sacramental functions, without giving you [*Maréchal*] any trouble or concern, and perfectly sheltered from all the imaginable arts, connivances, and machinations of Priestcraft."[15] Maréchal has written the proper word on the back of this letter: *impious*.

Father John Grassi wrote from Rome, September 21, 1817 (part of the letter being dated at Lyons, August 18), that he was sending this letter "by the Irishman, who came from Norfolk to solicit the creation of a new Bishoprick." In Grassi's letter the postcript declared:

I found several ecclesiastics very much surprised at hearing that the American Bishops are in such a dependence of Propaganda; for if they were only Vicars-Apostolic, it would not be extraordinary, but being now really Bishops, with their respective Dioceses, why must they depend from Propaganda? So many say here.[16]

Unfortunately for Father Grassi, Donaghey, to whom the letter was given for transit to Baltimore, did not respect the implied confidence, for we find him writing thus to Cardinal Litta from Leghorn, before his departure for Norfolk, on October 28, 1817:

Most Reverend Eminence,

The good Reception which you were so gracious as to give me on all occasions when I had the Honor to wait on you in Rome, and the decided Protection which you afforded to the Petition which my Catholic Brethren in Norfolk, State of Virginia, entrusted to my care to be presented to His Holiness, shall ever be remembered by us with Gratitude and sincere Prayers for your eternal Felicity.

The Confidence which the greatness and Solidity of your Character has infused in me; and the lively interest that you take in any thing which regards the true Church, of which

---

14. Prop. Arch., *Scritt. rifer., Amer. Cent.*, vol. 5, f. 26.
15. BCA, Case—16—S2.
16. Prop. Arch., *Scritt. rifer., Amer. Cent.*, vol. 3, f. 479.

your Eminence is an enlightened Prelate and a firm Pillar, encourages me to reveal to you a circumstance which seems to strike at the foot of the *Propaganda Fide* which for the spiritual welfare of the Faithful in every Part of the Globe, is under your immediate Direction.

The Affair in Question relates to the enclosed letter which I found (unsealed) among many others which were given to me on the moment of my leaving Rome in a great hurry.

I am not acquainted with the writer of the letter alluded to; nor can I say to a certainty who gave it to me to bring to America; but what has induced me to send it to you, are the following Expressions therein contained, which indicate disposition to become independent of the Propaganda. "I found several Ecclesiastics very much surprised at hearing that the American Bishops are in such dependence of Propaganda; for if they were only Vicars Apostolick, it would not be extraordinary; but being now really Bishops with their respective Dioceses why must they depend from Propaganda?"

If the *Sentiments* expressed by the Person who wrote the letter (John Grassi) be contrary to the Discipline or Tenets of the Church, I trust that your Eminence will approve of my Devotion towards the Spouse of Christ, in making *them* known to you; but should *they* be not so, I am certain that your charitable Disposition will pardon my misplaced zeal; especially when you, most Reverend Lord, will consider that my motive, for transmitting to you this information, is wholly guided by the Principles of Religion which I profess and which I hope in the Almighty God, I may persevere in to the Hour of My Death.

The Prudence for which your reverend Eminence is so Praiseworthy, will no doubt induce you to keep my having written to you on this subject, as a Secret; because were it known that I have acted as I have done on this Occasion, it might be attended with serious Consequences to me.

I take the liberty to inform your Eminence that Mr. Edward Swords, an Irish Roman Catholic, is the Agent here of the Roman Catholics of Norfolk in Virginia, United States of America.

I have the honour, etc.[17]

There is no evidence to show that the Cardinal-Prefect took cognizance of Donaghey's act, but it is not improbable that the sentiment expressed by Grassi caused a closer watch upon the American correspondence.

Under date of September 13-14, 1817, there are in the Propa-

---
17. *Ibid.*, ff. 484-486.

ganda Archives, three testimonials in favor of Father Thomas Carbry. They are from Father Patrick Gibbons, ex-Provincial of the Dominicans in Ireland; Father Pietro Antonio de Pretis, Vicar of the Dominican Master-General, at Rome, and Father John B. Chiesa, Procurator of the Order at Rome. To the last of these Father Joseph Javalon, O.P., Prior of the Minerva, adds his attestation to the same effect, namely, that Father Carbry was a priest of excellent standing and full of zeal for the glory of God and the salvation of souls.[18] These testimonial letters may have been procured by Donaghey. If so, and if they are to be taken in conjunction with the letter sent by Cardinal Litta to Fernandez, on September 20, 1817, then it would appear that the Sacred Congregation was already far on the way towards the establishment of the bishopric which the Portuguese physician recommended for the Church in the Southland. The letter is left here advisedly in the original:

Illmo D. Joanni F. Oliveira Fernandez, Secretario Consilii Catholicae Congregationis Norfolkiensis in Virginia. Norfolkium. 20 Septembris, 1817.

Quae de statu catholicae istius congregationis, ejusque petitionibus Beatissimo Patri mihique exposita sunt ea ex litteris per D. Joannem Donaghey perlatis, Sacra haec Congregatio de Propaganda Fide libenter percepit, ac plurime commendavit tum vestram in catholica fide inviolate servanda firmitatem, tum vehemens studium, quo parati estis ea omnia munifice suppeditare, quae ad Dei cultum, Ecclesiae decus, ejusque ministrorum sustentationem sunt necessaria. Quod ad me attinet, studiose curabo, ut pia vestra, quae tamen ecclesiasticis legibus conformia sint, desideria compleantur. Verum si de episcopatu loquamur, quem isthic erigi postulastis, animadvertatur oportet, quod cum Virginae provincia Baltimorenesis dioecesis partem constituat, neque ecclesiasticae leges, neque aequitatis atque urbanitatis officia sinunt, ut illa inconsulto Baltimorensi Archiepiscopo, ad quem jure pertinet, distrahatur. Quare antequam ad hujusmodi dismembrationem procedatur, aequum esse putavimus eumdem praesulem audier, ejusque simul oculis subiicere, quo sicut illius diocesis tam ampla est, aliunde vero Virginia tam longe dissita ut vix ad illius curam possit incumbere, ita ad levandum a tanto onere antistitem, et ad aptius succurrendum spiritualibis catholicae istius Congregationis necessitatibus, maxime est profuturum, si in ista provincia episcopus constituatur. Quid hac de re archiepiscopus sentiat, attendam. Interim vero illi magnopere commendo, ut derelictam istam congregationem

---

18. *Ibid.*, ff. 489-492.

de idoneo pastore provideat, qui illi sacramenta et reliqua spiritualia subsidia ministret, cumque maxima illius pars ex Anglia descendat, congruum plane est, ut ex ipsa natione pastor deligatur, qui melius eorum linguam, atque indolem noscere potest. Ipsi praeterea perspectum facere haud desum, vota esse Vestra, ut ad hoc munus praeficiatur P. Thomas Carberis Hibernensis Ordinis Praedicatorum, qui nunc Neo-Eboraci moratur, ut scilicet praesul, nisi in contrarium habeat quidquam, illum pastorem vobis designet. Quod vero pertinet ad jura, quae istius Congregationis directores sibi vindicare praesumunt, quamquam ipsis ob ecclesiarum aedificationem, ac dotationem, juspatronatus denegari non possit, nihil tamen amplius sibi arrogare possunt, quam Sacri Canones ejusmodi patronis concedunt. Plura enim, quae a directoribus sancita sunt, ecclesiae legibus adversantur, nec quia saeculares ecclesiae sumptibus onerantur, licet iis praeesse pastoribus, eosque sibi subiectos facere. Quod Ecclesiae donatur, in dominium transit Ecclesiae, nec laici reputare amplius possunt ut suum, quod Deo consecrarunt. Quamobrem directores iis tantum juribus, atque honoribus contenti erunt, quos sacri canones jubent, ecclesiarumque patronis dare solent. Cumque tanta sit eorum pietas, et orthodoxae fidei adhaesio, non dubito, quin sese ecclesiasticis legibus sint plane conformaturi. Dum itaque illos etiam hortor in Domino, ut aequam animorum dispositionem, quam in sancta religione illibate servanda, et in sublevanda suis opibus ecclesia, constantissime foveant, Deumque O.M. precor, ut iis, ac Dominationi Tuae omnem bonorum copiam largiatur.[19]

This document may be briefly summarized as follows: the status of the Norfolk congregation as described by Fernandez and as presented by Donaghey to the Holy See and to Propaganda, was received with much joy, and Litta commended Fernandez on his zeal for the Catholic Faith. He assured the Norfolk leader that the wishes expressed in the Petition would be granted, as far as the laws of the Church permitted. As to the erection of an episcopal See in Virginia, the Archbishop of Baltimore would, of course, be first consulted, and, no doubt, Maréchal, realizing the vastness of his diocese and the great distance between him and Virginia, would be satisfied to be relieved of the burden of its spiritual government. Litta agreed with Fernandez that the pastor should be chosen from the nation which predominated in Norfolk at the time. He intended, moreover, to propose to Maréchal the appointment of Carbry. A distinction is drawn between the *jus patronatus* as claimed by the Norfolk trustees and that

---

19. *Ibid., Lettere*, vol. 298, ff. 540-541.

granted by Canon Law. They could be regarded as patrons in the canonical sense, providing all conditions were fulfilled, but that could not include the right of governing the spirituals in their congregation.

The Cardinal-Prefect wrote two letters the same day (September 20) to Maréchal, the second of which narrates the mission of Donaghey and the Petition of the Norfolk Catholics for a separate bishopric.[20] The Province of Virginia was "so far away" from the archiepiscopal See that, as Litta declared, it was not possible for Maréchal to care for so "vast" a diocese. The Virginia Catholics, therefore, sought to separate that State from the Baltimore Diocese in order to enjoy an episcopal See of their own. They had plans for the support of a bishop, the maintenance of pastors, the creation of a diocesan seminary, and Catholic schools. Litta apparently considered the Norfolk congregation as partially abandoned by the Archbishop, and the order is given that a priest be sent to them as soon as possible. Ireland was English to Propaganda: "Since the greater part of the congregation are Englishmen, no one would be more acceptable to them than a pastor taken from that nation." Litta therefore proposed the Irish Dominican Thomas Carbry, about whom he had received excellent testimonials. He hoped that Maréchal would agree to the appointment of Carbry for the Norfolk post.

Evidently Propaganda felt certain that Maréchal would welcome the dismemberment of his diocese; and it might seem that Carbry's appointment as pastor at Norfolk was preliminary to his nomination as bishop of the new See, were it not that later documentary evidence shows that Propaganda never seriously considered him for the mitre.

Once Archbishop Maréchal knew that the burden of the Diocese of Baltimore had been placed upon his shoulders by the Holy See, he took up the problems facing his episcopate with alacrity. On September 25, 1817, two letters left his hands, one for Simon Felix Gallagher, the other to Robert Browne, demanding firmly, but gently, their submission to his authority.[21] The consequences of these letters have an indirect bearing upon the Norfolk situation, since up to that time, these two priests were regarded by all the malcontents in the country as fighting in their name for ecclesiastical independence. Browne submitted, or feigned submission. Gallagher became contumacious. On October 21, 1817,

---

20. BCA, Special Case B—J3.
21. Prop. Arch., *Scritt. rifer., Amer. Cent.*, vol. 3, ff. 164-165.

Maréchal wrote to Litta that the decision of July 9, in favor of Neale had given great joy to the bishops of the United States, to whom he had sent copies of the document. In spite of the unfortunate weakness which had ruined the reputation of Dr. Gallagher, Maréchal informed Litta that the Norfolk trustees were anxious to have Dr. Gallagher as their bishop: *Votre Eminence peut juger par cet échantillon de l'extravagance et du délire de ces gens-là.*[22] This timely apostolic letter did much to lessen the tension between Propaganda and Baltimore and it came at a fortunate time, for Litta was then reading the paragraph which Donaghey had copied from Grassi's letter to the Archbishop and had sent to Propaganda with his own sinister interpretation.

The Bulls for Maréchal's consecration arrived on November 10, 1817,[23] and on the fifth, Father James Whitfield, who had just arrived in New York from England, wrote to the Archbishop-elect to say that Bishop Connolly had accepted his invitation to be one of the assisting prelates at that solemn function. On the fourteenth of December, Bishop Cheverus, with Bishop Connolly and Father De Barth as assistants, consecrated Maréchal in St. Peter's Church, Baltimore. The sermon was preached by the Augustinian Father Hurley.[24]

Shea says that one of the earliest acts of the new Archbishop was the publication for the first time of the synodal acts of 1791, to which he appended the Agreement or Regulations of 1810. These disciplinary acts had formed the basis of the normal church life during the thirty-odd years of the established hierarchy. To these Maréchal added a minute of regulations of his own "in regard to the conditional baptism of converts in all cases; directing priests to use all endeavors to induce parties intending to marry to prepare by a good confession, and also to avoid marrying persons belonging to other congregations. He also prescribed rules for mixed marriages; censured severely the attendance by Catholics at Protestant services; directed that absolution should not be given too hastily; he forbade the erection of any church without the consent of the Archbishop. He warned the clergy and people against receiving strange priests, and gave directions in regard to cemeteries and the mode of distributing the Holy Oils. He concludes by directing that Mass should be offered regularly

---

22. BCA, Case—21A—L7.
23. BCA, Case—21A—H7.
24. Prop. Arch., *Scritt. rifer., Amer. Cent.* vol. 3, f. 495. Shea (*Op. cit.,* vol. iii, p. 40) gives the date as December fourth. The certificate of Cheverus and Connolly is signed December 16, 1817.

in commemoration of deceased archbishops of Baltimore, the requiem for Archbishop Neale to be offered on the 18th of June in the following year."[25]

On January 3, 1818, Archbishop Maréchal wrote to his friend, Cardinal Dugnani, telling him that when the Bulls of his nomination had arrived, he was fully determined to refuse the episcopate, but his friends had assured him that to do so would be to throw the whole American Church into disorder: *sans jéter l'Eglise des Etats Unis dans un abyme de difficultés,* not to speak of casting a shadow upon his loyal obedience to the Holy See. The interest Dugnani had shown in his career years before, when he was Director of the Seminary in Lyons, induced Maréchal to hope that the Eminent Cardinal would use his influence at Rome for the good of the American Church. Dr. Gallagher, he feared, would do untold harm to ecclesiastical discipline unless the Pope himself pronounced against him the severest censures of the Holy See. Donaghey had achieved fame in Norfolk and among the rebellious trustees of the land by his celebrated visit to Rome: *C'est ici un mystère inexplicable comment un homme comme lui perdu dans l'esprit public, a pu attirer l'attention de la S. Congregation et lui en imposer par une multitude de pièces et de promesses mensongères.*[26] After all, Maréchal added, Donaghey was nothing more than the agent of a certain Portuguese physician of Norfolk. The trustees were incontestably the most dangerous enemies the Church had in the United States.

It is in this letter that Maréchal first voices his suspicion that a certain religious employed by Propaganda in the task of translating the documents sent by the bishops of the United States was in league with the malcontents here. How, else, he asks Dugnani, can it be possible for a few rebellious priests and a handful of rebellious laymen to deceive the Sacred Congregation?

Cardinal Litta's mistake in accepting Donaghey's estimate of Fernandez and his letter to the Portuguese, of September 9, 1817, gave the trustees a dangerous weapon against the authority of the Archbishop of Baltimore. Early in January, 1818, Fernandez wrote an insulting letter to Maréchal, based upon Litta's apparent admission of the possibility of patronage, announcing the appeal to Rome for a separate bishopric.[27] In the meantime, Fernandez

---

25. Shea, *op. cit.,* vol. iii, pp. 41-42. A copy of this scarce little pamphlet is in the Library of the American Catholic Historical Society, Philadelphia.
26. Prop. Arch., *Scritt. rifer., Amer. Cent.,* vol. 4, ff. 40-42.
27. BCA, Case—16—S1.

asked for the nomination of Father Thomas Carbry, who was then residing in New York City, as pastor of the Norfolk congregation: "The Trustees, likewise, anxious to see peace and harmony restored to this congregation beg leave to request that you would condescend in removing the Reverend James Lucas from this place; after restoring to this church (which he has so unproperly abandoned) all the ornaments, articles and books, which belong to it."[28]

On February 21, 1818, in reply to a letter from Cardinal Dugnani, Maréchal wrote again to that prelate on American Catholic affairs in general.[29] The rumor was abroad at the time that Donaghey had succeeded in obtaining from Cardinal Litta a document recognizing the Norfolk Trustees as possessing the *jus patronatus*. If that be so, Maréchal wrote, then a firebrand has been thrown into the diocese: *Si cela est ainsi, voilà un tison jetté dans le diocèse, qui ne peut causer qu'une grande incendie, par l'abus qu'en feront ceux qui l'ont obtenu.* He begged Dugnani to understand that the schismatic movement at Norfolk was then far more serious than that of Charleston. In the latter city, he had only two refractory priests to subdue; in Norfolk, it was a question of the ecclesiastical right asserted by the trustees of naming their own pastor. Should such a right be granted to the Norfolk group, it would be a cause of disorder in every congregation of the United States: *et vu le génie du Peuple de ce pays, deviendra l'obstacle le plus considerable au progrès de la religion.* Then follows a detailed account of the Norfolk schism. Maréchal showed a keen knowledge of the underlying causes of the trouble. Fernandez's pamphlet he calls a salmagundi of errors. Fernandez himself was the *grand moteur* of all the evil. Maréchal tells Dugnani that the suspicion is growing stronger in the United States that whoever has charge of translating the official documents at the Propaganda is responsible for the ease with which Cardinal Litta, its Prefect, can be deceived by emissaries from America: *quelques mauvais sujets* ["moines" *erased*] *employés dans les bureaux de la S. Cong. et qui sachant l'anglois, sont les instruments secrets de toutes ces misères si fatales à la religion dans ce pays-cy.* This serious accusation remained for several years in Maréchal's mind; and later he acted with the conviction that such was the case.

---

28. It would appear from one of Maréchal's letters that the Archbishop had not seen the *Letter* of Fernandez (February 1, 1818—BCA, Case —16—S2).
29. Prop. Arch., *Scritt. rifer., Amer. Cent.,* vol. 4, ff. 67-70.

An interesting paragraph on the Norfolk situation will be found in Bishop Connolly's *Relatio* of February 25, 1818, to Cardinal Litta.[30] Bishop Connolly held the theory that the best solution for Church government in the country was to erect episcopal Sees immediately in all the seventeen States of the Union. The Irish were scattered through all the States "of this Confederacy and make their religion known everywhere." Bishops should be granted "to whatever State here is willing to build a Cathedral," or has petitioned "for a Bishop as Norfolk has done."[31] Connolly relates the fact that when a rumor reached Norfolk that Donaghey had not succeeded, Jasper Moran left the Church with his seven children and joined the Protestants. Connolly urged the erection of the Diocese of Virginia and proposed to Litta as its first bishop his former pupil at the Minerva, Father Thomas Carbry: *lo raccommendo caldamente a V. Emza.*[32] The following day (February 26), Connolly wrote again (both letters were to go by his friend Mr. James Irvine), explaining the difficulty the bishops had in not being able to incorporate Church property in some of the States. Had the trustees at Norfolk wished to do so, he says, they could have had Archbishop Neale condemned legally for his stand on the Church property there: *fossero ricorsi alli tribunali di questo paese, sarebbe sicuramente condannato l'archivescovo come prevaricatore delle Leggi Civili.*[33]

Maréchal's letter of October 21, 1817, to Litta was answered by the Cardinal-Prefect on April 1, 1818.[34] The reply is in French and is much more friendly in tone than any of Litta's previous letters.

"With regard to the affairs of Virginia," he writes, "it is true that we have had here a messenger from Norfolk who presented a project for the creation of a new See, promising to give all the necessary support; but in the plans, there are many absurd ideas, which are contrary to the spirit and to the discipline of the Church. This deputy seemed to accept the reflections made to him here, and he departed with a letter by which your advice is asked on the project of the new See and on their complaints against the pastor who, they say, has abandoned them. But God knows whether in place of his abandoning them, they have not driven him from his charge. They request another pastor, not

---

30. *Ibid.*, ff. 71-77.
31. Bayley, *History of the Catholic Church etc.*, p. 71. New York, 1853.
32. Shea, *op. cit.*, vol. iii., p. 48.
33. Prop. Arch., *Scritt. rifer., Amer. Cent.*, vol. 5, ff. 24-28.
34. BCA, Special Case B—K5.

Dr. Gallagher, but a Dominican [*Carbry*]. On all these things you will give us your advice, and I beg of you to do so in all frankness. I assure you that no decision will be made here except in the light of your counsel and after mature consideration."

Litta then explained his own attitude towards Donaghey in this way: that to persons coming from so great a distance, offering what was presumably substantial assistance in the work of the Church, something more than mere courtesy should be given. Undoubtedly, Donaghey made a favorable impression on the Cardinal-Prefect, and it is not an idle conjecture to imagine the effect of his visit in circles like the Minerva and the Irish College, where he would find warm support for his project, particularly when that project was being blocked by a French ecclesiastic, as Maréchal was considered.

Father John Grassi had a splendid chance to explain Maréchal's stand in the Virginia project, and as Litta says in the letter, his conversations with the former Jesuit Superior on American Church affairs were eagerly sought and enjoyed. Unfortunately, another ecclesiastical question was just then beginning to disturb the amicable relations between Grassi and Maréchal.[35]

On April 9, 1818, Connolly wrote to Maréchal an evasive answer regarding Carbry's affiliation with the turbulent Norfolkians, and urging him to have the Irish Dominican appointed Bishop of the See of Virginia.[36]

At the end of March, 1818, Archbishop Maréchal started out on a personal visitation of his diocese. He was accompanied by Father James Whitfield. The first series of congregations visited included Baltimore, Georgetown, Washington, Alexandria, Port Tobacco, St. Thomas' Manor, Newport, and other places. On June 11, they left Baltimore for Norfolk and Charleston. Norfolk was visited on June 12, and the Archbishop confirmed some eighty Catholics who had been prepared by Father Lucas. Shea says that Archbishop Maréchal's visit to Norfolk "was undertaken in the hope that he would be able to recall the obstinate to a sense of duty. He convened a meeting of the pewholders, but of fifty-five, nearly one-fourth refused to attend, while others protested and left the room." Maréchal remained there about ten days, but "finding all his efforts useless, he left Norfolk" (June 22). And this, in spite of Fernandez' accusation against Archbishop Neale

---
35. Grassi was preparing at this time to publish his *Notizie varie.* Cf. CHR, vol. v, p. 301.
36. BCA, Case 14—T3; Shea, *op. cit.*, vol. iii, p. 55.

of neglecting to do the one thing that might have brought peace to the congregation, a pastoral visit to the city.[37] During Maréchal's visit, Fernandez published a broadside: *To the Members of the Roman Catholic Congregation, of Norfolk, and the Public,* invoking the law upon those who "shall tresspass upon the said premises [*of the Church*]":

WHEREAS at the General Meeting of the Members and Pew Owners of the Roman Catholic Congregation of Norfolk, lawfully convoked and assembled, held on the 28th day of December, the Mayor of the Borough, W. B. LAMB Esq. being present, to appoint trustees, and to take into consideration some other important matters: It was *unanimously Resolved,*

1st. That the Civil Power of our Roman Catholic Congregation resides only in all the Members (who support our Church) publicly and lawfully convoked and assembled.

Resolved, 2d. That any decision from whatever Member it may proceed if not from a regular Meeting, lawfully and publicly convoked and assembled, is of itself surreptitious and of course null.

Resolved, 3d. That it being a fact that, the Prelates of the Church, as well as the Pastors, or any Clergyman or Clergymen invested with ecclesiastical dignity, have no other but Spiritual authority, and by no means upon the temporal concerns of the Church: any order from the Mo. Rev'd. Archbishop either directly or indirectly, through the Rev. *Mr. James Lucas* is null and void.

Resolved, 4th. Accordingly, that all the Rev'd. Mr. *Lucas'* dispositions and efforts (no matter authorized by the Rev. Archbishop, or any other member or members of the Congregation, not publicly and lawfully assembled) are hereby declared of no effect.

Whereas, the same Rev. Mr. Lucas, having treated with contempt all the insinuations of the Trustees (duly and lawfully elected by the Congregation aforesaid), not only refusing to open the door of the Church, to rent out the Pews, sending insolent letters to the Trustees, and above all, abandoning the Church, and stripping it in the darkness of night of its ornaments, committing the irregularity and sacrilege of carrying the Sacrament without decency and respect due on similar occasions, from the Church to his dwelling, without any threat or insult from the Trustees, only to excite animosity and schism among

---

37. Shea, *op. cit.,* vol. iii, pp. 43-48. Cf. *Diary of Archbishop Maréchal* (1818-1820) in the *Records* ACHS, vol. xi, pp. 417-451. At Alexandria, Va., he met Rev. Messrs De Theux and Van Quickenborne. (Cf. *Records,* vol. xxii, pp. 247-265.)

its Members!——The Trustees having assembled on the 4th day of January, 1817, to decide about their future conduct towards the Rev. *James Lucas,* after considering his improper and unaccountable behaviour, particularly in not having complied with the laws of this State—

Resolved, 1st. That the Rev. *James Lucas,* having abandoned the Church, violating the duties of a Pastor, a conduct in opposition to the Spirit of the Gospel, Maxims of the Holy Fathers, and the Canons of the said Councils of the Church, treating with disrespect the Board of Trustees lawfully elected, depositories of the power and views of this Congregation, and moreover, by not having complied with the Laws of our State, in consequence of which is amenable to law: he is hereby declared no PASTOR OF THIS ROMAN CATHOLIC CONGREGATION OF NORFOLK.

Resolved, 2ndly. That the Rev. *James Lucas,* not having forwarded the keys of the Church, politely demanded, the gates as well as the doors of the Church, be immediately locked up, and the windows fastened.

Resolved, 3rdly. That a Copy of these Resolutions be forwarded by the Secretary of this Board to the Rev. *James Lucas,* as well as to the Most Rev. Archbishop, requesting him (in case of its being his pleasure) to appoint a Pastor for this Congregation, to receive afterwards from the Trustees his collation, agreeable to the rights of patronage they enjoy as supporters of their Church.

Whereas, on the Meeting of the 16th March of the present year, held to meditate on the present situation of the Spiritual affairs of the Congregation, that (notwithstanding the utmost lawful and unintermitted exertions of the Trustees to obtain that peace and tranquility of mind, and enjoyment of the blessings of Religion) have resulted from the criminal obstinacy of the late *Rev. Archbishop L. Neale,* as well from the stubborn systematic contumacy of his most Reverend successor, in not conforming with the maxims of the natural, divine and canonic right, by acting in opposition to the fundamental law of the United States, and particularly of the State of Virginia—and moreover to the kind and polite insinuation of the Cardinal Prefect of *the Propaganda;* desirous besides to clear themselves and the Holy Religion they profess from any criminal attempts, which at a future period, *certain clerical Societies* may form under the false appearance of promoting the true Religion of our Saviour, against the peace of the people—the political union of these United States. They (the Trustees), wishing to cut short the evil that they have so far attempted to heal, by soft, polite, contemporizing, Christian means, having themselves repeatedly addressed to the most Rev. Archbishop *Neale* and *Mareshalle,* without any other result than a more scandalous induration of heart; they came unanimously to the following resolutions:

1st. That this Roman Catholic Congregation, being not composed of converted idolaters or infidels but all ancient Catholics, born of ancient Catholic families, and the present Rev. Archbishop having been neither requested, voted for or acknowledged by this Congregation, and having moreover acted towards us rather as the chief of a party, than as a mild Christian Pastor is from this, rejected by the Congregation as unworthy of being our Prelate.

2d. That adhering to our Christian principles of religion, in the acknowledgment of the Roman Pontiff as our spiritual chief and supreme Pastor, a detailed and humble postulation be addressed to His Holiness to provide for our Spiritual relief, by granting us a prelate of our choice for our state, or a Pastor for our Congregation.

The Trustees therefore, of the Roman Catholic Congregation, having understood, that an improper meeting of the Catholics of this town has been invited; apprehensive that the principal object will be under the specious and plausible pretence of promoting peace and the good of the congregation to obtain by force or any other unwarrantable method, the Roman Catholic Church in this Borough at present under their care, beg leave to apprize the public, that the said Church having been confided to their protection by the Roman Catholic Congregation, has been put under the particular charge of *Thomas Reilly,* Esq. to be kept free from injury or molestation, UNTIL A WORTHY PASTOR, APPROVED BY SAID TRUSTEES IS OBTAINED FOR SAID CONGREGATION.

Any person or persons, therefore who shall trespass upon the said premises, in any way, SHALL BE HELD RESPONSIBLE IN DAMAGES AT LAW.

By order of the Trustees,

ALEXANDER OLIVEIRA,
Secretary of the Board.[38]

About this time (June 6, 1818), Propaganda had decided to follow Maréchal's advice not to erect Virginia into a separate bishopric, but agreed to create a See at Charleston with the Carolinas and Georgia as a separate diocese. Maréchal had suggested to the Holy See the erection of a Vicariate-Apostolic for the Carolinas and Georgia, subject directly to Rome, but Litta disapproved the plan, because the bishops of the United States formed a regular hierarchy, and a Vicariate might disturb the order of the

---

38. BCA, Case—21A—T5.

Church (*miscere cum iis Vicarios Aplicos. ab Archiepiscopo independentes inductum ordinem quodammodo perverteret*).[39] The Cardinal-Prefect again emphasized Rome's action regarding the Norfolk situation: the *jus patronatus* had not been conferred on the Catholics there; it was only decreed that if they were to build a church and endow it, the Sacred Congregation would grant them the right of patronage within the limits of Canon Law: *Quod vero attinet ad Norfolcenses Virginiae Catholicos, nunquam eis collatum est jus aliquod Patronatus, sed tantummodo scriptum, quod si ipsi aedificent, ac dotent Ecclesias, ut facera pollicebantur, non aliud jus eis posse competere, nisi illud, quod Sacri Canones admittunt, scilicet Patronatus.* Litta requested the Archbishop not to neglect this portion of his charge; the more diseased it was, the more it should excite his solicitude; he should cure its wounds and lead it gently and patiently (*leniter ac longanimiter*) back to the right path.[40]

Before leaving Norfolk, Maréchal drafted a letter to Lucas stating that he would be justified in excommunicating Fernandez, Reilly, Donaghey, and the others, for the impious principles they held and disseminated, for their usurpation of the property of the Church, and for their public insults to himself; but he did not wish to take this extreme measures with the rebels. He forbade Father Lucas, however, to admit them to the Sacraments, until they had repented and had repaired the scandals they had given.[41] Evidently, in reply to this threat of excommunication, Fernandez issued a second broadside: *To the Roman Catholics of Norfolk,* on June 25, 1818:

> The present Trustees, fearful that a confusion similar to that which happened in the assembly of the 20th, will prevent them (in the one advertised for this day) to inform the assistants of their former proceedings, as well as for the wrong plans you are to adopt, beg leave to offer to your prudent and calm reflections the following observations:
>
> > Is it your intention to appoint or elect Trustees? You may, no doubt, do it for the temporal management of the affairs appertaining to the Bermuda-street chapel; and we shall be happy if you do all, as it is to be expected from your sound judgments.
> >
> > Or is it your intentions to appoint them from among the

---

39. BCA, Case—Special B—K7.
40. BCA, Case—21A—T2.
41. Shea, *op. cit.*, vol. iii, p. 48 note.

whole Catholics?—We presume you are in a hurry, without having observed the principal aim in question.

Who is your Pastor? Who has appointed or elected him?

Let us proceed to facts—You presume, no doubt, that your resolutions shall have a permanent effect. We are willing to admit of it, though neither the meeting of the 20th, nor that announced for this day, has been called by the Trustees, consequently is not lawful; for the Archbishop of Baltimore has as much right to call a meeting for temporal affairs of the congregation, as you to form a caucus to depose the President of the U. States.

But admitting that, by the very reason you cannot deny, the general meeting of the congregation convoked on the 28th Dec. 1816, was lawful, because assembled at the request of the Trustees—the only two who resisted to and protested against the proceedings of the late Archbishop and Mr. Lucas!

The Resolutions unanimously adopted, were consonant with Ecclesiastical Laws, and with vital principles which form the basis of our Social Compact. The new Trustees were unanimously elected, and desired to proceed to business.

They advertised a day for the Pews to be rented, and the Rev. J. Lucas, then Pastor, refusing to acknowledge the power in the Trustees to interfere and decide on the temporal affairs of the Congregation, had denied to open the Church, both for the meeting as well as for the renting of the Pews.

That the late Archbishop himself was wrong, it is now acknowledged by yourselves as well as by the present Archbishop.

We then had a Pastor, we had Divine Service, and a Congregation whom it was our only object to call to an understanding about our rights and privileges of our Clergyman.

But the Rev. J. Lucas by his precipitation brought over us all the evils we have suffered, and which we are apprehensive will last for a long time to come.

The Rev. J. Lucas has abandoned our Church; has stripped it of its ornaments; carried the sacrament to his dwelling, and afterwards to a frame house in Bermuda-street. For what purpose, God Almighty knows!!—Was it for the good of the Congregation?—Was it to bring us to peace and concord?—or was it to raise the standard of discord between the Members?

Which of the Trustees has said a word to him? they have never had with him any communication but by writing. Let him shew it: has he ever received any insult in the Church, or without, after their nomination? None—on the contrary, the Rev. J. Lucas' behaviour, and of some of his followers, have been the most scandalous. Here our Church remained exposed to an insult. Who could avoid, that any ill-intentioned man, in order to excite animosity against us; or to cast ridicule on our Religion, would attempt in the darkness of night, (similarly to the Rev. J. Lucas when he took away from the Church what he pleased) any insult, such as to destroy the Altar, or any other bad deed?

The Trustees, after such unforeseen and unexpected proceedings, came to the resolution,

1st. To lock up the Church.

2d. To acknowledge the Rev. J. Lucas no more Pastor of the Congregation.

Now, Gentlemen, if one of the most conspicuous amongst you, has decided (and without favour) that the General Meeting of the 28th December 1816, was legal, who can deny that the resolution of their Trustees, was likewise binding on the whole of the Congregation? Why then force us now to acknowledge again as Pastor, a man who has dishonoured and disgraced so openly his character and our religion?

If you, *jure an injuria,* thought then proper to continue with him, you are free, you can pay and support both him and the Chapel he has erected. But to return to the Church he has abandoned and defiled, we cannot; we shall not consent to admit it.

Besides, Gentlemen, by the very reason that you are Catholics, and freemen, we are persuaded, you will not give up your right of electing your own Pastor; or if you have chosen the Rev. J. Lucas, you will not be so despotical or inconsistent as to attempt to force us to the trial of another insult; or to surrender to a man a power which neither is your own, nor can be by him carried into execution, but for a total ruin of your own rights and independence.

Should it, however, be your pleasure to proceed to a new election, we will continue to hold the management of the affairs of the Congregation 'till the decision of the Holy See, to which we have appealed, and to which we have no doubt that you will cheerfully submit, if agreeable, or resist if not analogous to your wishes; for such is the construction of the ecclesiastical rights to be always submitted to temporal power.

You may therefore act as you may think proper; but in an active manner we from this moment most solemnly protest against your decisions, contrary to ours, and of course hold you responsible before God and man by any act of violence or usurpation that may in future take place.

By order of the Trustees,

A. OLIVEIRA, Secty.[42]

---

42. BCA, Case—21A—T4.

So far as Rome was concerned, the Archbishop was now certain that his wishes would be carried out to the letter. The Carolinas and Georgia were to be created into a separate bishopric with the See at Charleston. Propaganda had asked him to present the names of priests worthy of the episcopal dignity. All it suggested in this regard was that among the names there should be those of some Irish clergymen (*non exceptis Anglis*), since the majority of the Catholics in the Southland belonged to that race. Virginia was not, however, to be separated from the Diocese of Baltimore. The pamphlet of Fernandez was recognized as heretical and had been given to the Sacred Congregation of the Index for examination. Appeals from priests and laymen in his diocese would no longer be decided upon, until first Maréchal's side of the case was heard (*nihilque in posterum circa subditorum reclamationes decernetur, quin Amplitudo Tua prius audiatur*). Bishop Connolly had been requested by Propaganda to give Dr. Gallagher a refuge in the Diocese of New York, in order that Charleston might be free from his disturbing influence.[43] With these decisions as a working basis, Archbishop Maréchal saw his way clear towards a more compact system of ecclesiastical discipline in his diocese. Cheverus had suggested to Cardinal Litta either the appointment of Maréchal as Apostolic Delegate for the United States with power to settle in the first instance all conflicts between the trustees and the bishops, or the visit of Cardinal Litta himself or of some other ecclesiastic to the United States for the purpose of studying personally the conditions of the Church here.[44] Fortunately, this was not done by the Holy See. Apart from the fact that the temper of the times would hardly have permitted the centralization into Maréchal's hands of such extensive powers, the abrogation of the right of appeal to a superior court was inconsistent with the Church's age-long policy; and indeed, to judge the Archbishop by his own correspondence to Rome, he would not have welcomed such a fearful charge as the *sollicitudo omnium ecclesiarum* of the United States. The conflicts within his own diocese were appalling in their complexity; and while they may seem simple to us, from our vantage of a century's retrospect, they boded at the time the destruction of the Faith.

Dr. Gallagher, at that time one of the most learned priests in the American missions, had caused a schism which only a genius like John England was able to heal; and it now began to

---

43. Litta to Neale, July 11, 1818, Prop. Arch., *Letters,* vol. 299, f. 382.
44. BCA, Case—14—J2.

look as if the Norfolk Church had welcomed an equally dangerous genius in Thomas Carbry.

The action of the Norfolk trustees in urging Carbry to come to their city was well-known at the time; and on July 17, 1818, Maréchal wrote to the Irish Dominican suspending him from all activity within the Baltimore Diocese and threatening him with excommunication in case he ministered to the misguided rebels in Norfolk.[45] Bishop Connolly, who supported Carbry for the proposed Virginia bishopric, was informed by Propaganda (July 25, 1818) that Maréchal's wish not to separate that State from his diocese had been granted.[46] In the matter of lay trusteeship, Propaganda was much encouraged by the fact that the civil law of New York[47] had been changed to prevent the disposal of Church property by the trustees without the consent of the congregation under the presidency of the bishop: *Questa disposizione contribuirà molto a troncare gli abusi introdotti nell' amministrazione dei beni temporali della chiesa.*

Carbry had not been idle on his own account. As early as July 30, 1817, he had written to Propaganda a long letter on the "evil" conditions in the Diocese of Baltimore.[48] This he followed up on February 26, 1818, with a report on the conditions of things in the American Church in general; and on November 22, 1818, he wrote at length thirteen pages on the sad situation of the Church in the Carolinas. The threat of excommunication, however, seems to have held him back from accepting the post the trustees offered him, until the summer of the next year.

It was about this time that Maréchal began the survey of conditions in the diocese which resulted in his *Report* of October 16, 1818. A circular letter was sent to all the clergy in the diocese accompanied by a *questionnaire*, which shows the thoroughness of his methods.

"Divine Providence having permitted," he writes to the clergy, "that I should be charged with the administration of this Diocess, it is a sacred duty on me to get acquainted with the present state of all the Catholic congregations that are in it. To obtain this important knowledge I find myself under the necessity of troubling you with this letter persuaded that you will cheerfully transmit to me all the information in your power, which you judge any

---
45. BCA, Case—21—03.
46. Prop. Arch., *Lettere*, vol. 299, f. 402.
47. Zollmann, *op. cit.*, p. 95.
48. Prop. Arch., *Scritt. rifer., Amer. Cent.*, vol. 3, ff. 469-472.

value to me, when called upon, to cooperate with your zeal in promoting the Glory of Almighty God and the sanctification of the flock committed to your Pastoral solicitude. Although communications on this interesting subject will be at all times, very acceptable to me, yet in order to spare you trouble, I thought proper to send you a series of questions to which, for the present, it will be sufficient to answer with precision and perspicuity."[49]

This *Questionnaire* was as follows:

QUESTIONNAIRE
Main Congregations

Questions	Answers	Questions	Answers
1. What is about the extent of the territory it embraces?		2. How many Catholics in it?	
3. How many communicants had you last Easter?		4. Have you a church? Is it a wooden or brick building and what are its dimensions?	
5. Who is the legal owner of it?		6. Is it provided with all the sacred vessels, vestments, and necessities for the decent celebration of Divine worship?	
7. Is there a house annexed to the church, or are you obliged to board with some decent private family?		8. Do you administer the temporals of your church, or is it in the hands of Trustees? If the latter case, do harmony and peace exist between you and them?	
9. Does the congregation provide for your maintenance or have you some other means of living?			
10. Are you sufficient alone for the service of the congregation, or do you wish to have an assistant Priest?		11. In the latter case would the members of your congregation be willing to contribute to his decent support?	
12. How long since the sacrament of confirmation has been administered in it?		13. How many about, approach the sacred table every time you keep church on Sundays?	
14. What are the vices most prevalent in your congregation?			
16. Have you some families in your Congregation conspicuous by their zeal, piety or fortune; which are they?		15. Do you keep registers of Baptisms and Matrimony?	
18. What is your age? Are you strong and healthy? How long since you attended this congregation?		17. Do you experience any particular difficulties in the exercise of your sacred duties of ministry? And in what do they consist?	

Minor Congregations Which You Attend

Questions	Answers	Questions	Answers
How many? What is their name?		What is the approximate number of Catholics in every one of them?	
Where and at what distance from the place of your residence are they situated?		Is there any so important that it would require a resident clergyman?	
Do you celebrate mass in private houses or have you churches in each congregation?		How many communicants had you last Easter in every one of them?	
		How often do you visit that congregation?[50]	

Archbishop Maréchal had now gathered through a personal visitation of his diocese and from the answers sent in by the priests

---
49. BCA, Case—22B—M1.
50. *Ibid.*

to his *Questionnaire* sufficient information regarding the state of the Church under his jurisdiction to send a detailed report or *Relatio* to the Sacred Congregation de Propaganda Fide.

This remarkable document is of supreme importance for the history of the Catholic Church in the United States for the period 1815-1820. In the part which is of value for the Norfolk episode (after discussing the various causes of disorder in the American Church), Maréchal gives a keen analysis of the schismatic movement. Norfolk was a striking example of the evils of that kind of trusteeism which was the basis for these schisms: *Ita se res habet Norfolkio, ubi Doctor Oliveira Fernandez et duo Hiberni* [Donaghey and Moran?] *omni religione destituti, ab ecclesia ejecerunt piissimum suum pastorem Dominum Lucas et omnes suos concives Catholicos.* Maréchal hoped for the speedy erection of Charleston into a bishopric, but he had no one to recommend for the See. An English priest would be preferable to one from either France or Ireland: "Verum certum mihi videtur quod sacerdos natione Anglus, huic gravi officio adimplendo melius conveniret. . . . longe foret acceptior populis quam aut Gallus aut Hibernus aut vir ex alia natione oriundus."[51]

Since Maréchal did not discuss in this *Relatio* the project of the Virginia bishopric, he must have concluded that the danger of dismembering his diocese was past. But Dr. Connolly had not given up hopes of placing his former pupil Carbry among the American bishops. On October 31, 1818, he wrote to Maréchal approving the plan of erecting a See at Charleston: "I approve the plan of erecting Charleston into a bishoprick, and wish that every one of the seventeen United States had each a Bishop." He then recommended Carbry in the warmest terms for Charleston.[52] On November 18, 1818, Dr. Connolly wrote to Cardinal Litta, mentioning to him the wish as expressed to Maréchal "that each of these United States had its own bishop, as the best means for steadily propagating religion in them." He believed that the two Carolinas with Georgia and the Mississippi territories would require "in less than twenty years hence" eight bishops. He again recommended Carbry to the Cardinal-Prefect for the Charleston See.

It was this effort to place Carbry in the new See that caused Maréchal to send the Jesuit Fathers Benedict Fenwick and James Wallace, to Charleston to gain control of the church there against

---
51. CHR, vol. 1, p.449.
52. Bayley, *op. cit.*, p. 72; Shea, *op. cit.*, vol. iii p. 55; BCA, Case—14—T4.

any intrusion. Maréchal had made inquiries, after receiving Propaganda's letter of September 20, 1817, about Father Carbry; and, as he writes in his *Pastoral Letter to the Roman Catholics of Norfolk* (September 28, 1819):

"Soon after, a variety of reports concerning this clergyman reached us from different quarters, which gave us great uneasiness; fortunately the certain knowledge which we had, that he was in close intimacy with the few turbulent men of Norfolk who have been the cause of so much distress to you, and especially with the impious author of the writings above mentioned [*Fernandez*]. After mature reflections made in the presence of Almighty God, we believe that we could not conscientiously commit the care of souls to a character at least so dubious, and therefore refused to appoint him, lest he should prove a baneful acquisition to our diocese."[53]

Father Carbry's letter of November 22, 1818, to Father Faraldi, the Prior of the Minerva, Rome, would seem at first sight to contain arguments in favor of Maréchal's assertion that the Irish Dominican had assumed the leadership of the malcontents in the Diocese of Baltimore. Donaghey had brought messages from Faraldi to Carbry the previous year, and the latter decided to write in order to describe the serious conditions of American Church affairs. Donaghey's visit to Rome, he says, was for the purpose of explaining to the Sacred Congregation the religious conditions of the Southland, and especially to make known to the Roman officials the difference between the genius of the American people and that of the Europeans. Donaghey saw Rome with the eyes of an eagle (*con occhi d'aquila*) and on his return gave his friends in the United States a keen picture of Roman conditions. His main object in going abroad was to secure a bishop for Virginia, but Cardinal Litta gave him "sweet promises and graceful delays," *dolci promessi e procrastinazioni eleganti,* as he said when he returned. Nothing succeeds he says in Rome, except with money; and sooner or later the Norfolk Catholics would have to look elsewhere to obtain a bishop, independently of Rome, where everything was being managed by the Sulpicians and Jesuits, who were being supported by foreign ambassadors, particularly by the French ambassador and the English representative at Rome.

There follows in this document a paragraph which must have startled Carbry's correspondent. It is no less than the announce-

---

53. BCA, Case—22B—L1.

ment that there was a general feeling in the Southland that the Holy See should no longer be considered, and that "if a priest could be found, who would consent to go to Utrecht to be consecrated by the Archbishop of that city, all his expenses would be paid and they would give him a hearty welcome. None could be more acceptable to the American government, since the aims of the Holy Alliance were suspected; it was believed that its purpose was to stifle liberty in this country and the rights of the human race by imposing on all nations the yoke of servitude. . .
Jealousy was abroad in these parts against a Court, which depends upon the governments of Europe, having the right to name the bishops there. . . Various Senators have expressed to me their disquiet on this point, and they in Rome can be certain that in spite of all they may say, the present system will not last much longer. At the present time all the bishops in this country, with one exception, are Frenchmen, unpopular with the people on account of their language and their customs which are different from those of this nation. . . The confusion created by the late Archbishop Neale of Baltimore has been much augmented by his successor Maréchal, by sending to some cities of the Southern States certain French priests, in spite of the most obstinate opposition and even in spite of their expulsion from the churches; and also the Archbishop himself [*while?*] in the State of Virginia gave occasion to a flood of pamphlets, issued against the Sulpicians and Jesuits, and against the Archbishop himself, accusing him of cunning, falsehood, and hypocrisy, with great scandal to Religion and great bitterness of spirit. . . Processes and law-suits before the courts are threatened, and means are going to be taken to present petitions to Congress and to the Assemblies of the different States, in order that no ecclesiastic of whatsoever grade will be permitted to exercise any function in the Republic, unless elected by the people, conformably to the fundamental constitution of these States, as in the case with other religious bodies, outside the Catholic Church."

This remarkable letter might seem at first sight to implicate Father Carbry in the schismatic movement which had control of the Virginia congregation. But there is a general tone about the Irish Dominican's *exposé* of the whole situation that bespeaks for him a sincere desire to place the conditions here frankly before his friend in Rome. The relations between Rome and the American Church were not completely satisfactory at any time up to this period. Rome was not to blame, since the Holy See and the

Sacred Congregation were obliged to depend upon the ecclesiastics here for the proper information on Church affairs; and it would be hard to uphold the thesis that either Carroll or Neale were ever eager to furnish the supreme authorities at Rome all the information possible. There is the suggestion of an aloofness on the part of all who counted for something in the jurisdiction of the American Church from 1784 to Maréchal's time; and this aloofness gave an attractive chance to men like Browne and Gallagher for their intrigues. Father Carbry saw the situation clearly. He was not a young priest at the time. His years of splendid priestly labor in Ireland had matured his judgment and had given him that conservative outlook on Church matters without which it is impossible to judge cautiously the elements involved. When, for instance, in this letter, he says to Faraldi that the "conduct of Rome in allowing the See of Philadelphia to remain vacant for five years, on account perhaps of certain intrigues," and that De Barth's election to that See would ultimately ruin the Church in Philadelphia, he was expressing the popular sentiment of the Catholics here at the time. But this is not so much criticism on Rome's methods as upon the general looseness of contact between Rome and America. The real conclusion of his letter, though unexpressed out of prudence and tact, is that unless the ecclesiastical authorities in the United States realize more keenly their subordinate jurisdiction to Propaganda, "in twenty years, either there will be few Catholics in the Republic, or they will be divided into two sects: one calling itself American Catholics, the other Roman Papists, and perhaps there will be two bishops in every city, where now one is found."

One important observation on this letter seems to be demanded by its very thorough delineation of Church affairs in the United States. No man with the ambitious design of securing a promotion to the episcopate, would have struck out so boldly at the dangerous condition of the times. At the end of the letter he begs Faraldi to pardon him the utter frankness with which he has written. His object is to bring peace to the Church in America, and it will be seen later that, once his letter was made known at Rome, while it was most valuable for the guidance of the Sacred Congregation, it certainly settled Somaglia's decision of December 5, 1818, in regard to Carbry: *Non est ratio cur amplius de P. Carbery sermo fiat.*[54]

---

54. *Pastoral Letter* Maréchal, p. 73.

The next important document in the effort of the Norfolk rebels to set up an independent Church is an open letter, anonymous, printed as a broadside towards the end of December, 1818, and presented to Thomas Jefferson and to the members of Congress then in session. Robert Browne, who sent a translation of the letter to Rome, says that it was presented likewise to the Governors of all the States, to all the members of State Legislatures, to all the Judges, and to all who held any position of prominence in the United States:

Sir:
Although a stranger, the patriotic exertions, which distinguished your conduct in vindicating the rights of your country have made your name familiar to me. But your wisdom in fixing those rights upon principles, which will shed unceasing blessings upon millions as yet unborn, shall forever endear your character to every benevolent heart. Under this conviction I feel encouraged to submit with all deference and respect to the consideration of so luminous a mind, a subject, which at some future day must be deserving the attention of those whom Providence may call to the general government of those States. Religion has been always deemed a necessary auxiliary to the sound and enlightened policy of every State. To derive from it those salutary benefits, it is calculated to bestow, and to obviate those evils that might arise from a collision of those religious and civil institutions, which are alike the work of man, the various governments that have prevailed in the world have endeavoured to assimilate the outward character of those institutions.

The simple faith of the Gospel is easily reconciled to every form of government, but its votaries in their divisions have adopted dissimilar systems of religious polity, and different modes of appointing their ministers of worship. I need not remind you that the ministers of religion have much influence over the flocks committed to their care. This influence is the more extensive in proportion as their government differs from the government of the state. The church government, which is only of human institution is gradually identified with its faith, especially when it differs widely from that of the state, and when it is the interest, as it generally is, under such circumstances of the clergy to confound the one with the other. Being men they are often actuated by other motives than those of religion, especially if from ignorance they conceive it a duty, or if those passions, of which they cannot divest themselves, exercise an undue influence over their reason. This becomes still more serious and perhaps dangerous, when men educated and impressed with different ideas of governments, have opinions predilections and prejudices shaped according to the early impressions, which they received, and which no ordinary exertion can remove. When this frame of mind is passively guided by submission to a foreign government, conformable to its selfish policy, which must sometimes differ from that of the state: when that foreign government is dependent on, and subservient to all the great powers of Europe: and when it singly, or the other powers through its instrumentality can gratify the ambition of the aspiring, direct the zeal of the enthusiast, or mould at will all those various sentiments, which spring from Religion ill or well understood, I apprehend that it then becomes a duty incumbent on the heads of the state, to temper the influence of that foreign power, so far as to prevent it from becoming injurious to the commonwealth. You will perceive that these observations point directly to the polity of the Roman Catholic Religion as now existing in America. The Bishops are appointed by the Pope, and the subaltern Clergy by the Bishops. This you must observe is as temporal an act, as the appointment of the magistracy in any state. The Pope entirely depends on the British and other European Governments for his existence as a temporal Prince, and to what advantage those governments may hereafter turn this influence, you can estimate better than most men. Bearing in mind those preliminary observations, please to fix your attention on the following circumstances and facts. All the Catholic Bishops in the United States except one are Frenchmen and of a society called Sulpicians, Royalists by education, by religion and by principle: conscientiously attached to the head of their body residing in Paris, and blindly devoted to the views of the French Cabinet, which is now only a branch of that of St. James: united with the Bishops and Clergy of Canada by the solemn bonds of identity of association, indissolubility of brotherhood and community of property, notwithstanding whatever they may pretend to the contrary. Insinuating and intriguing, artful and hypocritical as the Jesuits, of whom Dr. Robinson gives a finished and masterly picture at the end of his life of Charles V. but at present much more dexterous and able, this Society having lost its most gifted members during the interval of its suppression.

Of all the Societies that ever appeared in the Christian world, none knew how to combine with the outward appearance of religious austerity so keen a regard for temporal interest, and so insatiable a thirst for riches as the Jesuits. Not to mention their indefatigable exertions in opulent and prosperous countries; they knew how to accumulate wealth, in the poorest and even in those where prosperity only appeared in perspective. In Sweden and Denmark they never intruded themselves, because the poverty of those northern regions offered no prospect of future prosperity, while the most severe and sanguinary laws could not prevent their establishment in the more opulent and rising kingdom of Britain. With an intuitive glance, they contemplated the future greatness of America and accordingly contrived to procure an establishment there under the auspices of Lord Baltimore, and as in every other country, into which they crept, they nested themselves on the threshold of your government, since you became an independent nation.

The first colonists his Lordship could procure, being an aggregation of such Catholics as he could find, many were naturally unmarried, and the good Fathers did not fail to persuade all those who died without families, to bequeath their property and lands to the churches, which they appropriated to the Society. Whether an inquiry into the titles of those lands, which the Society now holds, and if found to have been bequeathed to the churches, they should be restored to them, is an affair that regards more a Court of Equity, than the subject of this address. The success of this system has attracted the attention of the crafty Sulpicians, who are actually in open hostility with the Catholic congregations of some of the southern States, about the churches and their revenues, while both are the fruit of the piety of the people. Whether the law of mortmain obtains in America I know not, but it has been introduced into every Kingdom in Europe, instructed as they have been by experience of the danger of allowing property to accumulate in such hands, and it should be a question of political prudence whether it ought not be established in those rising States. It must be obvious to every thinking man, that where such uncommon and vigorous exertions are making by a body that never dies to accumulate property, which may be at the disposal of men residing in foreign and eventually hostile countries to this, some regulation is indispensable, and that corporations either unknown to the law, or closely connected, and depending upon superiors residing beyond the seas, should be discountenanced.

I beg leave to observe that one of those gentlemen sulpicians of the French metropolis, by name Du Burg, went to New Orleans a few years back to endeavour to turn out an old Spanish Clergyman resident Pastor in that city for many years, because the brotherhood of Baltimore understood that the Catholic Church there was richly endowed. His plan miscarried from the opposition even of the French inhabitants, and from some local circumstances which he endeavoured to overcome by going to Rome, but could not succeed. However he got himself appointed to a new Bishoprick erected in the Missouri territory, which he calls the Diocess of St. Louis, after a French King, to keep alive there, the spirit of royalty, and to Frenchify the country by preserving among the inhabitants (the first settlers being French) the prejudices and partialities for their ancient country. Fame, says he, has a pension from the French Government.

It was observed by Mr. Lajunais in a late publication, who was I believe member of all their assemblies during their revolution, that among other retrenchments now necessary to the French Government in its embarrassed state, that those pensions given to their Clergy on foreign missions, *for political purposes* should be discontinued. I lately conversed with a gentleman, I was informed of some consideration and influence at St. Lewis, who told me his grandfather was a Frenchman, his father and himself born under the Spanish Government in that city, but that he still considered himself a Frenchman, and a Catholic of that church. Indeed it is remarked in Europe, that only the third, or fourth generation of Frenchmen establishing themselves in foreign countries, glide into the opinions, habits and feelings of their adopted country. It is unnecessary for me to make any observations, to point out the bearings, or to reason upon the conclusions to which the above facts lead, in submitting them to an intuitive mind like yours.

The different religionists of these countries, if I am well informed, already elect the ministers of their faith of whatever grade or dignity. Besides this system having a merit of being perfectly conformable to the fundamental and vital principles of the American constitution, it is in itself most just and reasonable, that those who are most interested in the good conduct of their Pastors, and remunerate them for their labours, should have a right of selecting those whom they deem most suitable to their wishes and in their judgment most deserving of their confidence. This was also the discipline and practice of the Catholic Church for near a thousand years, nor was it tamely resigned by the people without many a violent struggle, and until an unnatural connection between the church and the state, overwhelmed and extinguished their civil and religious rights. This right is recognized even now by the Court of Rome in conceding to the King of England the title of interfering in the appointment of Catholic Bishops in Ireland. The Pope affects to establish, that this right, which originally belonged to the people, may be now transferred to their governors. Upon the accuracy of this reasoning it is needless to remark any further, than that he lays down a fundamental principle of this government in Europe, upon which he is unwilling to act in America, because so advised by the emissaries of the Sulpicians at Paris and at Rome, or because his Ministers tell him, if such a concession should be required by the government of the United States, he might be allowed some equivalent in return, which only betrays an ignorance of the principles which guides the policy of those countries. But whatever the views of the court of Rome may be, in its conduct towards the Catholics of North America, who now insist upon this right, as originally belonging to them; as conformable to the fundamental principles of the constitution; and as acted upon by other religionists in this country; here are the words, in which he admits the principle in Europe.

"Quare, Venerabiles Fratres, perspicuum et evidens est nihil nos effecisse aliud, nisi ut eam rationem ipsam prudentiae innixam stabiliter cum Gubernio Britannico retinendam decerneremus quam Romani Potifices Predecessores Nostri, antequam etiam nominationes Episcoporum Principibus indulgerentur quam maxime posset tuendam esse, pro eorum sapientia, judicarunt. Nititur ea (ratio) scilicet principio illo quod alter ex ilustrioribus Praedecessoribus Nostris S Leo Magnus expressit ut nullis invitis et non petentibus ordinetur, ne Civitas Episcopum non optatum aut contemnat aut oderit.—Quod quidem principium et si populum proprie spectet, cujus postulationum eo tempore ratio in eligendis Episcopis habebatur, valere tamen, debitis concurrentibus circumstantiis, debet etiam cum de Principibus agitur."

From this admission it is evident, that nothing but intrigue can induce the court of Rome not to accede to the just demands of the Catholics of North America.

It only now remains to examine the objections to the enactment of a Law excluding all those from being Pastors or Ministers of congregations, or Bishops in any State of the Union, unless elected by the people of their persuasion. It cannot create any jealousy, or give any umbrage to the other religionists, as they all act as if such a law existed, and most of them have established it by their bye laws in almost the whole Union. The Catholics alone, I believe, are the only religionists, whose clergy are differently appointed, of whom 19-20th. are Irish and who are extremely anxious for such a law. Their complaints are loud and universal, that French, Dutch and German Clergymen are imposed upon them without their knowledge or consent, whose language they do not understand, and whose jargon in preaching they consider a burlesque upon their religion. Such a law cannot then meet the disapprobation of any religionist except of those, who are desirous to keep up a foreign influence, which may prove injurious to the State at some future period. This is already apprehended by the sensible Catholics, especially the Irish, who have been already the victims of French and Italian influence in the land of their birth. They have remarked with regret in Maryland and Pennsylvania where the Catholics are most numerous, that the eternal subject of the harangues of the foreign influenced Clergy in those States, is obedience to the Church, that is to themselves. They dread the influence of such doctrine upon ignorant and weak minds, and suspect that it is so incessantly inculcated for some sinister purpose. They remember to hear it constantly vociferated in Europe, that the French revolution, so odious to the legitimates has sprung from that of America, and that a durable peace could not be established on earth, while such a hotbed of democracy exists, and that this is the language of the Royalist Priests even in America. I have heard it remarked that such a law would be regarded as interfering with the liberty of Conscience, so sacred in this country. But I am satisfied that this is viewing the question in a very wrong light. It does not relate to any doctrine of religion, but merely to a municipal regulation, to which it is the duty of every Government to attend. It simply comes to this, whether a foreign power shall exercise a right over the Citizens, which only belongs to themselves, and impose persons upon them without their knowledge, and contrary to their wishes; or whether the State will pass a law to protect them in those rights, which are exercised by those, who have rejected the authority of that foreign power: or whether they will allow that foreign power to exercise an authority in this country, which it would not be allowed in any other, and enjoy an influence here which no foreign power ought to have within the State. No letter rescript or bull, issuing from the court of Rome, is allowed to be published in any Catholic State in the world, without the expressed consent and approbation of the Government, while in countries not Catholic, the most arbitrary and despotic laws are clandestinely enforced by the Clergy appointed by the Pope, without the knowledge of the governments in such States, and have been generally submitted to by the people for nearly two centuries, on account of the acrimonious spirit of religious intolerance, which generally prevailed, but since a more bland and benevolent temper has gradually arisen among Christians, the unlimited power of the court of Rome has been proportionably contracting. Such a law regards not what doctrine is taught, but whether the teachers be imposed upon the citizens contrary to their will, which is against true liberty, and whether those teachers hold political principles dangerous to the State, and which they may spread under the mask of religion. The other religionists have no connection with those of Europe, except in the identity of faith, but the Catholics have a common church polity with those of their communion all over the world, although under Catholic governments, that polity is regulated and governed by the municipal laws of the States, (and this is what they warmly desire to be similarly established by law in America) to prevent the evils, that may possibly arise from an abuse of foreign influence. Such cannot happen among other religionists, because in their church governments, they have nothing to do with those of other States, and it is conducted by free citizens born in those States, who have common principles and common interests with the people. In short viewing it on all sides, it is as in Catholic countries, more a question of policy than of religion. But it may be asked why they do not exclude those teachers of their own accord. This would be most assuredly the shortest way, if all men could view every object in the same light: if all were alike capable of forming a correct judgment upon all subjects: if all were equally prepared to divest themselves of prejudices, especially when these are of a long standing; cherished from habit, diversified by education, and by different manners of strangers to each other, by birth, by language and by country. You will see at a glance the difficulty, not to say impossibility of bringing order unity and harmony out of such heterogeneous materials, and that nothing but the sanction of law can make them subside in concord and peace, by closing every avenue against the influence of prejudices of passion and of foreign intrigue.

It is also said, and what may not be said by envy, or by ambition to blame men in power, that the discussion of such a law would occasion unpopularity. This might be possible among the ignorant or interested, but it certainly never could influence the thinking and wise nor should this weigh for a moment with any man, who sincerely wishes the tranquillity and safety of the Nation to rest for ever upon a firm and solid foundation. I cannot conceive how an able and honest statesman, can with consistency, with honour to himself, and justice to this country sit down cooly to calculate the quantum of obliquy he may possibly bring upon himself, in promoting a measure, which may avert not only a possible but also a probable and positive evil from this country.

France is now not only the Ally, but also the dependant of England as far as relates to the government and must continue so for half a century, and if we be allowed to assume that a war might break out between this country and Britain, the former will probably be compelled to become a party. Perhaps were she in condition to enter upon a war even her inclination, or at least that of her government would urge her to that evil, thus to rid herself of the friends of Napoleon and of his family. But allowing her to be indisposed to embark in a war with this country, Britain unless she joined with her cordially, might place the late Emperor in her embraces. His return from Elba tells the present Dynasty, how great its peril would be, and must in spite even of inclination, or interest become your enemy. She lacks not in soldiers, and England has ships. Would it then be wise to cherish in the heart of the country, or to dispose in the ranks of your army, a large body of men, who might be so far seduced by an hired, or mistaken Priesthood to countenance the enemies of your government in the interior, or to desert to the standard of the enemy on the frontiers. You have seen in the late war, the Clergy of those States in which your revolution began, seduced, as is supposed, by promises of ascendency, become the allies of that nation, which they once so enthusiastically opposed; and can it be supposed, that men of monarchical principles, and national attachments and prejudices could not be more easily arrayed against you, seduced by promises, and allured by privileges dignity and honours, whenever personal safety shall permit. But by placing the appointment in the hands of citizens by law, and citizens too to whom the recollection of past injuries has rendered the British name odious, you check the influence of foreign powers within your State, you will have a clergy among those religionists of their own choice who will command their confidence, and whose political principles will be in unison with their own, and with those of the country they have adopted.

The right of the people to choose their civil governors is the fundamental principle of your constitution, and the unbounded liberty of conscience is also another fundamental principle, and as the law guarantees and secures the right of election in the former case, so the latter is nugatory without it, and tends to excite a spirit of discord among the citizens, fomented and fanned by the policy, intrigue, and craft of foreign governments. How readily foreign politicians can avail themselves of such an order of things, we are instructed by the history of nations, and that some underplot of that nature is now acting in the world, we have some ground to suspect, when we reflect on the extraordinary phenomenon in the politics of Europe, of the Pope being restored to his temporal rank among the legitimates, and the order of the Jesuits being re-established through the influence of the English Cabinet, and that, notwithstanding the noise made about it in the House of Commons by Cox Hippesly, it has received the most marked attention in Washington from the English Ambassador, promising, that it would be indemnified by his Government for the losses it sustained from the British troops in their incursion to the capital.

Whatever the views of the British Government may be, in affording such countenance to the Pope and the Jesuits, while it is promoting a propaganda of Methodism as well in America as in the most distant regions (Catholic countries excepted) time will develop, but it must be evident to common sense, that some object is in contemplation, and that consequently it behoves the Pilots of every State to be vigilant, lest any power claiming unlimited authority over the minds and opinions of men, may not feel an interest, or be influenced by other powers, to favour such religious teachers and guides, who are likely to prove fit instruments in misleading the people upon points, where it may not be easy for the multitude to discriminate between religious and civil duties. The clearsighted and penetrating may discover the imposition, and resist, but the many are not so easily enlightened, and feuds, contention and discord may arise to the prejudice of good order and Christian charity, and religion in the hands of an ignorant misguided and corrupted Priesthood, will whenever it suits the views of politicians, become a bane and a scourge instead of a blessing bearing comfort and consolation to its votaries.

It is clear, that at all times, but more especially in those in which we live, and considered as the United States are, with an evil eye by the Kings, Nobility, and Clergy of Europe, that her own safety, her interest and sound policy should urge America to limit the power of every foreign government within her territory, even in matters of religion, so far as regards the teachers to be employed for the instruction of the people; and that none should be suffered to officiate in that capacity unless by the suffrages of such American citizens as profess the same religion, worship in the same congregation, and are united in the same faith, whatever that may be.

I am with respect, your
Most H'mble and Obt. Servt.[55]

Early in 1819, Maréchal received Propaganda's letter of December 5, 1818, justifying the Archbishop's support of Father Lucas, and saying as we have seen, that there need be no further necessity of discussing Father Carbry as prospective pastor of Norfolk.

---

55. BCA, case—12—T1.

CHAPTER V

ARCHBISHOP MARÉCHAL AND THE NORFOLK SCHISM (*Continued*).

The New Year, far from bringing peace to the distracted Catholics of the city, saw the disobedience of the few assume an importance far beyond the merits of the struggle between the authority of the Archbishop and the misguided rebels. If the Archivist of Propaganda a century ago had not preserved all the documents on the Norfolk schism, it would be difficult to believe to-day that the suggestion of a plan to place the Southland under Utrecht came so close to actual settlement. The first letter is one, apparently from South Carolina dated January 4, 1819, and sent to Father Carbry for transmission to Father Richard Hayes, O.F.M., of the Church of Adam and Eve, Dublin. Carbry added this postcript:

"The letter was sent to me, written on four large sheets; and as it might be too bulky in that form, I thought it best to copy it on a single sheet and send it to you. You have here the whole affair before your eyes, and open for your judgment. Whatever will be your decision (on the letter), if it be directed to me, it will be faithfully transmitted to its destination. This is all the interest I have in this business. If I were seeking my own advantage, I would not send this communication, since I am asked for at Rome as Bishop of Charleston by the Catholics of that city. But this advantage has no place in my heart; and besides I have no personal knowledge of these gentlemen, whose desire I transmit, nevertheless I agree gladly with their request, declaring as my opinion that they are ready and able to fulfil their agreement. If therefore I have a share of the candour and confidence of this affair, I have, it seems, a just right to your confidence and honour."[1]

The letter itself was not written by laymen; and since the only clergymen in South Carolina at the time capable of writing such a document were Browne and Gallagher, it is probable that either one or the other is the author. Maréchal knew of the intrigue in

---

1. Prop. Arch., *Scritt. rifer., Amer. Cent.*, vol. 4, No. 80.

the summer of 1819, when Bishop Burke of Halifax wrote to him that "some Priests have lately offered to receive the Rev. Mr. Hayes as Bishop, if he would go to Utrecht and get a consecration from the schismatical Bishop of that city."[2] Late in September, 1819, Cardinal Fontana's letter of June 26, 1819, reached Baltimore. The Cardinal-Prefect said: "I presume you are informed that some Catholicks (if however they can be so called) by the organ of Thomas Carbry, of the Order of St. Dominic, have sent letters to an Irish Priest, to whom they have made considerable offers, if he were willing to go to Utrecht, to have himself consecrated by its schismatical Bishop, then to go over to America and consecrate other prelates in every one of its States. But this Priest being struck with horror at the criminal project, has immediately given information of it to the Holy See."[3]

Father Richard Hayes, O.F.M., had become known in Rome and in the British Isles as one of the ablest antagonists of the Veto in Ireland. The Quarantotti Rescript of February 16, 1814, had aroused an intense indignation among those Catholics of the British Isles who were opposed to it. The action on the Rescript (May 3, 1814), by Dr. Troy, Archbishop of Dublin, its rejection by the Irish Bishops in their meeting at Maynooth (May 26-27, 1814), the revocation of the Rescript (June 25, 1814), Cardinal Litta's "Genoese Letter" of April 26, 1815, sanctioning the Veto, and the general fear that the Holy See might imprudently grant the right of the Veto over the Irish episcopate to the British Crown, all led up to the Aggregate Meeting in Dublin, of August 29, 1815, in which Daniel O'Connell led the party devoted to an uncompromising determination never to submit to such a grant.

"As a result of the meeting, three representatives were deputed to proceed to Rome, to make representations to the Holy See . . . Two of them, Sir Thomas Esmonde and Mr. Owen O'Connor, were laymen, and they refused to go; the third, Father Hayes, a Franciscan, went."[4] Father Hayes reached Rome on October 25, 1815, and before long he found himself in the thick of the fight for what was indeed the turning point in Catholic Emancipation. Cardinal Consalvi, as Secretary of State, was profoundly hated by the Irish, who believed that he "either betrayed or sold our Church to the British minister at Vienna . . . though a Car-

---

2. *Pastoral Letter* (Maréchal), p. 82.
3. *Ibid.*, pp. 84-85.
4. Ward, *Eve of the Catholic Emancipation*, vol. ii, p. 148.

dinal, this man is not a priest. He is a secular Cardinal, just fit for any bargain and sale; right glad, I presume"—it is Daniel O'Connell who speaks—"to have so good a thing to sell as the religion of Ireland. Quarantotti, and Cardinal Litta and the Pope himself are all, of course, foreigners."[5]

"The same tone of speaking was adopted by Father Hayes in Rome, which, considering the position and reputation of Cardinal Consalvi, and the great work he had accomplished for the Holy See, was, to say the least, unseemly."[6] Father Hayes was in the Pope's own city, and no sovereign of the time could have permitted so audacious an attack upon his Prime Minister without at least a warning. The friendship of Castlereagh, most hated of all English agents in Ireland, and Consalvi was an alliance abominable to the Irish in their fight for freedom; and in denouncing it, Father Hayes used language which gave serious offense in Rome. On May 18, 1817, he received an order to leave Rome within twenty-four hours and the Papal States within three days. On his refusal to comply with the order, he was expelled by force, accompanied by dragoons who took him as far as the border of Tuscany. He returned to Dublin on September 24, 1817. On February 21, 1818, in order to silence the bitter attack made upon the Holy See in Ireland as a result of Hayes' treatment, Pius VII wrote to the Irish Bishops with regard to the patriotic Franciscan.

That the name of Father Hayes was known by the end of the year, 1818, in every group of Irishmen of Europe and America can be taken for granted. Too often had it been said, as the Irish Bishops wrote in 1818: "It would seem to have been forgotten that the conduct and perseverance of the Roman Catholics of Ireland had entitled them to any share of regard, or even of favorable consideration—the martyrs of three centuries appear to be already forgotten, and the zealous perseverance of the present generation is not esteemed worthy of being taken into account."[7]

These things were spoken of by such groups of Irishmen as those at Norfolk and Charleston; and to them a figure like that of Hayes loomed large at the time in the age-long struggle between Ireland and England. It was a period of strong national feelings, made all the more intense by the fear that English diplomacy, aided by French Catholic influence at Rome, would

---

5. *Ibid.*, p. 149.
6. *Ibid.*, p. 157.
7. *Ibid.*, p. 158.

succeed in shaking the only institution in Ireland which had escaped slavery, the Episcopate.

Father Hayes was a gallant rebel against England, but a true and faithful priest of God, and on June 1, 1818, he publicly expressed his poignant regret that his conduct had offended the Holy See, and he humbly asked pardon of Pius VII.

To this priest, then, it was that the schismatic proposal was made to have himself consecrated Bishop of South Carolina, the purpose being that he would quickly provide Virginia with its own bishop. The letter to Hayes opens with the statement: "I see by the public journals of your country that you have been persecuted not only without motive but with cruelty by the Court of Rome, and that you have been ignominously abandoned by those whose agent you were . . . with this persuasion, I will hazard the submission to your consideration of a project which will ennoble your misfortunes and cover your enemies with humiliation and ignominy." The writer praises the noble soul of his correspondent and is certain that he will never disclose the project through perfidy. The project was to break down the *giunta di uomini di chiesa Francese* who were seeking to establish a tyranny over the Catholics here, by establishing an independent Catholic Church in the Southland. Hayes was asked to go to Utrecht after receiving this letter and to request consecration at the hands of the Archbishop. Then he was to come here as soon as possible (*al più presto possibile*). All his expenses would be paid if he agreed to consecrate bishops for other American cities; should he refuse this condition financial help would be dubious.[8] Then follows a long argumentation regarding the Primacy which is declared to be only a human institution. The Church in this country was only twenty years old, the writer continues, and was therefore in the same state as the early Church, without fixed laws and discipline. Canon law was impracticable here, because of its opposition to the laws of the land. The French had planned to set up a despotic Church government here under the rule of the Bourbons, and the Catholics of America insist upon the *Jus patronatus,* by which they can elect their own spiritual leaders, election being the basic and vital principle of the American Constitution, to which all have sworn allegiance. "At present all the bishops of

---

8. Shea makes the mistake (*op. cit.,* vol. iii, p. 49) of concluding that the Utrecht Plan was primarily designed for Norfolk. There was a close connection between the two cities, and there is no doubt that Norfolk would have been the first suffragan See in the American Jansenist Church.

the United States are French, except the Bishop of New York," and they send to the people here foreign priests who are not of their race. The Irish Catholics suffer on account of the ridicule heaped upon these French priests by the members of other religious denominations, and as a result they are falling away from the Faith. To remedy these evils, the Catholics here made representation to the Holy See, but owing to the influence of the French Ambassador, their pleas were not heard. The English who are the avowed enemies of the Irish clergy, also prevented justice being done by the Holy See. Hence, nothing remained but to appeal either to the Greek Church or to Utrecht, and it was earnestly hoped that Hayes would take pity on his compatriots in the United States, abandoned as they were by Rome and tyrannized over by French bishops, and proceed to Holland for consecration. He was also to bring five or six young men who have completed their studies for the priesthood. That these candidates for the new diocese should be men of sobriety, piety, and of good character was evident, but the indispensable quality needed for the American Church was the gift of eloquence. Hayes was then directed to send his answer through Father Carbry at New York.[9]

On April 14, 1819, Father Hayes denounced the conspiracy to Cardinal Litta, who was then Vicar of Rome, and also to His Holiness, Pope Pius VII. Litta had written to the young priest on September 12, 1818, announcing the Holy Father's pleasure at his prompt and obedient submission. "In this letter," Hayes writes, "Your Eminence, on the part of His Holiness, admonishes me to show at all times the sincerity of my sentiments regarding the Holy See. I did not think that I would have so soon an occasion to give an evident proof of the same. I am transmitting to Your Eminence a copy of a letter sent to me from America, in which you will see with much sorrow the conspiracy which has been created for the destruction of the Church in the United States." Father Hayes had communicated the contents of the letter to Archbishop Troy, and all the documents in question were despatched that day to Cardinal Fontana, Prefect of Propaganda Fide.

Maréchal was warned by Father Benedict Fenwick, S.J., as early as February 3, 1819, that such a conspiracy was being mooted about Charleston, and he advised the Archbishop to visit that city during the early part of the spring. On May 13, 1819,

---

9. Prop. Arch., *Scritt. rifer., Amer. Cent.*, vol. 4, No. 82.

in replying to the Archbishop's letter which "communicated to me the very disagreeable intelligence that you could not possibly visit us this year," Fenwick informed Maréchal that Browne was about to be sent to Rome for the purpose of obtaining "a new Diocess [to] be formed in these Southern States distinct from the Diocess of Baltimore." Good Father Fenwick had other things to bother him besides this, he says—"all heat and no rain; mosquitoes by ten millions both day and night. Heaven preserve us!"[10]

Meanwhile at Rome the Charleston letter sent by Carbry was given to Father O'Finan for judgment. On May 23, 1819, O'Finan wrote to the Cardinal-Prefect of Propaganda that he had examined the translation and the original. He could not understand why Father Carbry permitted himself to take a hand in such an impious undertaking, which, if successful, would reverse all hierarchical jurisdiction in the United States and bring Gallicanism into that Church. While in Dublin, Father Carbry bore an excellent reputation as an ecclesiastic of merit and as a learned man. Whatever the faults of Father Hayes were, Father O'Finan does not believe that he would accuse Carbry of such an atrocious suggestion in cold blood (*di sangue freddo*). The style of the letter, he adds, is altogether different from that of Father Hayes, being more eloquent and vibrant. It is interesting to note that O'Finan immediately adds the remark: "I hope to God that Dr. Gallagher has no part in it!" O'Finan then asks for any copies of Carbry's letters which may be in Propaganda, to compare the style, and he suggests that Archbishop Troy might help in deciding upon the authorship of the letter. O'Finan knew the situation of the Church in the United States rather well at the time, and he urged the Cardinal-Prefect to appoint a bishop for Charleston, lest Carbry or Gallagher be sent by the rebels to Utrecht.[11]

---

10. BCA, Case—12—R2.
11. Prop. Arch., *Scritt. rifer., Amer. Cent.,* vol. 4, No. 83. Maréchal's comment on the conspiracy, as given in his *Pastoral,* runs as follows: "This is the impure source from which Thomas Carbry attempted to procure a Bishop, who, with all his adherents, would have been as really separated from the Catholick Church, as any sectarian Bishop in the world. We are informed, moreover, that to deceive the ignorant, the plan was carefully to preserve, after the example of the schismatical Prelates of Utrecht, all the exterior practices of our Divine worship, and to call their sect: The Independent Catholick Church of the United States." Of Hayes he writes: "It is manifest that Thomas Carbry mistaking Rev. Mr. Hayes for an abandoned character, inimical to the Holy See, believed he would cheerfully accept the criminal proposals made to him. But fortunately he was disappointed. The Catholicks of the United States have just reason

Archbishop Maréchal attempted to break the deadlock in the Norfolk situation by sending (May, 1819) Father Nicholas Kerney, "a young Irish Clergyman distinguished by his great mildness, prudence and piety," as pastor of the congregation in Portsmouth and assistant-pastor to Father Lucas.[12] Kerney had hardly settled down before the news of his arrival was sent to Carbry. The Irish Dominican immediately set out by sail from New York for Norfolk, where he arrived early in June, 1819.[13] On June 8, 1919, Maréchal wrote a peremptory letter to Carbry summoning him to show by what authority he exercised the ministry in the Baltimore Diocese. On June 14, he wrote a firm, kindly letter to Dr. Connolly, informing him of this uncanonical intrusion of Carbry: "To a Prelate of such eminent piety and learning I will not undertake to prove the criminality of such proceedings. Your Lordship perceives at once that Mr. Carbry has rendered himself guilty, in the sight of God and of the Church, of the most enormous crime, and that he is now laying under the most terrible censures that can be inflicted on disorderly Clergymen."[14] Superficially it would appear that Father Carbry had accepted the leadership of the discontented Irish Catholics in the Archdiocese of Baltimore, and that his sudden departure from New York was a prearranged plan. His presence in Norfolk gave courage to the rebels, and on June 14, the trustees sent to Maréchal the following declaration of independence from his spiritual authority:

At a joint meeting of the Trustees of the Roman Catholic Congregation of Norfolk and Portsmouth, convened on the 14th day of June, 1819, to take into consideration a letter directed by the Rev. Archbishop of the Catholic Church of Baltimore, to the Norfolk Pastor, the Reverend Dr. Thomas Carbry, dated on the 8th instant, by which the Reverend Archbishop summons the Right Reverend Pastor to appear before or to send to him the authentic Title, in virtue of which the Right Reverend Dr. Carbry is exercising the functions of Pastor in Norfolk and Portsmouth which said Reverend Archbishop calls his Diocess. After mature consideration of the contents of the letter afore-

---

to congratulate the Rev. Mr. Hayes for having repelled with indignation the insulting offers of Thomas Carbry, and immediately denounced him to the Holy See: and we sincerely wish his meritorious conduct in this circumstance may expiate in the eyes of the Holy Father the irregularities of which His Holiness complains in the brief above mentioned."
12. BCA, Case—12—R3. Cf. *Records* ACHS, vol. xxii, pp. 254-255.
13. BCA, Case—12—R4.
14. *Ibid.*

said, the Trustees of the Norfolk and Portsmouth congregations immediately resolved:

First that the Priest James Lucas and the Reverend Archbishop Maréchal, after the resolutions passed by the Trustees of the Roman Catholic Congregation aforesaid on the 4th of Jan., 1817, and 16th of March of last year; being neither their Prelate and Pastor which resolutions were rendered public through the press; and distributed amongst the members of both Congregations, a protest shall be legally intimated to the Reverend Archbishop of the Catholic Church of Baltimore, that himself not being a lawful Prelate of this state, and still less of these congregations he has no right at all to interfere with these congregations or any of their religious matters, whatever. And likewise, with the Right Reverend Pastor thereof duly elected by the Congregation, approved of by His Holiness and communicated to us by his Eminence Cardinal Litta.

Resolved that besides the right inherent in them as Christians and patrons of their churches acknowledged by the Holy See, the impertinence of the demand of the Right Reverend Archbishop of the Catholic Church of Baltimore, being a most glaring violation of their civil rights and religious liberties and in direct opposition to the state laws of Virginia, an extract of the same laws, shall be forwarded to him by which he may see, that he has no authority to meddle with the choice of our Pastors or to interfere with the exercise of his sacred functions, resolved that the Reverend Archbishop of the Catholic Church of Baltimore, be reminded of the proceedings in former times, viz:

At Rome in the African church
{ St. Cyprian, Lib. 2. Ep. 2
St. Cyprian, Lib. 1. Ep. 4
Conc. Carth., 4th Can. 1. }

At Alex., etc., etc.

Likewise of the proceedings, etc., of the Archbishop of Goa towards the Catholics of Bombatin on the coast of Malabar and its results by Lord Minto's decision, the whole published by the House of Commons of July 13th, 1814, as well as of the sentiments of the present Pope, Pius VII, in his Bull to the Archbishop and Bishops of Ireland of the first of February, 1816, acknowledging the right of the people in the election of their Prelates, alledging the authority of his predecessor St. Leo the Great, viz., that no more be ordained Bishops without the consent and postulation of the flock lest an unwelcome intruder incur its contempt and hatred, as it has been unfortunately the case with the Reverend Amb. Maréchall in this and other cities of the different states of the union.

Resolved that should said Reverend Archbishop of the Catholic Church of Baltimore, proceed (which God forbid) to any public act or calumnious deed against either the Reverend Dr.

Thomas Carbry or any of the members of the congregation, all his illegal, absurd and impious proceedings, as well as the causes leading to them shall be rendered public through the press and himself held responsible to the laws of the state of Virginia.

Resolved that a copy of these resolutions signed by the President and Secretary of this board, be forwarded to the Reverend Archbishop of the Catholic Church of Baltimore.

Norfolk, June 14, 1819, and 43d year of the independence of the United States.

Thomas Reilly, *President*
John F. Oliveira Fernandez,
*acting as secretary of the Board of the Roman
Catholic Church and Congregation of Norfolk.*[15]

That Carbry's departure from New York was viewed somewhat in the nature of a flight from the bitter conflict which had disturbed the Catholics of that city after the arrival of Dr. Connolly, in 1815, is evident from the fact that a meeting was called by his friend, Father Charles Ffrench, O.P., on May 21, 1819, "to express our sorrow at the unexpected departure of the Very Rev. Dr. Carbry from New York." Resolutions were passed, and it was agreed that "it is with sentiments of the deepest regret that we have learned the departure of our beloved Pastor from among us. A departure which we consider an irreparable loss to a congregation that has long witnessed his exalted merits, revered his piety, and admired the splendour of his talents. His unaffecting piety put hypocrisy to the blush, and his inalterable friendship has given him a lasting claim to our sincere esteem." Even granting that this tribute came from leaders in the factionist conflict of New York, there must have been something particularly likeable about the man to have been the occasion of such a set of resolutions. Dr. Connolly was asked to use his influence with the Dominican to secure his return. These resolutions were published in the New York *Columbian* for May 24, 1819, and were reprinted in the Portsmouth *Herald* for June 16, 1819. The editorial note prefacing them said:

We most cheerfully comply with the request of the Trustees of the Roman Catholic Church in this Borough, to publish the following honorable testimonials in favor of their venerable

---

15. BCA, Case—21A—G2. To prove his right to take possession of the church at Norfolk, Carbry is said to have presented to the magistrates a letter from Bishop Connolly authorizing him to do so (BCA, Case —18—G29).

and pious Pastor, the Rev. Mr. CARBRY, who, at their solicitation, quitted a higher and more desirable situation, and came hither from motives of the purest benevolence to minister to the spiritual wants of a flock so long suffering under a state of disunion and contention. He has come among them as a stranger, and under circumstances peculiarly delicate and embarrassing. The congregation of the Church in this place had long remained in a divided state, and angry feelings prevailed where "peace and good will" should have reigned.—At such a time it was not expected that those high and essential qualifications for Church ministry which distinguish the Reverend Gentleman of whom we are speaking, nor yet the truly Christian meekness and humility of his character, as a man could bear him blameless—perhaps if an Angel from on high had condescended to the task which Doctor Carbry has undertaken to fulfil, his authority would have been disputed and he denounced.—It is unnecessary for us to say through whose agency this unhappy state of things has been produced, as it is far from our intention to become partizans in a question of this nature. We trust, however, that the time is rapidly approaching when its baleful effects shall be dissipated and forgotten, like a noxious vapor, flitting before the all powerful rays of truth and reason, leaving no trace of its existence to disturb the good feelings of a single bosom. We may say, too, that the preaching of Doctor Carbry has been attended with the happiest effects in opening the eyes of all denominations of Christians who have too long been accustomed to associate the Catholic faith with bigotry, intolerance, and idolatrous superstition: they have heard him again and again with pleasure, and expatiated on the liberal and enlightened doctrines which he proclaims, no less than on the impressive and eloquent manner of his delivery.—It is under the ministry of such men as this that the Catholic religion appears in its genuine state. It is only when administered by a corrupt and despotic Priesthood, (who exists as an engine to keep the human mind in slavery), that it becomes odious and intolerable. In this land of freedom and equal rights, it ought to be established upon the pure principles of its institution, and not one solitary blot be permitted to mar its beauties. The Congregations are bound by social and political as well as by religious ties, indignantly to spurn from them every minion of a foreign system of tyranny, and to crush the embryo monster of usurpation before it is warmed into existence by bigotry and superstition.[16]

Then follows a letter written to Father Carbry by the trustees of St. Patrick's Cathedral, New York, dated June 6, 1819:

---

16. *Ibid.*

Rev. Sir,

Your sudden and in some measure unexpected departure deprived us of an opportunity of expressing to you the painful feelings excited by your determination of separating from us; but, to you and to ourselves should we be guilty of the highest injustice, were we any longer to suspend expressing our heartfelt gratitude that your unfeigned attachment to our interests so highly merits.

Your zeal, piety, and goodness; your unceasing perseverance in promoting a respect for religion; your unremitted attention in performing the various duties incumbent on you; your ardent exertions to render our congregation tranquil and happy, your cheerfulness in doing good, and the pleasure you manifestly felt in affording consolation to the distressed must render you eternally dear to our memory.—In an advanced stage of life, and approaching the regions of bliss, we behold in you an anxious wish to propagate the doctrines of our Church, which the benign influence of your liberal and judicious sentiments has (if possible) more permanently and respectably established. The kindness you have evinced to the whole Catholic family is known and felt by all: believing as we do, that your honest character was by none better understood than by our most worthy Prelate. It is a consolation to us, to have it in our power to add, as we most confidently do: that there are no expressions of regard or esteem which we may use, no declaration of our sorrow and regret at being separated from you, in which he does not most cordially unite and sympathise with us.

We offer you, Rev. Sir, our congratulations, that the Almighty has been pleased to take you under his special protection, during your late perilous voyage.—To Him our gratitude and our homage is due, for this additional mark of his favor. Should it ever happen that good fortune would again send you to us, we venture to assure you, that your reception would be such as might be anticipated, justly anticipated, from the fervent esteem and affection, inspired by a recollection of the many kind offices you have performed towards us, and cemented by the beneficial effects which they produce.

And now, Rev. Sir, in bidding you adieu, permit us to unite our prayers for your temporal happiness, during the remainder of your life, and when you shall have quitted this valley of misery, may you be translated into the presence of our Redeemer, there to plead the cause of your afflicted, but most affectionate friends.[17]

These are important papers in the career of Father Carbry,

---

17. *Ibid.*

whose life from now until his death has so many singular aspects that grave doubts arise about his sanity. Certainly the complaints against him for erratic conduct, from the very men who had welcomed him as the head of their schismatic congregation, began to reach Maréchal within a few weeks after his arrival at Norfolk. On May 31, 1819, James Herron wrote to the Archbishop accusing Carbry of impiety, and yet on June 2, 1819, Father Lucas wrote that the rebellious trustees had spoken openly of Carbry as their future bishop.[18]

By this time Browne was on his way to Rome via Bordeaux for the purpose of securing a bishopric for Charleston. Cardinal Litta was then in close touch with Norfolk affairs and wrote to Maréchal on May 31, 1819, asking him to investigate the Jansenist schism in that city. By this time, the anti-French attitude had also reached its peak in Philadelphia, and on June 14, Augustine Fagan, the Secretary of the Board of Trustees at St. Mary's Church, Philadelphia, wrote to Father MacCormack, the Guardian of St. Isidore's Convent, in Rome, at the advice of Dr. Connolly, asking MacCormack to present the Petition which he was sending to the Holy Father and to "use every means in your power to promote the object of it—which is to defeat the designs of a French Jesuitical faction who seem as anxious to possess themselves of our churches and church livings here, as ever the English were in the land of our forefathers."[19] The Petition repeats much that is already familiar to us in the Norfolk and Charleston documents, but it goes a step further in its boldness. Unless the Holy See realizes that the Irish Catholics in this country will not obey French pastors, placed over them by French bishops who have not the good of the Church at heart, but only the aggrandizement of their national prestige, then a "Convention of delegates from all the Catholic Congregations in the United States," especially those of Charleston, Norfolk, and Philadelphia, would be called to consider the means necessary to remedy this evil (*una Convenzione di delegati da tutte le Congni. Cattoliche degli Stati Uniti, per divisarne un remedio*).[20] Father John Ryan, O.P., who had witnessed the beginning of the trial of the racial troubles here, wrote from Lisbon on December 14, 1819, this concise statement of the situation:

In truth the Catholics of the United States consider the

---
18. BCA, Case—17—I5.
19. BCA, Case—18—H1.
20. *Ibid.*

Archbp. and his advisers as engaged in a systematic plan, for the exclusion from the Church of America, of every clergyman who is not a native of France. The pertinacy with which this system is continued, together with the ridicule, and contempt excited among the various sectarians in America by the attempts of these foreigners to preach in the English language, has already goaded the Catholics to such a state of irritation that consequences truly alarming are but too likely to result from this conflict, between the ambition of the Frenchmen on one side, and the indignation of the people on the other. The laws of the United States, give each denomination of Christians, an undoubted right to *elect* their clergy. Your Grace will perceive how injuriously the exercise of such a right, might operate against the essential spirit which pervades the discipline of the Catholic Church. This consideration has served hitherto, in restraining the American Catholics, from any serious attempts to avail themselves of this legal right. How far it may continue to restrain them, must depend on the prudence, and moderation of their Prelates, and on the promptitude of the Holy See, in removing all reasonable causes of discontent.[21]

On June 19, 1819, Maréchal informed Propaganda of Carbry's intrusion into his diocese. The Irish Dominican had presented himself to a magistrate in Norfolk, had secured legal recognition as pastor of the Catholic Church there, and had celebrated Mass in the church interdicted by Archbishop Neale. When Maréchal asked him by what authority he was ministering in Norfolk, he replied that such authority was not needed in the independent United States, but only in Europe where Catholics were living under tyrants.

Fernandez' pamphlet was doing much harm at the time, and this, connected with Carbry's action, had practically closed all avenues to peace between Baltimore and the Norfolk rebels. Carbry had cited before a magistrate of the city the person who handed him Maréchal's letter of June 8, and the Mayor told Fernandez that he considered the Archbishop's letter a violation of the State Constitution. By this time (June 23, 1819) Father Benedict Fenwick in Charleston, began "strongly to suspect that there exists a deep-laid, extensive and undermining plan in which Browne and Carbry act as principals, O'Driscoll, Fernandez and others as seconds, who have for their object the dismembering of the Diocese, and to promote the success of which Browne is gone to Rome. Should he succeed, I would not give one pinch

---

21. Guilday, *Carroll*, p. 680.

of snuff for the respectability of the Catholic Religion in these Southern States."[22] Those who were being attacked in this manner by the Irish were not silent, as can be well understood, and there is a strong hint of the *impasse* to which Catholic life was rapidly moving, in cities like New York, where one leader of the pro-French element, Father Malou, described the Irish to Bishop Plessis of Quebec (June 23, 1819) as *la canaille irlandaise*.[23]

The fears expressed in Father Fenwick's last letter that the Holy See might yield to the Virginia rebels seemed at first to merge into actuality when Maréchal received Fontana's letter of June 26, 1819, in which the Cardinal-Prefect decided upon the erection of a new See for the Carolinas and Georgia, and upon one also for Virginia. The creation of these two suffragan dioceses would bring peace to the distracted Church of the Southern States, Fontana wrote, and he had no doubt that Maréchal would willingly make the sacrifice for the good of the Church.[24] Maryland was a large enough territory for any one bishop (*satis uberem ad excolendam Domini vineam tibi copiam praebet*). On July 3, 1819, Fontana wrote to Dr. Connolly, asking for private information regarding Father Carbry, especially about his stand on the unity of the Church and the primacy of the Supreme Pontiff. Curiously enough, in his letter to Fontana of July 30, 1819, Maréchal calls Browne a Dominican and urges the Cardinal-Prefect to ask "the Superior of the Dominicans not to permit Mr. Browne to return to the United States." Bishop Cheverus of Boston had been watching the trend of events from the vantage point of a city where no difficulty similar to that of New York, Philadelphia, and the South, was to be found among his people. He had advised Maréchal on various occasions during the past two years (1817-19) that the erection of a See in Charleston might solve the problem and on more than one occasion he wrote strongly against choosing a French priest for the post. His own candidate for Charleston, strange to say, was his own successor, Benedict Fenwick.[25] Cheverus gives us the first hint of his diagnosis of Carbry's actions on July 16, 1819, when he writes to Maréchal that the Dominican does not seem sane to him.[26]

---

22. BCA, Case—18—H31.
23. Cf. Zweirlein, *Les premières nominations episcopales aux Etats-Unis* (Mélanges Moeller, vol. ii, p. 540. Louvain, 1914).
24. BCA, Case—Special B—L4.
25. BCA, Case—14—J26.
26. BCA, Case—14—J30.

The climax of all this complicated and confusing situation came in June, 1819, when in a special meeting of the officials of Propaganda the status of the Church in Virginia, the two Carolinas and Georgia, was taken up for consideration and final decision. The Sacred Congregation now realized more clearly than any of the American Churchmen the danger to the authority of the Church in case the Utrecht plan was to be successfully pursued by the disobedient groups in the South. It realized also how easily such a scheme could be carried out; and how, once an historical fact, it would be well-nigh impossible to root out the schism thus caused. Schism seldom stays schismatic; the step through its portals to heresy being easy.

The *Atti* for 1819 contain a printed account of the resolutions taken by the Sacred Congregation on these American difficulties. The entire history of the schism at Norfolk is given accurately and without sparing the important detail that in two cases Propaganda had to reverse its decision after having heard the true story from Baltimore. In regard to the erection of a See in Virginia, Maréchal had given on December 26, 1817, his five reasons for objecting to such a plan. First, Norfolk was a little city, with probably only two hundred and fifty Catholics; secondly, it was not far from Baltimore, being about a day's journey; thirdly, it had a priest who was sufficient for the spiritual care of these Catholics; fourthly, Bishop Connolly would be left alone, if Father Carbry were taken away; fifthly, the Diocese of Baltimore would remain divided, Virginia being between Maryland and the territory south and west of the Carolinas.

To settle the problem, Propaganda arrived at the decision that bishoprics should be established in Virginia and the Carolinas, and as soon as possible, lest Father Carbry or Dr. Gallagher be induced to attempt a schismatic Church. Archbishop Maréchal had refused his consent to the Virginia See, but there was more reason for a bishopric in that State, Propaganda felt, than in Charleston. Father Grassi, a former Superior of the Jesuits in the United States, had been consulted and in his judgment a bishop in Virginia was more necessary than in Boston. Archbishop Carroll had also thought of appealing to Rome for a See in Virginia. Father Grassi urged that the residence of the bishop be placed rather in Richmond, the capital of the State, than in Norfolk. Others, however, believed that the new See should be placed in Washington, on account of the political and diplomatic standing of the national capital. If the bishop were to reside in

Washington, he could have an easy access to the Government and he might serve as a Nuncio or Minister of the Holy See. The greatest difficulty consisted in finding the proper ecclesiastics to occupy these two new Sees. The Irish were in the majority in the Southern States, and French and English clergymen were not popular with them. So runs the document.

Two priests are now mentioned in the document as worthy of the episcopal dignity for Virginia—Father Francis O'Finan, O.P., formerly Prior of San Clemente, and Father Simon Harrigan, O.P., the Prior of Santa Maria della Pace. Besides these, five other priests were mentioned, Father Rice, O.S.A.; Father Thomas Murphy, formerly Rector of the Seminary in Waterford and Dean of Maynooth; Father Nicholas Foran, formerly professor of theology in the Seminary at Waterford; Father Kelly of Ossory; John England, of Cork: *il più bravo, il più attivo, il più eloquente di tutto quel Clero;* and Father Edmund Nowlan, of Ossory.

The decrees passed on August 2, 1819, postulated the erection of the See of Charleston, but deferred the Virginia episcopate until the Archbishop of Baltimore had been heard from, not only on the creation of the See itself, but also on the questions involved therein; namely, should the diocese of Virginia include the District of Columbia or should the See be in Norfolk, Richmond, or Washington.

Meanwhile Maréchal had carried the war into the camp of the enemy. On August 7, 1819, Fernandez received the following report from his agent in Baltimore:

> On my presenting your papers to the Archbishop of Baltimore, he answered me that he does not wish to have any communication with Dr. Fernandez, Mr. Reilly and their association. Nor will he receive any letters from them. He moreover added that in conformity with the laws of the Catholic Church, he had written a letter to a certain Priest named Thomas Carbry to know from him who had appointed him Roman Catholic Pastor of Norfolk and from whom he had received the spiritual powers which he now exercises in that town. From that Priest alone the Archbishop will receive an answer.[27]

On August 11, 1819, Fenwick wrote to the Archbishop calling his attention to the "infamous, anonymous printed letter addressed to Thos. Jefferson, Esquire . . . I am persuaded either Fernandez or O'Driscoll is the author of it. I have not been able to

---
27. *Ibid.*

obtain a copy; otherwise, I would send one to your Grace." Gallagher's submission to Maréchal's authority (August 20, 1819) lessened the danger of the Utrecht plan, because he had by this time lost caste completely in the American Church, on account of excessive intemperance. Propaganda wrote to Archbishop Troy on August 28, 1819, asking for information about Father James Cowan, the Provincial of the Franciscans in Ireland, whom the Sacred Congregation was considering for one of the Southern Sees. The same day letters were sent to the Bishop of Cork, asking information about John England, and to the Bishop of Ossory about Patrick Kelly, for the same purpose.

Maréchal received the news of the creation of the See of Charleston in Fontana's letter of September 11, 1819. He was also informed that after weighing seriously all the objections against the creation of the Diocese of Virginia, Propaganda had decided to act against his wishes and had decided to divide further the Baltimore diocese, but it was not settled whether the new See should be in Norfolk, Richmond, or Washington: *Quamobrem Sacra Congregatio nimirum expedire putat,ut Virginiae quoque Episcopus instituatur, sed nondum satis compertum est, utrum satius sit illius sedem Norfolkii, an Richmondii, an demum Washingtoniae statuere.*[28] A kindly word was added to assure the Archbishop that he should not sorrow over the loss of Virginia (*Neque est, cur doleas, si tua Dioecesis Marylandiae finibus circumscripta maneat*).

If there had been any serious consideration of Father Carbry for the See of Richmond, that possibility was past. Propaganda had the suspicion that he was not only the author of the letter sent to Hayes, but that he was also responsible for the evils which had disturbed the Church in New York (*post tot excitatos Neo-Eboraci tumultus*).[29] Father Faraldi, the former Provincial of the Dominicans, was asked by Propaganda on September 13, 1819, to use his influence with Carbry to leave America (*esortandolo a riparare lo scandalo e abbandonare l'America, se non vuole rendersi reo degli eterni supplizi*).[30] Some days later (September 18) Propaganda made a similar appeal to Father John Gaddi, Vicar General of the Order of St. Dominic, asking him to write a paternal letter to the Irish Dominican at Norfolk, exhorting him to leave America. The same day Propaganda wrote to Father

---

28. BCA, Case—Special B—L5.
29. *Ibid.*
30. Prop. Arch., *Scritt. rifer., Amer. Cent.*, vol. 4, ff. 209-211.

Settimio Rotelli, Vicar General of the Order of St. Augustine, recounting the evils created by Browne who was a member of that community and asking him to prevent Browne's return to America.

Maréchal, then occupied with his *Pastoral Letter to the Roman Catholics of Norfolk,* found himself in a quandary. Cardinal Litta had learned by experience the true situation of the Church here. He had made mistakes of judgment and of policy, but he admitted these both to Neale and to Maréchal the moment they had presented the exact status of affairs. If blame there be, it is not altogether his; and in any judgment of Propaganda's action other factors must be weighed in the evidence: on the one hand, Litta's sincere fatherly interest in the progress of the Catholic Church here, a desire to keep peace among the slender forces of the Catholics here even at the price of compromises that were within the Canon Law of the Church; and on the other, the dilatoriness and negligence of both Archbishops in furnishing Rome with accurate information. This latter factor amounts almost to an accusation of bad judgment, and with hardly any exception, all the American bishops fall under it during the first three decades of the organized hierarchy (1790-1820). Unfortunately, Litta had been taken from the Prefectship of the Sacred Congregation and had been made Cardinal-Vicar of Rome (1818). His successor, Cardinal Fontana, did not inspire confidence in Maréchal's heart. "It is indeed true," he writes to Litta on September 18, 1819, "that His Eminence Cardinal Fontana merits in every respect my entire confidence by the extent of his knowledge, his great zeal and his admirable piety. But the essential point is to know this country well in order to be able to take precisely the means necessary for the needs of our churches and above all not to allow oneself to be led by fears or false hopes which two or three bad Irish priests, with a small number of their compatriots, try to inspire by their conduct and their writings."

Litta was on his guard against this danger, and Maréchal hoped that Fontana would be equally perspicacious. The letter from which the above quotation is taken then enters into a description of the deplorable conduct of some of the Irish clergy. Unfortunately, even if what Maréchal has written in this letter as well as in his *Relation* be the result of racial prejudice, there is no answer available, for it was just at that time the scandal in Augusta shook the nascent American Church to its foundation; John Egan's marriage in Richmond before the Protestant bishop must have brought the fear of God to the hearts of those of his compatriots, cleric and lay, who had considered him as a partisan with themselves against the Archbishop's authority.[31] Maréchal told Litta that his only hope was in the formation of a national clergy and that it was towards this end he was directing all his efforts. Meanwhile, Father Carbry's conduct in Norfolk had brought discredit upon himself and his adherents, and on September 27, the trustees placed an advertisement in the Norfolk newspapers warning the Catholics of the city against him.[32]

The Irish-French conflict for control of the Church in the country was now a public affair. Maréchal's position as metropolitan focussed the struggle around himself. In all the American cities where Irishmen were, the factional sentiments of the Southland found supporters. To Cheverus in Boston, all this was but an echo of Church affairs many centuries before, and it is with delicate shrewdness that he writes to the Archbishop urging him not to flinch in the face of the danger of a general schism but to maintain with "Ambrosian firmness" his hold upon ecclesiastical authority.[33] De Neuville, the French Ambassador, also wrote to him from New York at this time (October 14): *Je vois d'un coté scandal, de l'autre je ne puis m'empêcher de voir insubordination ou au moins l'oubli de subordination.*[34]

If Maréchal's *Pastoral Letter* was published shortly after the date it bears (September 28, 1819), then its place in the mass of documentary material which exists for the story of the Church in Virginia during these five years (1815-1820) comes at this time. The *Pastoral Letter* makes eighty-five printed pages and is a direct answer to Fernandez' *Letter* of 1816. It is not separated into chapters, but the main divisions are quite logical. After referring to the "consolation of spending several days with you last year," Maréchal enters at once into the problem at issue between the canonical authority of the Church and "the few individuals who have brought so many calamities on your Congregation." He praises the faithful Catholics for their courage in building another church for divine service when they realized that the original property could not be recovered even "by legal process." The conduct of the usurpers had shocked even "our Protestant brethren whom we had the pleasure of visiting in Norfolk." The

---

31. *Ibid.*, vol. 4, ff. 121-123.
32. BCA, Case—17—I6.
33. BCA, Case—14—J31.
34. BCA, Case—19—Q6.

principal point at issue he explained as follows: "They now strive by every means in their power, to prove to you that their conduct is perfectly consonant with the principles of the Catholic Faith—that in this country you can lawfully, after the example of other religious sects, assume the right of choosing and rejecting your Pastors—that the power which the Catholic bishops of the United States claim, is an authorized usurpation, founded on superstition and unjustice." Then follows a dissertation on the doctrine of hierarchical jurisdiction and power and the history of the ecclesiastical government from the time of the Apostles to the Council of Trent and thence to the present (1819). Maréchal mentions "the unfortunate old Priest (Carbry) whom they have hired to officiate as their Pastor" and explains lucidly the difference between the liberty of the election of "magistrates and other civil officers" and that of the spiritual shepherds of Christ's flock. The objection that the Holy See had allowed to princes and to powerful laymen in the past powers dangerously near to that of granting jurisdiction to these spiritual leaders was then explained with a sincerity and candor which must have done much to offset the stand of the Norfolk opponents. A salutary lesson follows, drawn from the days of the Constitutional Clergy of France. The action of the Catholic Committee in England and Dr. Milner's firm stand were given as examples of the Church's doctrine and discipline in the election of bishops and in the appointment of pastors. Pius VII had won so magnificent a victory over "that unfortunately great man, who lately held France, and all the continental nations of Europe bound down to his throne"; yet Napoleon's "unbounded power could never attain that object. In vain did he lead his intrepid legions to the gates of Rome; in vain did he disperse the noble families of that great city which he suspected were opposed to his ambitious designs; in vain did the thunder of his cannon shake the Pontifical throne to its basis; the Vicar of Jesus Christ remained inflexible, for he knew his duty. The tyrant ordered Pius VII into exile. But that great and venerable Pontiff, chose rather to be incarcerated in a dungeon than to make a concession which he foresaw would be chiefly employed to tear asunder the bonds of Catholic unity. And shall a few obscure men in Norfolk, with an old prevaricating Priest at their head, entertain the same hope, which the powerful Emperor of France could never realize?"

The *jus patronatus* had been so variously treated in the many pamphlets and letters of the day that Maréchal gave a detailed exposition of its origin, history, and meaning.

However, he said, let us suppose this privilege were conceded to the present generation. Who would be the electors? Would every man, who merely bears the name of Catholick, be admitted to give in his vote, whatever may be his impiety and the immorality of his life? Or would the privilege be restrained to those only whose conduct is pious and edifying? Shall the drunkard, the impure, the professed libertine, and he who hardly knows the elements of his religion, and lives in an open transgression of her laws, be allowed to choose the ministers of Jesus Christ, together with the sober, the chaste, the enlightened and regular Catholick who punctually fulfils all the commandments of God and the Church? It is evident that in a matter of a nature so sacred, a discrimination ought to be made; and would not this first and necessary step be obnoxious to insuperable difficulties? Upon whom would the choice most probably fall? Would it fall on the modest and pious clergyman, who spends his days in instructing the poor and ignorant; in carrying the last consolations of religion to dying Christians; in reconciling repenting sinners to the offended Majesty of God in the tribunal of Pennance,—who every day in his private oratory and the altar, raises his pure hands to God to draw down the blessing of Heaven on his flock—who mounts the pulpit, not to please his auditory and glean from the world the pitiful reward of praise; but to instruct, exhort and move—who consecrates his intervals of leisure, not to idle visits and frivolous conversation, but to meditation and studies suitable to his state of life? The merits of such a clergyman being generally unknown or not sufficiently felt, he would very likely not be elected; and yet *him has the Lord chosen*. The gay and sprightly companion—he who at home spends his time in idleness or frivolous occupations—who, in the societies of worldlings which he habitually frequents, can command their attention by some light accomplishment—who can preach a fashionable discourse, or pronounce a vapid declamation which he probably had not even the slender merit of composing, this man will unite the votes of the multitude. In vain might a few pious and sensible Catholicks raise their voices against his election; they would be drowned in the general clamour. Under such a pastor what would become of the unfortunate congregation? Instead of exhibiting the endearing spectacle of sincere religion and piety, it would soon present disgusting scenes of irreligion and immorality.

The *Letter* and the broadsides of Fernandez are then discussed and the proper epithet applied to the "impious author." Father Carbry's usurped powers are described for what they were worth:

What is truly incredible in this land of liberty, this same Thomas Carbry and his associates, who have lately disseminated so many foul writings, who dared to advise the *civil* authorities to be on their guard against the *spiritual* jurisdiction of His Holiness as of a foreign government; who poured forth such virulent abuse against our venerable predecessor and ourselves, at last arrived to that degree of extravagance as to summon us by an attorney at law, to receive their disgusting and insolent letters. We have frequently blessed Divine Providence, that we live under a free and just government. But we never felt the advantage more strongly than in this conjecture. For were we under an absolute one, and these impious men could induce its ministers to support their measures, the Catholick Bishops of the United States would soon be thrown into dungeons, and their flocks dispersed, unless they submitted to their abominable, new fangled canon laws. The general features of their writings, and the tenor of their conduct exhibit persecution under its most hideous and fearful forms. But let them remember that her shafts in this country are blunted and shivered on the aegis of American Liberty, and fall harmless at the feet of their intended victims.

Maréchal's *Pastoral Letter* is the historical turning-point in the schismatic movement in America of these years, (1815-1821). Father Carbry found himself discredited with all peace-loving citizens in Norfolk. O'Driscoll the leader of the Charleston feudists, lay dying in November, 1819.[35] Peace was beginning to appear in New York Catholic circles, an armed truce, it is true. But rebellion and insubordination were not yet uprooted in the American Church. Unknown except to a few here at the time, there arrived in New York on December 10, 1819, Philadelphia's evil genius for the next decade, Father William Hogan.

---

35. BCA, Case—20—T29.

CHAPTER VI

THE ERECTION OF THE SEE OF RICHMOND

The conferring of the pallium on Maréchal by Father Anthony Kohlmann, at St. Peter's pro-Cathedral, Baltimore, on December 19, 1819, gave to that prelate increased powers and influence in his great fight for Church authority in America.[1]

Dr. Henry Conwell's acceptance of the long vacant See of Philadelphia was acknowledged by the Sacred Congregation on January 29, 1820. There remained but the appointment of the bishop to the new See at Charleston, and John England's selection for this post (June, 1820) was a harbinger of peace and spiritual progress in the Southern States.

There remained then the problem of Virginia. Father James Neill, S.J. wrote on February 10, 1820, to Father John Grassi, S.J., who was then in Rome, that Father Carbry had established an "Independent American Catholick Church" in Norfolk, but that his project was derided by all the respectable Protestants of the city. Carbry seems to have realized his failure, for we find him in Richmond, treating with the trustees who were opposing Father Baxter's authority and proposing to them "to have himself appointed Bishop of Virginia." In fact he had stated "to many that he is already raised to that dignity by the Catholics of Norfolk, Petersburg, and other towns of this Commonwealth."[2]

Propaganda finally decided to act, in spite of Maréchal's well-known desire to keep Virginia as part of his diocese; and on May 20, 1820, a decree was passed to the effect that the Holy Father be asked to create Virginia into a separate diocese, suffragan to Baltimore, with Richmond (*quae praecipua Virginiae urbs est*) as the episcopal See. The new diocese was not, however, to include the District of Columbia.

Father Patrick Kelly, of the Diocese of Ossory, Ireland, (*virum pietate, prudentia, studio, atque doctrina plurime commendatum*) was chosen as Richmond's first bishop. The two priests mentioned in an official document (June 5) of the Propaganda Archives for the new Sees are John England and Patrick Kelly.

---

1. Shea, *op. cit.*, vol. iii, p. 51.
2. BCA, Case—17—B10.

Dr. Kelly had made an excellent scholastic reputation for himself at the Irish College at Lisbon. He taught for some years in the Seminary of Ossory, where he was afterwards Rector. He was revered by all as a priest and was distinguished for uprightness and solidity of character. Many thought him rather tenacious in his political sentiments and somewhat inflexible in his opinions (*tantochè sembra tantavolta duro ed inflessibile*). He was a good preacher, was forty years old, and of a strong constitution. In all, he was *attissimo al vescovato*.[3]

On June 25, 1820, Pius VII granted the petition and ordered the official documents to be prepared for this settlement of Virginia's Catholic life. Apparently no official message of this decision was sent to Archbishop Maréchal at this time; but the Baltimore prelate was being kept rather well informed of all the decisions by Father William Taylor of New York who had gone abroad as the bearer of a petition from the group of New York Catholics actively opposed to Bishop Connolly's regime. On March 2, 1820, Taylor wrote from Genoa to the Archbishop that at Lyons he had had a pleasant interview with Archbishop Plessis of Quebec. From his conversation with Plessis, Taylor says: "I could infer that some unprincipled person has industriously misrepresented the state of the Catholic Religion in America and has given an unfavourable description of the French Bishops and clergy, in that country, at the Court of Rome." Fontana had told Plessis that "the people do not like to have French Bishops in that country;" and Taylor, who has the air of privately grooming himself for the episcopate, adds: "I shall, you may depend on it, connect this unblushing calumny with its source and give it a complete refutation before my departure from Rome."[4]

On July 1, 1820, the Sacred Congregation announced to Cardinal Consalvi, the action of the Holy See regarding the South; two new Sees had been formed: one in Charleston, to embrace the two Carolinas and Georgia, with John England of Cork as its bishop; the other in Richmond, to embrace Virginia, with Patrick Kelly, as its bishop.[5] Consalvi was requested to prepare the necessary official documents. About this time also (June 24, 1820), Fontana had written to Bishop-elect England recommending

---

3. Prop. Arch., *Scritt. rifer., Amer. Cent.*, vol. 4, unfolioed. At the time of his election to Richmond he was president of St. John's College, Kilkenny, Ireland. Cf. Murphy, *History of the Catholic Schools of Kilkenny.*
4. BCA. Case—20—R9.
5. Prop. Arch., *Scritt. rifer., Amer. Cent.*, vol. 4 unfolioed.

to his paternal care Father Robert Browne, who was then in Rome. The Holy See had removed the suspension Maréchal had placed upon Browne and had restored him to sacerdotal functions, except within the Diocese of Baltimore.[6] He was about to return to the United States and would be helpful to England in the Diocese of Charleston which he knew so well.

Taylor who wrote from Rome on July 8, 1820, gives Maréchal the news of his two suffragan Sees. "Of the geography of the United States," he writes, "they are very ignorant here. Cardinal Fontana whose judgment is much seriously affected by years, told me it was their intention to erect Virginia into a Bishoprick and to have the Bishop reside at Hartford. I told his Eminence that Hartford was in Connecticut, that Richmond was considered the Capital of Virginia; and it was only by producing the map of America that I convinced His Eminence of this *geographical heresy*. I could not describe to Your Grace the censurable and unchristian conduct of the Irish Friars here; they have attempted even to protect the unprincipled Carbry, who has been invited to Rome to render an account of his conduct."[7]

On June 22, 1820, Father John Rice, O.S.A., who had become involved in the Norfolk schism during Donaghey's visit to Rome, wrote to Bishop-elect Kelly informing him of his election to the See of Richmond. In reply to this letter Dr. Kelly says:

Birchfield, Kilkenny, July 16, 1820.

Reverend and Dr. Friend:

I received a day or two ago your very unwelcome favour of the 22nd ult. in which you congratulate me on my elevation to the See of Virginia in America: jocosely, I suppose, as anyone's elevation to any see however accomplished he be and howsoever well acquainted with the state of religion in his church is matter of condolence rather than of congratulation: how much more is that of me who have no pretensions to any of those accomplishments natural or acquired which dignify the Bishop and who, besides, am an utter stranger to the state of religion not only in that church to which you say I am called, but even in that of which I am now a member. Your letter especially in this affair of my exaltation has been to me a source of more serious uneasiness that I recollect to have experienced since the night previous to my receiving the Subdeaconship. I am determined, however, to suffer the will of God to have its course and earnestly hope that, if my exaltation contribute not to the

---

6. Ibid., *Lettere*, vol. 301. f. 443.
7. Ibid., f. 444.

sanctification of God's name and the coming of his Kingdom, he will by some means or other prevent its taking place.

The letter to which you allude in the first paragraph of your letter is, I suppose, that which you wrote some time last year to Father Nowlan. If any inconveniences have arisen to you from that communication, I must candidly confess, it ought, as far as my knowledge goes, to be laid at my door, and not at his. For as soon as he received that letter he sent for me and gave it to me to read. Having read it, I felt offended at it, though I do not now recollect what it was in particular that provoked me: but I believe it was the report you mentioned in that letter, as then afloat in Rome, of my going or having gone to America, and your desire to know whether this supposed journey of mine originated in misunderstanding with my Bishop or not. After I read the letter, Father Nowlan asked me what did I think of it. I answered peevishly: it does not concern me as I am neither going nor have gone nor do I desire to go to America nor did it ever enter my head to intrigue for a mitre. What answer, said he, shall I make Father Rice? None at all on my part, said I. So that if Father Nowlan have not since answered your letter and I cannot affirm whether he has or not, the omission ought to be attributed to me rather than him. Morrisey too was at that time in Rome and it occurred to me that he might have given birth to the report with a view to injure Dr. Marum, on that account I mentioned the circumstance to his Lordship: but I have not since heard whether he made any use of the information or not. Perhaps this naked but true statement may serve to clear up what you cannot explain in the conduct of Father Nowlan. With respect to my ability to bring out with me three young clergy qualified as you deem requisite, I feel no hesitation in saying I could lead forth with me four times that number if necessary, were the means at hand of bearing their expenses out and places there provided for them on their arrival. So that if the church of Virginia require the auxiliaries you mention, you should lose no time in applying to the Propaganda for the necessary aid. Any young man proposing to go with me will be opposed by his relatives as I myself expect to be opposed strongly by mine, so that no help can be drawn from those quarters. I have not yet thought of how my own expenses are to be supplied. Adieu and believe me,

Your afft. friend and servant.[8]

The Father Edmond Nowlan mentioned in the letter had also been recommended for one of the new American Sees.

---

8. Printed in the CHR, vol. VI, pp. 259-260, from the Prop. Arch., *Scritt. rifer., Amer. Cent.,* vol. 40, No. 160.

On July 22, 1820, Propaganda wrote to Bishop-elect Kelly, recounting to him the sad state of the Church in Virginia, the opposition of Maréchal to the new See, his own duty to proceed immediately to his diocese, the case of Carbry who was to be dealt with gently but firmly, the doctrines of Fernandez, with whom he should act with prudence and caution, and recommending that the trustees be treated rather with persuasion than with strictness. Fontana advised him to go to Norfolk first and to reside there until a place was prepared for him at Richmond.[9]

Another letter, dated August 31, 1820, from Dr. Kelly to Father Rice, gives us an insight into the character of the newly-elected Bishop:

Rev. and Dear Friend,

On the 13th of July last I received and on the 16th, I answered your, as I called it in my answer, unwelcome favour of the 22d of June. I had not the precaution to postpay my letter; it was, of course, returned to me in a few days from the foreign office. As soon as I received it, I resealed it, repaired my commission and committed it to the post: so that I hope you have already received it. On the 12th inst. I received the Apostolic letters dismembering the Archdiocese of Baltimore, erecting the State of Virginia into the church of Richmond and constituting me its Bishop. I began, of course, immediately to prepare for my consecration. It was determined it should take place on the 24th. in St. James' Chapel. Every thing having been ready for that day, Episcopal consecration was conferred by Dr. Troy, pontifically officiating on me, assisted by Drs. Murray & Marum in the presence of Drs. Keating & Doyle with an immense crowd of Clergy and Laity. I felt much satisfaction after the ceremony; because I went through it far better than I expected.

As yet I have had no communication with Dr. England. Rumour has it that he received his bull on the 12th and that his consecration will not take place untill the 21st of Septr. It is likely I shall be then in Cork when every thing will be arranged for our departure. I shall urge that we set out as early as may be in October provided always I shall by that time have heard from you and shall have obtained from the Propaganda the necessary Viatic. I hope you have already made application to the Sacred College as I requested in my last letter: if not, you must see you should lose no time in making the application. I think I shall need about an hundred pounds. I am at present pennyless and cannot reckon upon any thing as my own to meet the expences of my voyage except what may

---

9. *Ibid., Lettere,* vol. 301, f. 532.

result from the sale of my horse and furniture. My friends, no doubt, are able to lend me what I'll want: but their aversion to my departure at all is such that I should like very much to be relieved from the necessity of applying to them. I have received no additional information concerning the state of things in Norfolk beyond what you mentioned in your letter and what his Eminence the Cardinal Prefect communicated in a letter which accompanied my apostolic letters. This circumstance creates me much uneasiness and will, I am certain, keep me restless untill I shall have set out on my journey. Should you have heard any thing since your last letter or should you then have forgotten any thing that might tend to my forming a right notion of the difficulties I shall have to contend with, be pleased to communicate it to yr. affe. friend & Servant.

P. S. Father Nowlan says he answered yr. letter of 1819 and I believe he has the post receipt for it.[10]

Bishop Kelly was consecrated on August 24, 1820, in St. James Chapel, Dublin, with Archbishop Troy as consecrator, and Archbishop Murray and Bishop Marum as assistants.[11]

On September 21, 1820, Bishop Kelly took part in the consecration of Dr. England at the Cork Cathedral.

Propaganda furnished Bishop Kelly with the means necessary for his voyage to Virginia by sending him a subsidy of one hundred Irish pounds on November 11, 1820. This same day three letters were dispatched by Propaganda, one to the Catholics of Charleston, one to the Catholics of Norfolk, and one to Maréchal.[12] The letter to the congregation at Charleston announced the election of Dr. England as their Bishop with the hope that he would be satisfactory (*illum vobis satis gratum acceptumque esse futurum*).[13] To the Norfolk congregation, with the announcement of Dr. Kelly's coming, there is a long exhortation to unity in the Faith and discipline of the Church to the Catholics of that city. The letter to Maréchal is a straight-forward document. Propaganda recognized the sincerity of Maréchal's opposition to the dismemberment of his diocese, but against the Archbishop's wishes and for the good of religion, Virginia was separated from Baltimore; and the Sacred Congregation hoped that Maréchal would accept the decision of the Holy See and would receive

---

10. Prop. Arch., *Scritt. rifer., Amer. Cent.*, vol. 4, ff. 163-165.
11. Shea says that Dr. Kelly took the oath of allegiance to the King of England at his consecration (*Op. cit.*, vol. iii, p. 79).
12. Prop. Arch., *Lettere*, vol. 201, f. 855.
13. *Ibid.*, f. 861.

the new suffragan bishops cordially and with brotherly harmony.[14]

Shea who calls the separation of the Southland from Baltimore a "hasty and inconsiderate action," emphasizes the obvious fact that the creation of the two suffragan Sees had divided the actually remaining Diocese of Baltimore into two parts, far distant from each other: Maryland and the District of Columbia in the North, and Alabama and Mississippi in the Southwest.[15] But this was not the real issue at stake between Maréchal and Fontana. In the earliest of his letters recommending the erection of Charleston, Maréchal expressed the wish that the new See should include these territories, since Charleston and Savannah were terminals from which the immigration westward was proceeding. The issue was the dismemberment of his diocese against his expressed wish and against his oft-repeated statement that Virginia could not support a bishop in the dignity such an office demanded. Moreover he had little patience with Fontana who, he believed, allowed himself to be frightened by imaginary dangers of a schismatic and independent American Church. Maréchal's contempt for the Norfolk rebels never wavered, and he felt poignantly the slight to his episcopal dignity in the fact that Fontana dealt directly with a little group of Irish rebels, led by the unworthy Portuguese, Fernandez. He feared, as Cheverus also feared, that the new bishops (Conwell, England and Kelly) would come to America, imbued with prejudice against the hierarchy here, but he was willing to cooperate with them if he found them amenable to reason and anxious to labor for the good of the Church.[16] Maréchal knew also the temper of the rebellious factions in his diocese. It was an easy step from opposition to a pastor, regularly appointed, on account of personal feelings, to opposition to a bishop, appointed by Rome, on these or other grounds.[17]

On October 17, 1820, Maréchal wrote again to Fontana protesting against the creation of the Virginia Diocese. What will be the surprise here, he asks, on the part of Catholics to see a diocese as large as several kingdoms of Europe suddenly reduced to the limits of a diocese in Italy, and especially since there was no possible way of securing support for a bishop in Virginia?[18]

On October 17, 1820, in a letter to Pedicini, Secretary of the

---

14. BCA, Case—32C—K7.
15. *Op. cit.*, vol. iii, p. 58.
16. BCA, Case—14—K39.
17. BCA, Case—14—K49.
18. BCA, Case—22—D2.

Sacred Congregation, Maréchal makes the charge that his letters to Propaganda were being intercepted by priests in Rome who were misusing them to the detriment of the Church here.[19]

The experienced Archbishop Plessis, of Quebec had given Maréchal a very valuable hint (October 5, 1820) in suggesting that much wasted effort could be avoided if the Baltimore metropolitan followed the system used by the English bishops, that of having an accredited agent in Rome; and he recommended for this post, the Rector of the Venerable English College, Dr. Gradwell.[20]

The cordiality asked by Propaganda for the new bishops had an unfortunate beginning. On November 20, 1820, Malou informed Maréchal of Father Browne's arrival in New York, with letters from Dr. England, reinstating him in the exercise of his sacerdotal functions.[21] On November 21, 1820, Dr. Conwell arrived in Baltimore, and though we have no record of the interview between the Archbishop and himself, it is presumable that the Irish-French controversy was fully discussed. Dr. Conwell seems to have received a very favorable impression of Maréchal, for in the years following his arrival in Philadelphia, his correspondence with the Archbishop is confiding and reverential. Father Anthony Kohlmann sensed the popular feelings on the question of the new bishops and wrote to Maréchal, from Washington, on November 27, 1820, strongly advising the Archbishop to make no public protest against their coming.[22] All the Irish would desert the Church, he says, and would swell the ranks of the schismatics. Cheverus wrote from Bristol, Rhode Island, on November 29, 1820, advising silence on Maréchal's part. *La conduite de Propagande,* he says, *est inconcevable. . . rien ne semble leur avoir donné la moindre idée de nos missions. Ils verront bientôt, mais il sera trop tard, quels sont les veritables amis du St. Siège et de la Religion.* He is so disgusted, he says, with the present situation, that he would like to resign the See of Boston and go to St. Mary's Seminary, as a teacher.[23]

Browne, the *avant-courier* of Dr. England, as Benedict Fenwick calls him, arrived in Charleston at the end of November, and attended Mass the following Sunday in a pew with some of his former friends.[24]

---

19. BCA, Case—22—D3.
20. BCA, Case—21A—15.
21. BCA, Case—18—S44.
22. BCA, Case—17—W52.
23. BCA, Case—14—K39.
24. BCA, Case—16—P31.

A letter of consolation in his troubles came to Maréchal from Dr. Poynter, Vicar-Apostolic of the London District, dated December 5, 1820.[25]

Bishop Cheverus, who was greatly worried at this time about the faith of the Catholic boys at Harvard (*un miracle seul peut conserver la foi des chers jeunes gens à Cambridge*) wrote on December 6, 1820, that there was no hope for the Church in America while Propaganda regarded *les évêques et le clergé des Etats-Unis comme de bien pauvres êtres*.[26]

On December 14, 1820, Hogan wrote to Maréchal the first letter of a series of documents, pamphlets and brochures which belong to the schism in Philadelphia and which shocked the Church here to its foundations.

Before the year was out, Malou had announced to Maréchal the arrival of Dr. Kelly in New York (December 29, 1820) and intimated that his stay with Dr. Connolly would send him to the South an anti-French partisan. On January 7, 1821, Malou wrote again to say that Dr. Kelly had taken Father Ffrench's part in the New York trustee quarrel.[27]

The general situation at the time of Dr. Kelly's arrival is well described by Maréchal in a letter to Plessis, dated Baltimore, January 6, 1821. "I have none but disastrous news to give you," he writes. Propaganda had rejected the priests chosen for the vacant Sees by Maréchal and his suffragans and had sent Bishops from Ireland. Dr. Conwell had called to see Maréchal at Baltimore and Maréchal was impressed by his piety, and his energy despite his sixty-eight years. The attack made publicly upon him from the pulpit of St. Mary's, Philadelphia, the first Sunday he appeared in his cathedral, by Hogan, who was immediately suspended, had reawakened all the old troubles of that city. Rome had absolved Browne in spite of all his sacrileges and his schism, and that turbulent clergyman was then in Charleston awaiting Dr. England's arrival. Dr. Kelly was in New York; and Carbry and his faction were issuing defiant denials of his authority in Virginia. The *incroyables décrets du Saint Siège* had upset the confidence of many in Rome's prudence and caution. The American clergy and people are "frozen with fear." *Et comment pourrons-nous maintenir l'autorité après que la Propagande a aneanti notre jurisdiction, foulé aux pieds des lois de la discipline ecclésias-*

---

25. BCA, Case—19—N9.
26. BCA, Case—16—K40.
27. BCA, Case—18—J47.

tique et même de la simple justice naturelle, et prostitué sa dignité jusqu'au point de devenir le défenseur de prêtres fameux par leur crimes et l'executrice de leurs systemes d'impiété! Le clergé et le peuple américain sont glacés d'effroi![28] Plessis had appealed to Poynter to save the Church in America from the dreadful controversies with which Poynter and the other English Vicars-Apostolic were so familiar. But Propaganda refused to change its decision.

---

28. Cited by Zwierlein, *ut supra*, pp. 546-547.

CHAPTER VII

BISHOP PATRICK KELLY

When Dr. Kelly arrived in Baltimore to present his Bulls to his metropolitan, Maréchal read to him a solemn protest against the new See of Richmond:

> Although it would be entirely lawful for us to oppose the erection of the said see, whether we consider the wicked means by which it was obtained, or the scandals and calamities of every kind, which will undoubtedly be the result; yet fearing that the said enemies of the Church of Christ will take occasion even from our most justly founded opposition, to inflict the most serious injury on the Catholic religion, your Lordship may, as you judge best, proceed or not to take possession of the new see and diocese of Virginia according to the tenor of the Bulls transmitted to you. But to assure the tranquility of our conscience we hereby distinctly declare to your Lordship, that we in no wise give or yield our assent positively to this most unfortunate action of the Sacred Congregation de Propaganda Fide. If you carry it out, we are to be held free before God and the Church now and hereafter from all the evils and scandals which the Catholic religion suffers or may suffer from it in these United States.[1]

Maréchal wrote also to the Cardinal Fontana, appealing from his authority to that of the Sovereign Pontiff—"Therefore, most Eminent Cardinal," he concludes, "two vagabond friars, Browne and Carbry, concocting their schemes with other Irish friars living in Rome, have prevailed; and the Sacred Congregation, deceived by the absurd calumnies of such men, has made itself the instrument to carry out their impious schemes."[2]

Bishop Kelly left Baltimore for Norfolk on January 18, 1821, and reached the scene of his labors the following day. "It was a strange commentary," Shea writes, "on the statement made at Rome, that Norfolk was at such an immense distance from Baltimore that the Archbishop of Baltimore could not possibly attend it, to find that even in those days of comparatively slow travel

---

1. Shea, *op. cit.*, vol. iii, pp. 79-80.
2. *Ibid.*, p. 80.

the distance could be traversed in less than twenty-four hours.[3]

Bishop Kelly took possession of the original church in the city. Having studied in Lisbon, he had many points of contact with Fernandez and the young Portuguese priest whom Fernandez had "appointed" pastor. Consequently, as Lucas wrote to Maréchal on January 21, 1821, the Catholics who had remained faithful to the Church were taking umbrage at the courtesy Dr. Kelly was showing Fernandez, and were very much worried because the new bishop had restored Father Carbry to sacerdotal functions. *L'évêque ne nous consulte guère—il est environné du parti schismatique!* In February, Dr. Kelly placed a ban on the attendance at Father Lucas' temporary church, and issued an order stating that the Catholics of the city would only fulfil their obligation of Sunday Mass by coming to the church over which he and Father Carbry presided.[4] Lucas adds the interesting note that Dr. Kelly's first sermon was a rather eloquent one, on Hell. Of his own flock, he says: *Ils sont tous en larmes dans l'incertitude.* Father Lucas would have gone immediately to Baltimore, but he was under contract with the scholars of his little school who had paid their tuition fees up to June.[5]

Maréchal now believed that the cause of episcopal authority was lost, and there passed between himself and Cheverus several letters on the necessity of the Archbishop's immediate presence in Rome where his protests to the Holy See might be made verbally. Dr. Cheverus wanted an ecclesiastic in the country with the powers of an Apostolic Delegate, and he urged Maréchal to go to Rome, and to return with these extraordinary faculties: *Revenez-vous révêtu des pouvoirs qui mettent fin à la confusion de notre pauvre église des Etats-Unis.*[6] Cheverus himself would have come to Baltimore to discuss the question, but he felt such a visit might be imprudent, lest the Irish clergy see in it *quelque conspiration gallicane.*[7] On February 18, 1821, Lucas wrote that Baron de Neuville, the French Ambassador, had told him that the Nuncio at Paris told him that the Pope was contemplating the sending of a Nuncio to the United States to settle ecclesiastical troubles here.[8]

---

3. *Ibid.,* p. 81.
4. BCA, Case—18—142.
5. BCA, Case—22—D13.
6. BCA, Case—18—K41.
7. BCA, Case—18—K45.
8. Maréchal succeeded about this time in securing the talented services of Dr. Gradwell as his official agent to the Holy See (Cf. Zwierlein, *ut supra,* p. 551).

When Dr. Gradwell accepted the agency in Rome, Maréchal felt that at last by Gradwell's "long experience and great abilities an end will be put . . . to the disastrous measures, which the Propaganda, misled by Irish intrigues, has this many years not ceased to adopt."[9]

Father Lucas communicated to his flock Dr. Kelly's letter stating that his powers as pastor would cease from and after the first day of June, and the members of his congregation drafted the following Memorial, which was signed by some eighty persons and then presented to Dr. Kelly:

Norfolk, 25th May, 1821.

To the Rt. Revd. P. Kelly, Bishop of Virginia.
Most Revd. Sir,

The undersigned, members of the Roman Catholic Congregation, have heard with heartfelt sorrow the suspension of the Rev. Father Lucas from his Ecclesiastical functions from and after the first day of next month.

This unexpected measure would have been to them less mortifying, had it been warranted by the misconduct of that Clergyman; but as they are assured by you, that he has given no cause for censure, it is a gratification which brings with it many grateful remembrances of the Spiritual comfort and blessings he so generously bestowed upon his faithful flock in the days of affliction; and with bitterness in their heart, they exclaim: is a suspension, (which to them amounts to a curse) to be the reward of the piety, disinterestedness and zeal of a Clergyman who has preserved the orthodox Doctrine in its purity, and who has delivered into your hands that patrimony untainted!!

Among the reasons which might have concurred to avert this present calamity, and which a calm reflection will certainly point out to you, one is so vitally important to the welfare of a great part of the Congregation that it cannot be passed over in Silence: That is the difficulty, not to say the impossibility of many French members to be understood by you and vice versa.

The undersigned therefore impressed with the belief that your mission to this Country embraces the interest of the Church, as well as the welfare of the faithful, humbly beg and indulge themselves with the hope that, after having duly weighed these considerations, you will rescind the Suspension of the Rev. J. Lucas, that you will restore to him his powers and permit him to officiate in the brick Church as honorary assistant, and by that act of justice, you will promote the

---

9. Hughes, *op. cit.*, Doc., vol. i, pt. ii, p. 1049.

interest of the Church, and the advantage of Religion. God preserve you many years.[10]

Dr. Kelly replied to Mr. Magagnos, who had written the Memorial, on June 7, 1821, as follows:

Dr. Sir,

I have given the memorial you did me the honor of presenting me on Saturday last, as much consideration as I conceived to be due to a document signed by so many respectable persons all of whom are objects of my sincere pastoral affection and many of whom are entitled to my warm private friendship, and believe me, it is with regret I announce to you that the result of my deliberation is, that I do not deem it expedient at present to grant the prayer of the memorial. Do not understand me as approving the procedure you have adopted.

Had your memorial been confined to a simple statement of a Spiritual grievance and that I was permitted the exercise of my discretion in providing a suitable remedy, there would have been nothing objectionable in it; but your memorial goes a good deal farther: for it demands and as an act of justice too, which is not at all concerned in the business and under menace of temporal inconvenience in case of refusal, that I impart a share of the Spiritual authority with which I am officially entrusted to the Rev. Mr. Lucas.

Now, Sir, however warmly I may admire your feelings of private friendship towards that Rev. Gentleman and how strong so ever his claims to them may be, I must ever regret that they have borne you such lengths as to interfere with the freedom and purity of the exercise of the Episcopal office. This interference has ever been productive of the most disastrous consequences to Religion, and therefore discountenanced by ecclesiastical Superiors and cautiously avoided by persons lay as well as clerical, who were even but little acquainted with the nature and discipline of the Church.

I did hope that a little reflection on long prevailing dissentions, some attention to late occurrences and the obvious necessity of confirming or at least of not disturbing the peace we now enjoy, would have protected me from this uncanonical interference, even though there had been question of a Clergyman bound by the usual ties to the Diocess, and as accomplished as possible in ecclesiastical science, prudence and charity: but alas! I have

---

10. BCA, Case—22—E9. "Doctor Kelly on his arrival treated Mr. Lucas with severity, withdrew his faculties, and made him close his chapel. This strongly antagonized the Catholics against Doctor Kelly. The schismatic party which he pleased at first is now determined to wage war to the knife against him." (Maréchal to Plessis, Baltimore, April 28, 1821, in the *Records* ACHS, vol. xviii, p. 443).

been disappointed. My feelings of disappointment shall, however, diminish nothing of the truth, with which I shall ever continue, your affectionate father in Christ.[11]

✠ Pat. Kelly,
Bishop of Richmond.

On June 19, 1821, Mr. Magagnos answered Dr. Kelly in the name of the committee of four who acted for the congregation:

Most Revd. Sir,

We had the honor of receiving your answer to our petition and are highly gratified by the expression of your kindness: yet, from some observations it contains which wound our honor and character, we believe that you have misunderstood our motives or that we must have been deficient in something. Therefore we beg leave, in order to defend our reputation and repair our faults, to address you a 2nd. time, indulging ourselves with the hope that your paternal affection will easily forgive an unintentional error and more willingly grant a favor.

In December, 1815, the Rev. Mr. Lucas was appointed Pastor of this Congregation by the Archbishop of Baltimore who recommended him in these terms: "He is a gentleman in whom I have entire confidence." Since that epoch, his conduct has proved worthy of that confidence, and he has been exercising the functions of Pastor, until your Lordship took this Congregation under your particular care. He has received you as his Bishop with all possible marks of respect, obeyed all your orders, and done whatever you have desired him to do. You have lately withdrawn all his Spiritual powers and prohibited him to say mass.

In this afflicting circumstance, considering this prohibition and the withdrawing of his powers as unmerited and calculated to discourage the faithful whose confidence and esteem he enjoys, as a great disadvantage to some, and an irreparable loss to others; we united spontaneously to express our deep concern, unfeigned sorrow and regret, and (thinking we could not adopt a better plan) to present you "the prayer of a memorial," in which we intended simply to state a spiritual and heartfelt grievance for which we humbly suggested the only remedy we deemed suitable. It appeared to us just that a Priest acknowledged by your Lordship to have always acted as a good Clergyman, and who had been our lawful and faithful Pastor, should not be deprived of his spiritual powers or excluded from the Church. We thought him no less entitled to courtesy and hospitality than a Priest passing through this town, who on presenting his credentials, would be admitted into the Church, and permitted

---
11. *Ibid.*

the exercise of his spiritual powers. We believed that there could be no better motive nor stronger reason for presenting a request than its justice; and fully impressed with the justice of ours, we could not expect a refusal, and of course could not have expressed a "menace:" nor did we ever require that you should impart to the Rev. Mr. L. a share of your Spiritual Authority in such a manner as to cause you any loss or diminition thereof, having never wished to deprive your Lordship of anything, but on the contrary, to support and defend your authority.

These reasons and considerations, and not feelings of private friendship alone (since we would do the same for any other Clergyman) actuated us to present you our prayer. Had we thought it could interfere so as to impede the freedom, and sully the purity of the exercise of the Episcopal office; had we had the most distant idea that it could be productive of consequences in the least degree disastrous to Religion, we would have, as heretofore, most cautiously avoided every interference, being persuaded that it would have been discountenanced and reproved by our ecclesiastical Superior.

But, most Revd. Sir, serious reflection on long prevailing dissentions of which the Rev. Mr. L. and we have been the Victims and not the authors, great attention to late occurrences and the obvious necessity of confirming peace, induced us to present you our supplication. We enjoyed peace before your arrival, and in spite of violent exterior efforts to disturb, we preserved it, and for its sake, made innumerable sacrifices. We were always averse to a turbulent disposition which our heart condemns and the tenor of our past conduct disavows. We have too much respect for the canons of the Church, to have recourse to an interference in the least degree contrary to them, we know of no law violated by the presentation of a prayer addressed to you, in order to obtain what we think most conducive to our Spiritual welfare.

Besides, We believe the Rev. Mr. L. bound by the usual ties to the Diocess. Your Lordship found him and his Congregation in strict and intimate Communion with the Church and his Spiritual Superiors from whom he received his powers and mission. You justly called the little Chapel to which, for the sake of peace, we had retired, "the only seat of canonical jurisdiction." Then he was bound to the Diocess. The erection of an Episcopal See in Virginia, did certainly not loosen those ties, but only transferred to your Lordship the jurisdiction over Pastors and flocks. You have exercised it over him and us; he has yielded you complete obedience, and is yet determined to do so. We have willingly submitted to whatever you have prescribed; we have assisted and blindly obeyed you.

In fine, the judgment and confidence of three Archbishops, men whose reputation for exalted piety, consummate wisdom and keen penetration has been long and firmly established; five years' practice of every ecclesiastical virtue, every religious, moral and social duty that could command esteem and engage approbation, and facts we have witnessed during that time, prove beyond a possibility of doubt, that the Rev. Mr. L. is very far from being deficient in Ecclesiastical Science, prudence and charity; on the contrary, we believe him to be an ornament to the Church.

Now, Most Revd. Sir, We trust that these reflections added to those which in our first petition, we had the honor of submitting to your Lordship's consideration, will prove sufficient, and obtain for us the object of our Solicitude.

We also hope that they will convince you we had no bad motives, no sinister views, no intention to disturb the peace or violate the canons of the Church, and therefore that there is nothing objectionable in our request. And that being the case, its grant cannot be in any way an infringement on or a disparagement to your Authority, nor attended with any disadvantage whatever; but on the contrary will be a Salutary relief to our painful anxiety, a cause of great Spiritual joy, consolation and comfort, and be received with sincere gratitude as an inestimable blessing. We beseech you then for the 2nd time, to restore to Mr. L. his spiritual powers and permit him to officiate in the Church. As "objects of your sincere pastoral affections," we hope you will have for us the regard it entitles us to to grant us our prayer. We expect it from your kindness, rectitude and justice, as our Head, Pastor, and father in Christ, for whom we pray to the Almighty to grant a long life for the good of his Church, of Religion and of the faithful.[12]

Dr. Kelly answered on June 23:

Dear Sir,

As the matter contained in your communication of the 19th instant, had, before the presentation of your 1st. memorial, been submitted to me by the Rev. Mr. L. and of course duly and gravely considered by me, the reconsideration of it has produced no change in my determination.

I attributed no bad motives, no sinister views, no evil intention to you or to any of those respectable persons by whom you stated the former memorial to have been signed. In my reply to it, I considered the action, not the agents. That memorial stripped of its formal appendages, appeared to amount to this Simoniacal proposal: Give Mr. Lucas canonical approbation,

---

12. *Ibid.*

and the revenue of the Church shall be benefitted. As your communication to which I am now replying, similarly stripped appears to amount to this: Give Mr. L. canonical approbation, for he has merited it. Now, Sir, though God will, no doubt, suitably reward the Obedience and worth of the Rev. Mr. L.; yet canonical approbation is no more the object of merit than it is of Simoniacal traffic. The power of imparting it Ecclesiastical Superiors receive gratuitously and ought gratuitously exercise.

I shall not add another word, but conclude with assuring you that nothing was or is farther from my intention than to wound the honor or character of you or any of those in whose name you have acted and that I shall ever continue your affectionate Pastor.

✠P. Kelly.
Bishop of Richmond.[13]

Lest the Archbishop doubt the authenticity of the above letter, Lucas added to the copy he sent to Maréchal the statement: "Do not believe that this is not an exact copy of Dr. Kelly's letter. Walter Lacy copied it most attentively and I sent it again to be compared with the original. Every note of punctuation is strictly copied. I shall make no comment. Such writing speaks for itself. But the faithful can scarcely believe their eyes."

The last letter written by the memorialists to Dr. Kelly, dated June 27, 1821, was a gallant but fruitless attempt to save their pastor from expulsion:

> We have received the answer you have been pleased to give to our 2nd. Memorial and supplication, wherein we beseech you to restore to the Rev. Mr. L. his spiritual powers and to permit him to officiate in the Church.
>
> Though we have duly and gravely considered it, we remain thoroughly convinced that you must be impressed with the justice of our demand and of the reflections we have submitted to you; and that the reasons you make use of to support your refusal, are quite destitute of foundation: in fact, they are such as cannot persuade us of the justice of your arbitrary determination.
>
> We are not ignorant of the meaning of the word simony: we detest and abhor the crime and cannot conceive how you can impute to us any intention of committing it.
>
> We sincerely lament your determination to insult us, wound our feelings and injure our character; and in the deep sorrow of our hearts caused by such an example, and by the loss of

---

13. *Ibid.*

every hope of justice or favor from you, we confidently throw ourselves in the bosom of a just God, casting our Solicitude upon him, and fervently beseeching him to enlighten you for the Good of Religion, and to grant you a long life.

THE SAME MEMORIALISTS.[14]

Dr. Poynter wrote on June 6, 1821, from London encouraging Maréchal in his stand against the "Irish adventurers, who, encouraged and supported by Irish Trustees and others of independent and revolutionary principles, become the scandal of the Church in causing divisions among the people and raising opposition to Episcopal authority." Dr. Poynter might well hold out hopes to Maréchal with the American agency in Gradwell's hands; and the more news he received from Virginia, the clearer it became to him that Dr. Kelly would inevitably bring disaster on that Church.

On June 10, 1821, Walter de Lacy wrote to the Archbishop, asking for advice in the sorrowful situation Father Lucas' followers found themselves:

My Lord and venerable Father,

I recollect that on the arrival of Dr. Kelly you assured us, that although released from the immediate charge of us, You would ever take the deepest interest in our spiritual concerns; this assurance, your great piety, and truly pastoral regard for the faithful, emboldens me to lay before you the lamentable condition to which we are now reduced, and to implore your relief or assistance, or in case this cannot immediately be given, your sympathy, consolation and prayers, to enable us patiently to endure it until we can obtain a remedy.

You must know, my lord, that Dr. Kelly has lately withdrawn the powers given to the Rev. Mr. Lucas by the most Rev. Archbishop Carroll and continued to him by your venerable predecessor and yourself, which powers, even Dr. Kelly himself, when asked for the reason of so extraordinary a proceeding, clearly and frequently declared were never forfeited by even a shadow of misconduct or censure. By this arbitrary stretch of power the greater, perhaps the better, part of the faithful of this place and its vicinity, are deprived of the most salutary, the most sacred of the sacraments. Since many of them are totally unacquainted with his language, and he and his assistant with theirs: others (of whom I am one) who speak his language, cannot approach him with that confidence in the efficacy of his ministry, that filial obedience, those dispositions of the heart

---
14. *Ibid.*

which must ever accompany the holy rites of our church, in order to render them effectual. His conduct since the very day of his arrival has been calculated to inspire us with anything rather than confidence and veneration; for on that day he visited and made humiliating concessions to the authors and ministers of a schism. The baleful effects of which I fear will be long felt. He continued to treat them with every deference, every indulgence, every mark of confidence and communion, until now they encroached on his *personal* convenience; and even now, he continues to treat them with lenity and forbearance, but whether from motives of charity or fear I dare not say. I know that God delights in showing mercy to the repentant sinner, and that it is the duty of erring man to follow his divine example; but of *their* repentance we have seen no proof, no indication, although we have fervently prayed and ardently hoped for it. On the contrary, the faithful who have always adhered to the church and listened to the voice of her pastors, he has treated with marked neglect, severity, and I think I may add, injustice. Indeed so evident has this been to all, that the protestants, nay even the schismatics, loudly exclaim against it. To show you my lord that however improperly my countrymen may have acted on other occasions, on this, they have shown their characteristic love of justice and their veneration for our late pastor by voluntarily affixing their signatures to a most respectful petition, written in compliance with the importunities of the French people, the poor negroes (who are deprived of every consolation and instruction) and many respectable Americans; but he has refused to grant the petition, and his refusal has been accompanied by remarks, insinuations and un . . . (when I recollect that it is of a dignitary of the church I am speaking, I dare not finish the word) which render the refusal doubly painful.

Indeed such has been the conduct of the Rev. Gentleman, that it is difficult to believe, that the extinction of the schism, or the promotion of religion was the object of his mission; until differently taught by *his* example, we were ever led to believe it a sacred duty to sanctify the whole of the Sabbath, by our attendance at high Mass, vespers and other pious duties suitable to the day; but now, we need only attend one low mass, we have no vespers, no evening instruction for the negroes, who deeply deplore the privation, and who I fear will have great reason to do so, as they are totally abandoned to the corruption of our nature without one friendly hand to guide them; and to the temptations peculiar to their state, without the only effectual means of combatting and overcoming them. Dr. Kelly appears to think they have *no* souls, or, that their souls are not worth the trouble of saving.

In fact, it is impossible to reconcile his conduct with the established duties of a good pastor; for so far from making every effort for the recovery of the strayed sheep, he has dismissed *two faithful shepherds,* and thereby exposed a great portion of the flock to the insatiable appetite of the ravenous wolf. In this deplorable condition we know not what to do! The church commands us to frequent the sacraments. Dr. K. deprives us of the means of doing so. Our divine redeemer commands us to forgive and love our enemies. The Rt. Rev. Dr. lends all the weight and power of his episcopal office to promote the vengeance, and gratify the hatred of a few guilty men. Our God commands us to do good for evil. He who should lead us by example to the obedience of this command, has most strikingly, most publicly violated it.

If with every assistance of the Church, and every effort on the part of its pastors, it is difficult to resist the influence of evil example, govern our unruly passions, and perform our duties, alas! What is now to become of us? But I trust that God, and you, my lord, will not abandon us, although the pastor to whom we have been committed has betrayed his trust and turned us out of the fold.

Venerable father, if I have said anything which you may deem improper, do not, I beeseech you, attribute it to disrespect for the Church or its minister, but to a keen sense of the almost irreparable injury inflicted on us by the man; yet I know that error in *him* will not justify error in *me*. I therefore firmly resolve, with the assistance of divine grace, and the aid of your pious prayers (which I humbly beg) to follow the example of *our own* estimable pastor, patiently to resign myself to the will of God until it shall please him to extricate us from the difficuties into which we have lately been plunged.

May heaven preserve you many, many years, for the edification and blessing of your flock, is the ardent prayer of, most reverend father,   *Your most Obedient Humble Servant,*
                              WALTER DE LACY.

Norfolk,
   10th June, 1821.

P.S. I have written this on behalf of the rest of my family, as well as of myself. And I know of *many other* members of the congregation, my lord, whose sentiments exactly coincide with ours.[15]

The good effect of Gradwell's intelligent direction of American affairs in Rome is visible in his first long report from the Eternal City, dated June 23, 1821:

---

15. BCA, Case—21A—A6.

My Lord:

I wrote to your Grace on the 10th of February and since that time I have had no information from the Archdiocese of Baltimore, though it was very desirable, till about ten days ago. Bishop Poynter transmitted to me your Grace's letter of March 30th to his Lordship with a long and excellent letter of his own on the same subject. This happened very opportunely. I knew that a Congregation was to be held at Propaganda on Baltimore business on July 11th and had lately heard Cardinal Fontana complain that none of the three new suffragans has yet written and that there was no letter from your Grace. I chose an opportunity of mentioning the letter which I had received to the Cardinal, when he was at liberty to enter into conversation on the whole subject. At the request of his Eminence I immediately translated them into Italian but as one half of Dr. Poynter's letter, though most interesting to Propaganda, was of a private and confidential nature, shewing the origin and progress of the insults offered to your authority and the connection which this had with a persecution carried on in the same manner for some years against himself, I put this at his Eminence's request in a private memorial for the information of his Eminence alone. Knowing also that Abbate Inglese of Louisiana, now in Rome, was drawing up a report on the state of the American missions for the information of Propaganda, I also waited upon him and I have had two long conversations with him. He was not aware of the Irish politics and had not heard of Mr. Hogan's impudent conduct at Philadelphia. The letters therefore which I have received are most opportune and welcome and I trust they will do good. I flatter myself that a sketch of the conversations that have passed between Cardinal Fontana and myself on this subject will give you some comfort. I said: "America needs and now implores the same blessing which England has already received from your Eminence's protectorship, the defeat of a turbulent faction, and the restoration of right order in that afflicted church. We know how the good Cardinal Litta was beset by artful men and notwithstanding all his good qualities, how easily he was deluded by their arts. Choose good bishops, give them your confidence, and then let them act, and support their authority. They are the best and the most disinterested judges of the interests of their dioceses. But whenever Propaganda has listened to the appeals of suspended and bad priests or intriguers the country has been thrown into confusion to the great detriment of religion. England has felt this, Ireland feels it severely, and still more, the church of the United States. It is lamentable to see in the instances of New York and Philadelphia, the consequences of deciding here on important points without regarding the advice of the Bishops and of following the suggestions of turbulent men who excite confusion and raise a clamour in order to deceive Propaganda and then take advantage of it. This is a real conspiracy which it is material to comprehend and to resist. The system of trustee presentation to foundations is a most mischievous pretension. Whether it be done by laymen or Jesuits it tends to shake security and confidence in the stability of the ecclesiastical property to patronise bad priests and resist episcopal authority even to the length of sacrilege and schism. I beg that your Eminence will look well into the state of the American church and do promptly what your wisdom shall suggest to console the Archbishop and his clergy and to protect both their character and authority from the machinations of selfish regulars and intruding adventurers. Nothing but your Eminence's firmness in this plan can remedy the past or give hope for the future." The Cardinal has read those letters and last night he told me that three letters had arrived that morning at Propaganda from America, one of which was from your Grace. The Cardinal replied to me with great concern and many expressions of respect and pity for the prelates and clergy of Baltimore. He said, "Now I have a clue to the labyrinth. I had no hand in the nomination of the new bishops. It was done by Cardinal della Somaglia, during my illness and absence at Naples, about the same time that he passed the decree for England which his Holiness has long since revoked. What is done, is done. But I will do what I can to prevent further mischief, and to restore order. The case admits of no delay. With regard to Lay trustees, there is precedent against their claims, but the claims of the Jesuits are a stronger case, because they were the only clergy originally and were always the administrators of the property they claim till the time of their suppression. Part of the property was given by men of their own body to the Order. The order is now restored in America. They wear their habit, etc. In future nominations in the Episcopacy, all due attention shall be paid to the recommendations of the Archbishop and the merits of his clergy, and I wish to receive more frequent communications from the Archbishop as my guide in other matters relating to his province. I have now made improvements in the way of transacting the business of the S. Congreg. You see that we now sail with another wind. If I have health I hope to do some good in those distant missions."

This is a short sketch of our conversations. The business is now fairly before his Eminence and he takes an interest in it. I will take care to keep it alive in his memory, by occasional conversation, and by supplying him with all the information I receive. He is convinced that the French and native clergy have been undeservedly vilified, and have been ill treated. He has almost discarded the gentleman who has for many years had the chief management in the [?] of England and Anglo-American affairs. The Cardinal is a learned and prudent man and indefatigable in business as far as this weak state of his health permits. If Providence spares his life, he will restore order in the missions which have been unhappily thrown into confusion. His Holiness also, and the Secretary of State, Cardinal Consalvi, take a great interest in the Baltimore affairs, and I have had several conversations with Abbate Inglesi on the subject of all the North American missions. Knowing this, I have assiduously inculcated several important considerations on the Abbate's mind. The want of fixed co-residence, and fixed prebends has staggered the Roman canonists about the institution of a chapter for the present, though the object is a good one. But still I think an equivalent may be derived by means of Grand Vicars or Rural Deans, without clashing with the canons. His Holiness is in good health. I send this letter through the hands of Bishop Poynter.

I have the honor to remain your Grace's Obedient Servant,
ROBERT GRADWELL.

P.S. Dr. Poynter hopes that he will succeed with the Propaganda in favour of the establishment of a chapter in Baltimore notwithstanding the objections of the Roman canonists.

Forwarded with his best respects by Dr. Poynter.[16]

On July 21, 1821, the Cardinal-Prefect of Propaganda replied to Maréchal's various protests against the erection of the Virginia See, assuring him that he was wrong in suspecting that the intrigues of Browne and Carbry were decisive in so serious a matter, and declaring that the idea of the Diocese of Richmond went back to Archbishop Carroll's time. Propaganda was convinced that the troubles at Norfolk were due to the fact that there was no bishop at hand to guide the priests and people; nor could the Sacred Congregation see how the presence of a bishop there could do harm to religion, especially since Dr. Kelly was so excellent an ecclesiastic. Propaganda was inclined to follow Bishop Connolly's advice that each State should have a bishop.

Meanwhile a quarrel had broken out in May, 1821, between Dr. Kelly and Father Carbry, and the latter quitted Norfolk for Lake Drummond in North Carolina.[17] There is reason to believe that he went to Charleston to consult Bishop England. Eng-

---

16. BCA, Case—17—F8. Cf. Hughes, *op. cit.*, Doc. vol. i, pt. ii, pp. 1050-1051.
17. BCA, Case—18—J57.

land came to Norfolk on June 30, and remained until July 8, preaching three times in Dr. Kelly's church.[18] There is no mention of Carbry or of Lucas in his *Diurnal*. Lucas wrote a "secret" letter to Maréchal on July 5, 1821, telling the Archbishop of the rumors created in the little city by the presence of two Catholic bishops. Miss Joanna England, the bishop's sister, was with Dr. England, and it is to her he seems to credit the statement that both Dr. Kelly and her brother had been shamefully treated by the Archbishop. This is highly doubtful, since England wrote on July 6, 1821, from Norfolk, a rather cordial letter to Maréchal, saying that he had planned to leave by the steam packet the day before for Baltimore, "but was obliged by bad weather to put back." England's diagnosis of the Norfolk situation was far-sighted; he used this knowledge to urge upon Maréchal the necessity of a Provincial Council which would produce "a most desirable effect: the union and coöperation of the Bishops of these disturbed States."[19]

In the *Acta* of July 30, 1821, we recognize the larger question which was at issue between Baltimore and Rome, and which we have not discussed in these pages lest the story should become too confused, the independence the Holy See justly meant to maintain in the selection of bishops to the Sees of Christendom. This had always been a thorny problem between the nascent American Church and the Holy See. The direct election of John Carroll by the priests of the United States was permitted by the Holy See, unprecedented as such a privilege was at the time; but the saving clause, *pro una tantum vice*,[20] which Rome used, made her stand quite clear upon this, her own singular prerogative. In the *Acta* of July 30, Cardinal Cappellari upheld the Roman view of the problem and explained that the policy could not be accepted of allowing the metropolitan of Baltimore the exclusive right to nominate to new Sees in the United States. Rome always would consider seriously the fitness and capacity of any of the priests whose names were sent to the Holy See by the hierarchy of the United States, but its prerogative of absolute freedom could never be trammelled by the bishops here.

About the time Father Lucas was preparing definitively to leave Norfolk (August 2, 1821), Propaganda wrote to Dr. Kelly thanking him for his last letter (which is not in the Archives) in

---

18. *Diurnal*, p. 27.
19. BCA, Case—16—J6.
20. Guilday, *Carroll*, p. 359.

which that prelate had described the collapse of the schism shortly after his arrival. The Sacred Congregation was sorry that Maréchal had given him such a cool reception (*aegre autem accepi te ab archiepiscopo Baltimorensi duriuscule exceptum fuisse*), but it was not surprising (*id vero non miror*), since Maréchal had so strenuously opposed the Virginia diocese. Propaganda advised Dr. Kelly to show all due reverence to the metropolitan and also to remain in Norfolk until Richmond was prepared to receive him.[21]

The suddenness with which Maréchal made up his mind to go to Rome in person was not due altogether to the Virginia situation. Another problem had arisen shortly after his consecration and was then assuming a larger importance than the question of the suffragan See of Richmond. This problem does not enter into the story of Virginia, though in reality it should not be separated from any of the diocesan problems of the time, and, indeed would not be kept apart here, were it not that it would lead us entirely too far afield, namely, the controversy with the Society of Jesus over certain property holdings in Maryland. On October 14, 1821, Maréchal sailed from New York for France.[22]

At any rate, the Virginia question was treated while he was in Rome, and Maréchal "obtained a promise that Virginia should be placed under his care as administrator as soon as Dr. Kelly could be transferred to another diocese." Shea also says that when he complained at Rome "of the interference of the hierarchy of another country (Ireland) in the affairs of the Church in the United States, he was met with the sneering remark that the Archbishop of Baltimore and his suffragans had no right to nominate to vacant Sees. His reply was made in an appeal to the Pope: 'We freely confess that we have no right to present Bishops for the province of Baltimore. No such right has ever been granted to us by the Holy See. Therefore we do not possess it. Nay more, I and my suffragans, who have occupied episcopal sees in America for many years, sincerely desire to be free from so formidable a burden . . . Yet it is certain that they must be nominated by some one; but who, considering the distance of North America from the Roman See, is to present capable and worthy subjects? Surely the Irish Bishops cannot do so to advantage . . . The Irish Bishops have only an imperfect knowledge of our America, such as they glean from geographies and books of travel. Unacquainted with the disposition and cus-

---
21. BCA. Case—18—J59.
22. Hughes, *op. cit.*, Doc. vol. i, pt. ii, p. 1051.

toms of our Americans, it is utterly impossible for them to nominate men who suit our States.' "[23]

It would appear that Dr. Kelly had not waited for Maréchal's visit to Rome to secure, or to have secured for him, a change to another See. On October 3, 1821, Propaganda wrote to Dr. Connolly, Vicar-General of Waterford, Ireland, recommending Dr. Kelly in place of the late Bishop Robert Walsh of that See. The Sacred Congregation had decided to transfer Dr. Kelly *justis de causis* and no more opportune an occasion would present itself than the vacancy in Waterford-Lismore. On October 5, 1821, Cardinal Fontana wrote to Maréchal admitting that the Sacred Congregation had made a mistake in erecting the See of Richmond and that he had decided to ask the Holy Father to transfer Dr. Kelly to a See in Ireland. Virginia was to be returned to the Diocese of Baltimore. Fontana was delighted to tell Maréchal that the Holy See was sending him a beautiful chalice for the Cathedral in Baltimore.[24] The decision to transfer Dr. Kelly was made on September 27, and was due to the fact that Maréchal had not only not accepted the action of the Holy See but had continually declared that such action was inopportune, unpleasant, and even dishonorable to him as Archbishop of Baltimore (*non modo inopportunum, verum etiam molestum ac inhonorum tibi*).[25]

Archbishop Plessis had intervened in Maréchal's cause with the Sacred Congregation, and on November 17, 1821, Fontana replied to the metropolitan of Quebec in no uncertain terms about the rights of the Baltimore prelate:

The Right Reverend William Poynter, Vicar of London, communicated to us two requests which your grace sent to him in behalf of the Most Reverend Archbishop of Baltimore. The first treated about the election of the bishops; according to your report, this archbishop is very sorry, that the Sacred Congregation in electing the bishops in the United Provinces is listening to relations and reports of anyone, while it is the office of the metropolitan to consult other bishops, and to present to the Sacred Congregation the one, who is regarded by the common opinion as more worthy, so that the Sacred Congregation should not recede from this candidate whom the metropolitan proposes.

After this claim has been presented in the S. Congregation the Eminent Fathers gave opinion that this does not follow

---

23. Shea, *op. cit.*, vol. iii, pp. 67-68, 71-72.
24. BCA. Case—22—K4.
25. Cf. *Records* ACHS, vol. xviii, p. 443.

from the metropolitan rights of the Archbishop of Baltimore, nor can it be attributed to him by virtue of a special privilege. If there is question of the metropolitan rights, this claim is contrary both to the old and to the present discipline of the Church. According to the ancient discipline of the Western Church, of which now is the question, the metropolites have never possessed the right inherent in their dignity, to elect bishops, as it is evident from the many constitutions of the sacred canons as well as from the letters of St. Leo and St. Simplicius, the Roman Pontiffs. Again, according to the recent discipline of the same Church, it is well known that the election of the bishops (unless some special agreement be to the contrary) belongs altogether to the Apostolic See, especially in the missionary countries. Nor should it be objected in the Archbishop's statement that not he but the H. See is the elector, because then the metropolite would attribute to himself the right of presentation; whenever the H. See would be forced to elect only those presented by the archbishop, it would evidently amount to the same as if the archbishop were the elector.

Nor were the Cardinals of the opinion that such a right should be granted to the Baltimore Prelate as a special privilege: first not to make any innovations in ecclesiastic discipline; secondly that it should not serve as an example to other metropolites; finally lest the privilege would pass into a right with the progress of time. We are quite well aware of the Baltimore Archbishop's piety, prudence and attachment to the H. See, so that there could not be even a doubt that he would abuse this privilege, if granted. But as it is question of a privilege which had to pass to the successors, every danger must be avoided, lest the future metropolites should become masters of episcopal elections, and by and by, with time, emancipate themselves from the Apostolic See, lest factions and parties originate, and the way be opened to some bishop of not perfect orthodoxy.

Such being the case, the S. Congregation decided that the norm proposed by the archbishop cannot be admitted, but we want him to understand that the same S. Congregation in electing bishops in the provinces of the United States will always give particular attention, above all, to the recommendations of the Archbishop of Baltimore and other prelates; as it happened, indeed, in electing the four bishops, who were postulated by the excellent prelate Carroll, as well as in electing Archbishop Neale, Aloysius de Barth and Rev. Maréchal himself, also lately of the bishop of Cincinnati, all of them recommended recently by your Grace according to the proposition of the Baltimore metropolite and his suffragan bishops.[26]

---

26. Prop. Arch., *Lettere,* vol. 302, f. 516.

That same day (November 17), Fontana replied to Maréchal in a letter of the same tenor, assuring him that the Holy See had always listened to the American bishops regarding nominations to the new Sees. Naturally, Maréchal, who had Richmond in mind, could not accept this statement at its face value; but he had won a victory, while in Rome, and it was only a question of time before the "dismembered" part of his diocese would be returned to him. There is an interesting (though undated) letter of this time from Propaganda to Bishop Connolly of New York, urging him to accept Dr. Kelly as a coadjutor. The tradition is that Dr. Kelly had so openly condemned the State governments in this country for incorporating boards of trustees for Catholic churches, that Dr. Connolly was not willing to accept him as coadjutor lest trouble arise in New York. Bishop Du Bourg was worried at the time that Dr. Kelly might be sent to Louisiana.[27]

In spite of the disturbed condition of his diocese, Bishop Kelly gave every evidence of a zealous interest in the Church of Virginia. His deception in the case of Father Carbry and of the party that had clamored so long and so loudly for a separate diocese with one of their own race as bishop was a cruel blow to the prelate who believed he had acted for the best interests of religion in Virginia in refusing faculties to Father Lucas. "The very men," writes Shea, "who had clamoured for an Irish priest now turned against an Irish bishop, selected especially to see that their fancied wrongs were redressed. The old feud continued. There was a Bishop's party and a trustees' party, each endeavouring to secure possession of the church, till the civil authorities intervened, and twenty-one were arrested."[28]

There was little financial support for Bishop Kelly in these conditions, and he is said to have opened a school in order to maintain himself until the Holy See was able to help him. The Catholics in Norfolk numbered about three hundred; those in Richmond were but few; and in the other cities of the diocese, Martinsburg, Winchester, and Wheeling, they were accustomed to look to the priests of Maryland and Pennsylvania to visit them occasionally. At the end of the year 1821, Bishop Kelly sent

---

27. Cf. *Records* ACHS, vol. xxi, p. 197; *Spicilegium Ossoriense*, vol. 1, pp. 275-276; Hughes, *op. cit.*, Doc. vol. i, pt. ii, p. 959.
28. *Op. cit.*, vol. iii, pp. 81-82. Father Lucas came to Washington, D. C., and was pastor of St. Peter's Church. He soon became estranged from his people, and sought admission into the Society of Jesus, in July, 1825. He was stationed at Bohemia Manor in 1844. *Records* ACHS, vol. xxiv, p. 135.

Father James Walsh to Richmond, but after his departure with Bishop Kelly in 1822, the Catholics of Richmond were without a resident pastor.[29] Virginia became a sort of no-man's-land after Dr. Kelly's return to Ireland; the few scattered facts of its Catholic history during the next twenty years present a pitiable story of a struggle maintained by the children of the first congregation to preserve the Faith. "It is not the intention of the writer," said Dr. England in 1836, "to pass judgment upon others; but he thinks that amongst other mistakes, the opposition to the separate administration of this latter diocese, by causing its Bishop to return to Ireland as soon as he could obtain permission from the Holy See, has been by no means favorable to the maintenance of religion in the State of Virginia. This mistake is about to be remedied, but the past cannot be recalled."[30]

One of the most pathetic incidents in this long narrative of intrigue, animosity and mutual distrust, is that of Bishop Kelly's calling all the Catholic children over eight or nine years of age together just before his departure, and administering to them the Sacrament of Confirmation.

On January 28, 1822, by a special decree of the Sacred Congregation, Bishop Kelly was transferred from Richmond to the Diocese of Waterford-Lismore, in Ireland. The Virginia See was returned to the administration of Archbishop Maréchal. This decree received papal sanction on February 3, 1822, and on February 22, the Bull appointing Maréchal Administrator of Virginia was issued.[31] In June, 1822, Dr. Kelly left Norfolk for Ireland. He died at Waterford on October 8, 1829.[32]

There is a *General Description of the Metropolitan Province of Baltimore* for the years 1821-22, in the Propaganda Archives, and alongside each of the eight American Sees is placed a word to describe its state at the time. Opposite the See of Richmond, the word *confusio* is written.[33]

Such unfortunately is the key-word for the seven years treated in this sketch.

---

29. Keiley, *The Catholic Church in Richmond, Va.*, p. 7. Norfolk, 1874.
30. *Works* (Reynolds), vol. iii, p. 294.
31. BCA, Case—22—G19.
32. Carrigan, *History and Antiquities of the Diocese of Ossory*, vol. 1, p. 272-275. Dublin, 1905.
33. Hughes, *op. cit.*, Doc., vol. i, pt. ii, p. 959.

CONCLUSION

A final document for the history of Virginia at this time is an undated Latin Prospectus in the Propaganda Archives signed by Michael Joseph O'Fay, D.D., of Galway in Ireland, suggesting to the Holy See the establishment of a College in Virginia. "Of all the states in the United States," the document reads, "the largest and the most flourishing is Virginia, with its two million inhabitants and its size larger than all Italy. The capital is called Richmond, which is also the episcopal See, but it is now vacant and under the administration of the Archbishop of Baltimore. There are but few Catholics in this city, and these are so poor that they can scarcely support one priest. Norfolk, the second largest city, has two priests, and there is a fourth priest in a town called Martinsburg —*in allis locis, nulli Catholici, sacerdos nullus.*" The Virginians are praised for their "sublime nature," artistic culture, shrewdness and inquisitiveness. There is no Catholic College in the State, and one would be of immense benefit in bringing the knowledge of the Church to the Protestants, who would undoubtedly send their sons to be taught there. It was proposed therefore, in the name of some Irish priests then in residence in Rome to go to Virginia and found such a College, on condition that it be under the jurisdiction of the Sacred Congregation—*haud administrationi Archiepiscopi subjecti.* Apparently nothing ever came of Dr. O'Fay's proposal.

In one of the early numbers of the *Miscellany* (July 10, 1822), Bishop England announced the departure of "the late Bishop of Richmond." During his residence in the borough of Norfolk. Dr. England writes, Bishop Kelly's attention "to his pastoral duties was unremitting; and his success corresponding; the affection and regret of his former flock, accompany the Rt. Rev. Doctor Kelly. When he arrived in Norfolk, a disgraceful and unmeaning schism had rent, and was destroying the Catholic congregation. A gentleman, who was, we are informed, a good physician, unsuccessful merchant, and very bad but arrogant and dictatorial divine; one, who could swear before a court of justice to Church history, by the hour, and longer if the court would allow him to disgorge his undigested accumulation, was the principal fomentor of the mischief—his object was to make a republican Roman Catholic

Church; of which he was to be monarch. Do not stare, gentle reader, for indeed, he could reconcile contradictions. He was to do more; for although he never received spiritual jurisdiction himself, he could communicate it to others, and prove the absurdity of the maxim, which all wise men, himself excepted, had held, for at least two or three thousand years, if not longer, *Nemo potest dare quod non habet,* for he could give, what he had not. These things, and many wonders besides could he perform; and he actually did perform one mighty work: he nearly deprived the Catholics of Norfolk of their senses and of their religion; but, by the exertions of Doctor Kelly, they regained both. During the last summer, when the yellow fever raged in Norfolk, the bishop was constant in his attendance upon the sick, and during months, was every day amongst the infected, solacing, cheering, instructing, and administering sacraments to the diseased. Thus was he deservedly beloved, and justly respected; and the prayers and good wishes of the Catholics of Norfolk are the well earned return for his services. How much more pleasing and consoling a spectacle is this, than brawling and dissention? Until the regulations which have been made in Rome shall be notified, the Rev. Mr. Walsh of Richmond has been appointed to superintend the Diocess. The Rev. Messrs. Hore and Delany remain in Norfolk and Portsmouth; the Rev. Mr. Fitz Patrick is in Petersburg, and the Rev. Mr. Mahony in the western part of the state."

This statement was attacked by "Old Catholic" in the Norfolk *Herald* on August 7, 1822, in the following letter: "That the gentleman whom you attack was the principal fomenter of the collisions in the church at this place, is an assertion without any foundation. Though his deep learning and intimate knowledge of the history of the Church qualified him well for the task of exposing those usurpations which were the sole cause of the dissentions in the Catholic Congregation at this place. When these dissentions commenced, he had no agency at all in the temporal concerns of the Church. So far, reverend Sir, your information has been incorrect, or your fancy somewhat exuberant. I grant you, Sir, that his talents were often employed, during the time of strife, on the side of the *radicals,* in combatting the high handed measures of the bishop and his agent, whose object rather appeared to be, to secure the *fleece* than to save the sheep. He maintained the unpardonable doctrine, that as the *Congregations* were taxed for the support of their pastors, *the right belonged to them to elect their pastors;* at all events, to reject any who might not be agreeable to them. He furthermore maintained, that *all power over the funds,* and other temporal concerns of the Church, *ought to be vested in trustees appointed by the congregation,* who surely ought to have a voice in appropriating moneys contributed by themselves. But this doctrine did not suit the views of the bishop and pastor. It was only necessary that the pastor should please the bishop—no matter for the congregation; but, above all, that the sole control of the money matters should belong to the clergy."

Bishop England answered this letter in the *Miscellany* for August 21, 1822, and it is evident that he believed Jasper Moran to be the "Old Catholic" of the *Herald*. On September 11, 1822, the *Miscellany* announced that "Dr. Kelly, late Bishop of Richmond, now Bishop of Lismore and Waterford (Ireland), arrived at Liverpool, after a passage of twenty-five days from the United States. His arrival in Ireland, in the Ivanhoe, from Holyhead, is noticed in the Dublin *Morning Post* of the 16th July."

After the death of Maréchal, Archbishop Whitfield endeavored to have the vacant See of Richmond suppressed and the State of Virginia united again to the Archdiocese of Baltimore. A majority of the votes of the Second Provincial Council of 1833 was obtained, recommending this measure to the Holy See. Rome did not enter into the views of Whitfield. Upon his death in 1834, Archbishop Eccleston, "whose views accorded more with the spirit that governs the Holy See than did those of his two immediate predecessors," asked at the Third Provincial Council (1837), that Richmond be restored to the American hierarchy. The approval of the Holy See was given. Father Richard Whelan was chosen and was consecrated on March 21, 1841, as second Bishop of Richmond.

THE END

INDEX

Address to the Members, etc., 32
Alexandria, Catholics in (1794), xiv
Anti-Catholic laws, viii
Anti-Irish sentiment in Virginia, xviii, 60
Anti-French sentiment in Virginia, xvii, 52, 59-60
Antonelli, Cardinal, 2
Apostolic Delegate proposed (1820), 86
Appointment of Dr. Kelly, 128-129
Archives, Rome, Quebec, Baltimore, etc., ii
Axacan, v

Baltimore, Archdiocese of (1808), i
——, Lord, in Virginia, vii
Baxter, Father Roger, 62
Bohemia Manor Academy, 2
British Guiana, 4
Browne, Rev. Robert, O.S.A., 39, 43, 102, 107, 113, 126
Bruté, Bishop, xvi
Bushe, Father, James, xiv

Cappellari, Cardinal, 148
Carbry, Father Thomas, O.P., xvii, 49, 50, 53, 60, 72, 74, 77, 87, 102, 107, 109, 110-111, 113, 114, 120, 121-122
Carroll, Archbishop John, i, xi, xiv, xviii, 47, 142, 148
Castlereagh, Lord, 104
"Catholic Atheists," 7
—— Emancipation, vii, 103
Cauchie, Canon, ii
Chabrat, Bishop, xvi
Chalice for Baltimore Cathedral, 150
Charleston, Schism of, 34, 39; See of, 86, 89, 115
Cheverus, Cardinal, i, 34, 65, 75, 115, 131, 132, 135
Church discipline in the U. S., 75;
Government, problems of, i-ii
—— and State, 93-101
—— property laws, 6
Cisalpine Club, 28
Clergy-Corporation, 4, 9
Clorivière, Father, 9, 43
College of St. Omer, 2
Connolly, Bishop John, O.P., 75, 78, 86, 87, 89, 108, 110-111, 125
Consalvi, Cardinal, 103, 125

Convention of Irish - American Catholics, 113
Conwell, Bishop, 131
Councils of Baltimore, 9
Cowan, Father James, O.F.M., 118
Crypto-Catholicism, i

David, Bishop, xvi
De Barth, Father, 75
Delaney, Father, 155
Demerara, 2
De Neuville, 120, 135
Devotions, Catholic, in Virginia, 14
Dissensions among Catholics in Virginia, 33
District of Columbia, 124
Disorders in American Church, **72**
Diocese of Virginia, 74
Donaghey, John, xv, 16, 32, 53-59, 63, 70-71, 78-79, 90
Dubois, Bishop, xi, xvi, 9
Du Bourg, Bishop, xvi, 41, 65, 68, 95
Dugnani, Cardinal, 65, 76-77

Egan, John, 119
——, Bishop Michael, O.F.M., i
England, Miss Joanna, 148
——, Bishop John, ii, xvi, xviii-xix, 6, 86, 117, 124, 129, 147, 148, 154-155
Episcopal Church in Virginia, x
—— nominations in United States, 148-149, 152
—— Seminary at Norfolk, 57-58
Equality, religious, x

Fagan, Augustine, 113
Febronius, 29
Fernandez, Dr., J.F.O., xiv, xv, 11, 31, 60-62, 76-77, 80-82, 108-109;
letter of, 27-28, 43, 120
Fenwick, Father Benedict, S.J., 89, 106, 115, 131
Ffrench, Father Charles, O.P., 110, 132
Figueria, Rev. M. V., 70
Fitzgerald, Col., xiv
Fitzpatrick, Father, 155
Flaget, Bishop Benedict, i, xvi
Fontana, Cardinal, 106, 119, 134, **145**, 150-157
Foreign Clergy, in United States, 46, 97-98
Franklin, Father John, 62
Fredericksburg, Catholics in, 12

157

INDEX

French Clergy in United States, xvii, xviii-xx, 51, 106
——— Revolution, xx

Galton, Bishop, 3
Gallagher, Rev. Dr. Simon Felix, 39, 43, 86, 102, 116
"Genoese Letter," 103
Georgia, 89
Georgetown College, 5
Gortyna, Bishop of (Neale), 4
Gradwell, Dr. Robert, 136, 142, 144
Graessl, Bishop-elect Lawrence, 4
Grassi, Father John, S.J., 42, 62, 67-68, 70, 79, 116
Guale (Georgia), i

Harrigan, Father Simon, O.P., 117
Harvey, Sir John, viii
Hayes, Rev. Richard, O.F.M., 102
Heresy, "geographical," 126
Herron, James, 16, 33, 113
———, Walter, 33
Higgins, Eugene, xv, 10, 16, 32, 38, 41
Hogan, Rev. William, 28, 123, 132
Holy See, Appeal to the, 45, 62
Hore, Father, 155
Hughes, Archbishop John, 9
Hurley, Father Michael, O.S.A., 75

Immigration Catholic, into Virginia, xi
"Independent Catholick Church of the United States," iv, 29, 39, 105, 124
Inglesi, 147
Intolerance in Virginia, vii-x
Ireland, and Holy See, 104
Irish Catholic problems in United States, 113, 117, 119-120, 149, xvi, xviii, xix

Jamestown, iv
Jansenist Church in United States, 89-92
Jefferson, Thomas, 93-101; letter, 95, 101, 117
Jesuits, 79, 100, 149
Jus Patronatus, 7-8, 12, 30, 105, 109-110, 121-123

Kelly, Bishop Patrick, iv, x, 117, 124, 126-127, 128, 134-148, 152
Kerney, Father Nicholas, 108

Lacy, Father Michael, xiv, xvi, xxi-xxii, 31
———, Walter, 141, 144

Lawlor, John, xiii
Lay trusteeship, 5
Litta, Cardinal, 40, 43, 65, 68, 72-73, 77-78-79, 106, 119
Loyalism, in Virginia, x
Lucas, Rev. James, xxv, 9, 10, 34, 48, 135-142, 152

Magri, Rev. Dr., iv
Mahony, Father, 155
Malou, Father Peter, S.J., 115, 132
Maréchal, Archbishop Ambrose, iv, xviii, 34-35, 65-66, 69, 74-75, 76, 79, 87, 101-123, 103, 107-108, 112, 130, 134, 149; Pastoral Letter, 90, 119; *Report,* 87
Martinsburg, 152, 154
Maryland, priests in, i; settlement of, v; Catholicism in, 97
Miguel, Father Xavier, xi
Miscellany (Charleston), 154
Molyneux, Father Robert, S.J., 5
Mongrand, Father, xi
Moran, Jasper, xv, xxii, 32, 41, 43, 63
———, Thomas, xv
Mosheim, 29
Moseley, Alexander, xiv
Mulhollan, Bernard, 16, 32
McCormack, Rev. James, O.F.M., 113
McElroy, Rev. John, 62
McLaughlin, Denis, xiii

Neale, Father Francis, xiv
Neale, Archbishop Leonard, i, xiv, xviii, 10, 13, 23-24, 35-38, 62, 81
"No Popery," viii
Norfolk, Church in, xxi, 17-18, 30, 56-58, 63-101, 79, 102-123; principles of the Trustees, 30; clergy for, 58, 59; support of church in, 58; *To the Roman Catholics of,* 83, 84
Nowlan, Rev Edward, 127

Oath of Allegiance, vi
O'Brien, Rev Matthew, O.P., xxiv
O'Connell, Daniel, 103
O'Driscoll, Dr. Michael, 123
O'Fay, Rev. Michael, 154
O'Finan, Rev. Francis, O.P., 107, 117
Orista (South Carolina), i

Patronage, right of, iv, 47, 50-51
Persons, Rev. Robert, S.J., vi
Piatti Francis, xiii
Pius VI, 4
——— VII, 41, 66

Pombalism, 28
"Popery" in Virginia, vi
Propaganda Fide, Congregation of, xvi, 66-69
Provincial Councils of Baltimore, 9
"Popish recusants," ix, 132
Portsmouth, xi, 12
Poynter, Bishop, 133, 142, 150

Quarantotti Rescript, 103
Questionnaire (Marechal), 88

Regulations of 1810, 75
Relatio, of Bishop Connolly, 78
Religious liberty, in United States, x
Rice, Father John, O.S.A., 126
Ricci, Resurrection of Laurent, 8
Richmond, Church in, xii, 8, 12; erection of See of, 123, 124; Restoration of See, 156; Vacant See of, 153
Ryan, Rev. John, O.P., 113
———, Rev. Timothy, 62

San Domingo, Insurrection, xiv
Schism (Norfolk), 8, 101-122, *et passim*; (Philadelphia), 7; (Charlston), 53-55
Schools, in Virginia, 50
Secular-Regular controversy, xvi, 9
Sedella, Father Antonius, O.M. Cap., 95
Seminary, at Norfolk, 57-58
Seton, Mother, xxv
Shea, John Gilmary, cited, iv, xiv, 40-41, 130
Smyth, Father Patrick, xvi
Somaglia, Cardinal della, 92, 146
Spelleman, John, xiv
St. Croix, Island of, 52
St. Thomas' Manor, 4

Sulpicians, xvi, 95
Suppression of the Jesuits, 2
Swords, Edward, 71
Synodal Acts of 1791, 75

Taylor, Father William, 125
Temporalities, in Virginia, 48
Tessier, Father, xxiv, 10, 62
Tiernan, Luke, 17
Titus Oates Plot, viii
Transfer of Bishop Kelly, 153
Troy, Archbishop, of Dublin, 49, 106
Trustees, ii-iii, 9, 15-16, 55-57, 83-84, 100, 111-112

Utrecht Plan, 91, 102, 105-107, 116

Vestrymen, 15
Vicariate for Carolinas, 82
Villalobos, xv
Vindicatory Address (Moran), 38-39, 63
Virginia, Church in, 74, 78-79, 89, 116, 149; Petition for a bishop in, 49, 82; College in, 154
Visitation of Diocese (1818), 79-80
——— Convent, Georgetown, 5

Wallace, Father James, S.J., 89
Walsh, Father James, 153
Waterford-Lismore, Diocese of, x, 150
West Indies, Catholics in, 48
Wheeling, 152
Whitfield, Archbishop James, 34, 75, 156
Winchester, Virginia, 152
Wingfield, Edwin Maria, v
Winslade expedition, vi
Wynne, Rev. John J. S.J., 8